Praise f

Evaluating ALL Teachers of English Learners and Students With Disabilities

"This book is a must read for today's teachers and administrators. By viewing diverse students and their educators as assets, identifying research-based strategies, and offering practical examples, Staehr Fenner, Kozik, and Cooper provide a framework for rich instructional conversations that moves teacher evaluation from the blame game, that beats educators down, to a collaborative and informative process that empowers teaching effectiveness and student learning."

—Spencer Salend, Emeritus Professor of Educational Studies
State University of New York at New Paltz

"Teacher evaluation is perhaps the last vestige of segregated education; a situation that can only be remedied by thoughtful proposals for authentic change. In this ground-breaking text, Staehr Fenner, Kozik, and Cooper move the field forward by providing a theory and research based framework for preparing, evaluating and supporting teachers to effectively educate all students, including English language learners and students with disabilities. Rather than retrofitting typically used evaluation tools, the proposed framework embraces UDL by considering the principles and practices associated with effective inclusive schooling from the outset. Teachers, administrators, and teacher educators can easily use this framework to tailor their own processes for promoting professional development and teacher effectiveness."

—Leslie C. Soodak, Professor of Education
Pace University

"Educating the growing number of English Learners in PreK–12 educational settings can no longer be the sole responsibility of ESL and bilingual experts. All teachers and administrators must build new competencies in order to reach this diverse group of students and develop their full potential. In this context, what constitutes a fair and effective teacher evaluation system? In this book, the authors successfully outline an objective assessment framework that builds educators' individual and collective capacity to improve their practice not only with ELs but with all their students. A must read for teachers and evaluators alike."

—Rosa Aronson, Executive Director
TESOL International Association

"When teacher evaluations became part of our school accountability system I wondered how effective teaching of students with disabilities would be addressed. This book provides the answer! I am particularly impressed with how reflective practice is embedded within the process described in this book. It's a must-have for any teacher evaluator who wants to assess how teachers are teaching all students well within an inclusive classroom."

—Cheryl M. Jorgensen, Educational Consulting
Inclusive Education Consultant

"Drs. Staehr Fenner, Kozik, and Cooper have started an essential conversation. Schools serve increasingly diverse populations and in order to do that well, all aspects of the school culture must support inclusive practices. Teacher evaluation should include attention to the needs of ALL students and support evaluators to create an atmosphere of cohesiveness among general and special education teachers as they work together to improve learning outcomes for all students. I would recommend this text to anyone who evaluates teachers, the practical scenarios and look-fors will help evaluators think about how to best structure pre- and post-observations, as well as providing helpful guidelines for consideration during observations. There is great urgency to ensure that teacher evaluation doesn't move forward without inclusive attention to the needs of ALL students and the practices their teachers employ."

—Jessica A. McCord, Educational Consultant
Keystone Assessment

"This book is an invaluable resource that addresses a critical, national issue facing teacher evaluation systems as teachers and their evaluators grapple with determining how the standards of teaching practice – what teachers should know and be able to do – apply to general education classrooms with English Language and student with disabilities. The authors' four fundamental principles undergird a thoughtful, informative process supported by research, practitioner's voices, and common sense strategies to assess and enhance teacher effectiveness. This book provides a real service to teachers and evaluators by making the complexities of teacher evaluation a meaningful experience with profound benefit, not only for educators, but all students and the schools in which they are enrolled. "

—Lawrence T. White, Director of Educational Services
NYSUT

"This book is an essential tool for teachers, administrators, and parents who strive to level the playing field by providing every child with an equal opportunity to learn. The authors have addressed the important topics of what teachers need to know to create a positive learning environment for all students, including English learners and those with special needs. It includes evidence-based effective practices *that evaluators should look for in inclusive classrooms and professional development ideas to develop a community of learners. Teacher evaluation with diverse populations in our 21st century classrooms is challenging. Diane Staehr Fenner, Peter Kozik, and Ayanna Cooper have created a compendium of resources that many will find helpful."*

—Dolores Burton, Author
The Burton Group

"Staehr Fenner, Kozik, and Cooper have hit the mark! Educators, administrators, and evaluators now have a valuable resource to assist them as they navigate the world of teacher evaluation. Clearly, these authors have their fingers on the pulse of today's schools, excellently articulating the issues and challenges associated with educating diverse learners. They describe the conditions necessary for English learners and students with disabilities to meet with success while also articulating the factors that lead to an educators' success. Their chapters dedicated to the four principles of inclusive teacher evaluation provide the reader with a deeper understanding of the supporting research as well as practical strategies for implementation. The case examples, in addition to the tables, graphics, and sample documents are valuable in that readers can immediately replicate these strategies. Also, the quotations throughout the book illustrate the practicality of the material. I look forward to using this book in several of my teacher preparation courses as well with educators who are very much in need of guidance on this important issue."

—Kathleen M. Feeley
Long Island University

EVALUATING
— ALL —
TEACHERS
OF ENGLISH
LEARNERS AND
STUDENTS WITH
DISABILITIES

Supporting Great Teaching

DIANE STAEHR FENNER

PETER KOZIK

AYANNA COOPER

Foreword by Melanie Hobbs and Giselle Lundy-Ponce

CORWIN
A SAGE Company

FOR INFORMATION:

Corwin
A SAGE Company
2455 Teller Road
Thousand Oaks, California 91320
(800) 233-9936
www.corwin.com

SAGE Publications Ltd.
1 Oliver's Yard
55 City Road
London EC1Y 1SP
United Kingdom

SAGE Publications India Pvt. Ltd.
B 1/I 1 Mohan Cooperative Industrial Area
Mathura Road, New Delhi 110 044
India

SAGE Publications Asia-Pacific Pte. Ltd.
3 Church Street
#10-04 Samsung Hub
Singapore 049483

Acquisitions Editor: Dan Alpert
Associate Editor: Kimberly Greenberg
Editorial Assistant: Cesar Reyes
Production Editor: Amy Schroller
Copy Editor: Linda Gray
Typesetter: C&M Digitals (P) Ltd.
Proofreader: Pam Suwinsky
Indexer: Judy Hunt
Cover Designer: Janet Kiesel
Marketing Manager: Lisa Lysne

Printed in the United States of America

A catalog record of this book is available from the Library of Congress.

ISBN 978-1-4833-5857-4

This book is printed on acid-free paper.

SFI Certified Sourcing
www.sfiprogram.org
SFI-00453
SFI label applies to text stock

15 16 17 18 19 10 9 8 7 6 5 4 3 2 1

Contents

Foreword

When the American Federation of Teachers (AFT) began union-led work in 2010 on teacher development and evaluation systems, in partnership with two state federations, the New York State United Teachers (NYSUT) and the Rhode Island Federation of Teachers and Health Professionals (RIFTHP), we encountered little to no information on how these systems address the needs of English learners (ELs) and students with disabilities enrolled in general education classrooms. This initiative, the Educator Evaluation for Excellence in Teaching and Learning (E3TL) Consortium project, which involves the AFT, NYSUT, the RIFTHP, and labor-management teams from ten school districts across New York and Rhode Island, is primarily funded by an Investing in Innovation (i3) Fund grant from the U.S. Department of Education and by an AFT Innovation Fund grant.

The E3TL project's overarching goal is to establish state-of-the-art teacher development and evaluation systems. A unique characteristic of this project is that the particular learning needs of special populations (English learners and students with disabilities) are taken into account by identifying what teachers and evaluators need to know and be aware of when it comes to instructing ELs and students with disabilities in general education classrooms. From what we have observed, it is the only project of its kind in the nation.

Given that increasing numbers of ELs and students with disabilities spend the majority of their school day in general education classrooms, the members of the E3TL project realized that there is an urgent need for general education teachers to be evaluated appropriately and fairly. When we learned that our colleagues Diane Staehr Fenner, Peter Kozik, and Ayanna Cooper, were going to write this book, we were thrilled, and we cheered them on because the topic is virtually unexplored in the field.

The abilities and needs of these special student populations are not fully addressed by most teaching practice rubrics, yet these rubrics are becoming the norm nationwide for teacher evaluation systems (e.g., Danielson,

Marzano, and others). This poses a challenge. Teachers in inclusive settings serving ELs and students with disabilities require much more preparation, support, resources, and information than currently available using any rubric.

For example, ELs with very basic levels of English proficiency and students with disabilities with significant cognitive or speech and language impairments may need special considerations and accommodations in order to successfully participate in classroom instruction. Without the right supports to help teachers engage these students in grade-appropriate content through a variety of alternative methods, teacher evaluation in these classrooms runs the risk of just becoming a better "gotcha tool," in the commonsense words of teacher evaluation expert Angela Minnici (2014), who was the i3 project director when the grant was awarded for this work.

Consistent with the E3TL's goals, this book communicates a clear vision of effective teaching, accurately identifies and supports teachers on a continuum of performance, and provides accurate and rich data that can be used to guide and deploy resources to help all teachers develop and improve. Research indicates that fidelity of implementation is critical to the success of comprehensive teacher evaluation systems in improving teaching quality and increasing student achievement (Darling-Hammond, 2014). This book identifies quality implementation components of performance-based teacher evaluation systems to assist in scaling up and sustaining such systems across the country.

To address the needs of ELs and students with disabilities in general education classrooms, this book addresses three components that were developed through the work of the E3TL project:

1. It provides considerations for effective practice in the teaching of ELs and students with disabilities (these were incorporated as an addendum in the teaching standards rubrics used by NYSUT and the RIFTHP). The considerations highlight what's needed to help provide a positive learning environment that capitalizes on the diverse linguistic, social, cultural, and intellectual needs of the student body in all aspects of language and content acquisition. Additionally, the considerations within the rubrics outline the conditions necessary for ELs and students with disabilities to be successful learners in general education classrooms *and* the supports general education teachers must have access to in order to be successful. These considerations are particularly important in assisting both teachers and evaluators in understanding what it means and what it takes to be an effective teacher of ELs and students with disabilities.

2. It provides a set of shared values for effective instruction of ELs and students with disabilities (originally presented in an issue brief written by this book's authors, commissioned by the E3TL). The values state that schools and classrooms can better promote the success of all students by working to provide equal access for all learners, supporting student individuality and diversity, using responsive teaching strategies, and forming a culture of collaboration.

3. It discusses the professional development needed for evaluators and teachers working with ELs and students with disabilities. It focuses on evidence-based practices, what evaluators should look for in inclusive classrooms, essential supports that general education teachers need, and the issues evaluators and teachers should be aware of when educating ELs and students with disabilities.

The AFT, NYSUT, and the RIFTHP did not embark on this E3TL project in isolation. We convened a committee composed of national experts and practitioners (teachers and administrators) from participating districts to examine their teaching standards rubrics and provide guidance on effective teaching practices for general education teachers with ELs and students with disabilities enrolled in their classrooms. Three of those experts who worked diligently with us are the authors of this much-needed book.

One of the lessons learned is that any multifaceted teacher evaluation and development system cannot be implemented with fidelity without a well-thought-out process and the requisite amount of investment, expertise, collaboration, and consistent tweaking.

As teacher evaluation systems evolve, we expect to see more guidance for school districts and state departments of education on what teachers and evaluators should consider when it comes to effective teaching involving special populations. In the meantime, we predict that trailblazing efforts such as our E3TL project and this book will inspire schools and union leaders to make their teacher evaluation process as inclusive as possible and to provide teachers and other educators with the guidance, resources, and preparation they need to help *all* students succeed.

—*Melanie Hobbs and Giselle Lundy-Ponce,*
American Federation of Teachers

Acknowledgments

Diane Staehr Fenner: This book exemplifies what can happen when individuals who represent different perspectives collaborate effectively and focus on student learning. I would first like to thank my coauthors Peter Kozik and Ayanna Cooper for agreeing to write this book with me that grew out of our initial project with the American Federation of Teachers. I would also like to recognize Giselle Lundy-Ponce, Melanie Hobbs, Diane August, Spencer Salend, and Catharine Whittaker for helping to shape my thinking on teacher evaluation that is inclusive of all learners. A heartfelt thanks to Ellen Street for helping out with some references and also to Sydney Snyder for providing input on the organization of the book.

I am especially thankful for Corwin's senior acquisitions editor Dan Alpert for immediately affirming that teacher evaluation inclusive of ELs and students with disabilities was a much-needed topic in the field when I proposed the idea him. Dan has offered many insights into the direction of this book, and I would like to thank him for his many layers of support. In addition, I would like to say thank you to the Corwin team, including Kimberly Greenberg, Stephanie Trkay, and Cesar Reyes for supporting our work through all aspects of the publication process and to Linda Gray and Amy Schroller for their attention to detail and patience while editing the book.

Peter Kozik: There are many mentors and thoughtful educators I would like to acknowledge as having contributed to my thinking for this book: Gerald Mager, Matt Giugno, Wilma Jozwiak, and the many educators on the Task Force for Quality Inclusive Schooling, as well as my colleagues Iris Maxon and Steven Wirt, who implemented the task force, a 15-year attempt to provide educational equity for students with disabilities in New York State. In addition, I want to honor the advocacy of Lisa Prosser, Ben's mom, and John Shamlian, Haley's dad, and the many parents and students whom I've tried to serve within the system. Also, I want to acknowledge the "white hairs" who represent for me public education working hard in the interest of all students: David Dineen, Marilyn Dominick, and

Clifford Crooks as well as Rick Cowles, the best assistant principal with whom I've served. I also want to thank Robin Hecht for her continued support of good teaching and the contributions she made to developing the scenarios in this book. Thank you, finally, to Diane, Ayanna, Spencer Salend, and Melanie Hobbs who have helped guide my thinking over the last five years.

Ayanna Cooper: To my coauthors Diane and Peter, I could not have imagined we would continue this adventurous journey together, advocating for ELs and students with disabilities, since we first worked together a few years ago. *Mahalo!* I am also grateful for the opportunity to share the voices of dedicated educators as part of this book. A special thank-you goes to Craig Martin, Cherrilynn Woods-Washington, Lynette Jackson, Julie Carroll, Brenda Colonna, Celeste Hentz, Elizabeth McNally, and Margo Williams. I appreciate you sharing your personal perspectives and experiences working with diverse student populations.

About the Authors

 **Diane Staehr Fenner** is the president of DSF Consulting, LLC, a woman-owned small business dedicated to the achievement of English learners (ELs) through professional development, curriculum design, research, and technical assistance. Clients include the American Federation of Teachers, the Center for Applied Linguistics, the National Education Association, the Peace Corps, state departments of education, school districts, and the U.S. Department of Education. Dr. Staehr Fenner frequently partners with the American Institutes for Research on projects that support ELs. She serves as the council for the Accreditation of Educator Preparation (CAEP) program coordinator for TESOL International Association. Prior to forming DSF Consulting, Dr. Staehr Fenner gained research and EL policy experience at George Washington University's Center for Excellence and Equity in Education. Her instructional background includes a decade as an ESOL teacher, dual-language assessment teacher, and ESOL assessment specialist in Fairfax County Public Schools, Virginia. She writes a blog that provides practical information and strategies for teachers of ELs for the Colorín Colorado website. Her first book published by Corwin Press was *Advocating for English Learners: A Guide for Educators* (2014). She also coauthored *Preparing Effective Teachers of English Language Learners* with Natalie Kuhlman (TESOL International Association, 2012). Dr. Staehr Fenner is a frequent speaker about EL education at conferences across the nation. However, her most important role is that of Mommy to Zoe, age 10; Maya, age eight; and Carson, age five.

Peter Kozik is a former social studies and English language arts teacher, adult GED instructor, community college teacher, teacher center director, chairperson of special education, director of special education, and RK–12 public school principal with over 30 years of experience in the field of education. From 2002 to 2011, he served as the research coordinator and then the project coordinator for the New York State Higher Education Support Center, located at Syracuse University, and as the chairperson for the New York Task Force on Quality Inclusive Schooling, a consortium of 75 colleges and universities in New York State with teacher preparation programs focused on the inclusion of students with disabilities in the K–12 general education curriculum. He is currently an assistant professor of education at Keuka College in the Finger Lakes region of New York State where he teaches undergraduate courses in Adolescent Integrated Methods, Youth-at-Risk in American Schools, and Assessment in Inclusive Schools, as well as graduate courses in literacy leadership and in teaching writing PreK–12. He and his life partner, Carolanne, a professor of nursing at Upstate Medical University in Syracuse, New York, codirect the Knapsack Consulting Group, which provides organizational and professional development for religious, not-for-profit, educational, and health care entities. They have raised five children, ten dogs, nine cats, and four chickens in South Onondaga, New York.

Ayanna Cooper is an independent consultant who specializes in building the capacity of *all* educators who serve English learners. By working closely with districts and state departments of education, she is able to aid in improving outcomes for English learners, their families, and their teachers. Her professional experiences include teaching English as a second language (ESL), instructional coaching, supervising urban ESL teacher candidates, and serving as the K–12 director for an English learner public school program. Ayanna has also worked on various projects and has been an invited speaker for the American Federation of Teachers (AFT) and the National Education Association (NEA). She has an extensive background in teaching courses for both preservice and inservice educators of English learners. Most recently, she has served as the associate program chair for the TESOL International Association 2015 International Convention & English Language Expo in Toronto, Ontario. Ayanna has designed and facilitated professional development nationwide for educators on a number of topics, including use of the World-Class Instructional Design and Assessment (WIDA) ELD Standards and Assessments, differentiated instruction, and interpreting English language proficiency data. She has written articles and blog posts and has served on a number of committees dedicated to teaching and advocating for culturally and linguistically diverse learners. This is her first publication with Corwin.

I dedicate this book to my husband David and children Zoe, Maya, and Carson. I also dedicate this book to teachers who are striving for equitable instruction of all learners.

—Diane Staehr Fenner

My work on this book is dedicated to my family and the love we share and to my friend, Francis Burke.

—Peter Kozik

I dedicate this book to my husband Ronnie, children Ronnie and Breanna Cooper, and to my mother Deborah Wornum. Thank you for your continued support, words of encouragement, and especially your patience. I would also like to dedicate this book in memory of my grandmother Edith E. McClannahan.

—Ayanna Cooper

Introduction

As school districts implement teacher evaluation systems in schools, evaluators and teachers need access to current thinking on evidence-based practices for educating English learners (ELs) and students with disabilities, particularly in general education classrooms. The growing number of ELs and students with disabilities represents a significant percentage of the PreK–12 student population. Taken together, these students' strengths as well as challenges must be considered not only in instruction and assessment but also as an integral part of teacher evaluation systems.

Evaluators and teachers need to understand the complex concepts of culture and second language acquisition as well the principles of universal design for learning and the use of accommodations that might be apparent in classrooms that include these learners. At the same time, evaluators must be aware of the value of collaboration and professional coteaching relationships for these student populations in the teacher evaluation process. Without these central understandings, evaluators cannot adequately evaluate the teaching of diverse learners they witness.

This book, applicable as a companion to any teacher evaluation system, is designed for evaluators, for teachers, and for professional developers at all levels in PreK–12 education and for administrative leadership programs and policymakers who are interested in strengthening the implementation of teacher evaluation systems to include all learners. As the nationwide implementation of teacher evaluation systems continues, the need for this book only increases. Since the book is designed for the full inclusion of *all* learners, the book's practical appeal will ultimately increase quality access to the general education curriculum for ELs and for students with disabilities.

The topic of evaluating teaching in inclusive classrooms for ELs and students with disabilities is presented in a detailed and comprehensive manner and is based on case studies that could be used in any setting. The case study scenarios provide sample conversations from pre- and post-observations as well as descriptions of classroom environments, events and activities, and teaching. The case studies can be used in schools and in undergraduate and graduate programs, as well as by professional developers to describe and discuss the teacher evaluation process in school faculty, team, and grade-level meetings to examine evidence-based practice for reaching and teaching all learners. The book examines the unique strengths and challenges that each group of students presents separately in classrooms but also finds commonality in characteristics shared by effective teachers of both groups of diverse learners.

The book's eight chapters are framed within relevant research and also contain practical applications for teachers as well as evaluators. Many of the chapters contain quotations from evaluators in the field. Chapters 1 through 3 first prepare a solid foundation for recognizing the urgency to effectively teach ELs and students with disabilities so as to provide teachers and evaluators a shared frame of reference. Then, Chapters 4 through 7 highlight areas in which ELs and students with disabilities have faced inequitable education by providing a deeper examination of the four new principles of inclusive teacher evaluation that address each of these areas. Each chapter in Chapters 4 through 7 follows a similar organizational structure to define and apply one principle per chapter. Chapter 8 focuses on embodying the four principles through the coaching of teachers of diverse learners. The following overview of the chapters provides an orientation to the content and structure of the book.

Chapter 1. Need for an Inclusive Teacher Evaluation Framework: This chapter creates a sense of urgency around the need to include ELs and students with special needs in the teacher evaluation process. It provides demographics on both groups of students as well as these students' achievement gaps. It also shares insights into research and current practices in terms of teacher evaluation taking place in the United States today. This chapter concludes with four principles of inclusive teacher evaluation framing successful teacher evaluation systems that empower teachers to become better practitioners for ELs and students with disabilities. These principles are exemplified and woven throughout the remainder of the book.

Chapter 2. Foundations of Education of English Learners: This chapter builds a basic foundation for EL education. It sets the tone for inclusively educating ELs by highlighting relevant legislation that sets a precedent for the effective education of ELs. The chapter also provides a research-based view of second language acquisition as well as current practices for educating ELs in various settings (e.g., dual language, bilingual education, sheltered English immersion, English for speakers of other languages support, etc.). The chapter serves to orient the reader to examples of effective practice in teaching a wide variety of ELs who are in classrooms across the United States.

Chapter 3. Foundations of Education of Students With Disabilities: In this chapter, a brief historical overview of law and regulation regarding students with disabilities is followed by an effort to connect public mandates with evaluation systems for students with disabilities and the argument for inclusive classrooms. Perspectives of students with disabilities are considered, as is literature regarding effective classroom practices for this population of students and the evidence for including all learners, PreK–12. Necessary preconditions for schools and school districts for the successful achievement of students with disabilities are described and examined. Professional development as well as the structures necessary for the success of this population of student are described. Twenty-first-century skills are examined for their impact on the achievement of students with disabilities.

Chapter 4. Principle 1: Committing to Equal Access for All Learners: This chapter focuses on the components of Principle 1. The chapter first underscores the need for this principle, which provides a foundation for inclusive teacher evaluation of all diverse students and also specifically for ELs and students with disabilities. The chapter focuses on the process of using Principle 1 to begin teacher evaluation, describing how and when to incorporate Principle 1 into an inclusive teacher evaluation system. The chapter then provides specific sample "look-fors" for teachers of ELs, for teachers of students with disabilities, and for teachers of both groups of students to support the use of Principle 1. A sample rubric from Rhode Island shows how Principle 1 can be operationalized in an authentic teacher evaluation system. Scenarios follow that highlight dialogues between teachers and evaluators that exemplify how Principle 1 could unfold. Chapter 1 ends with questions that educators can use to reflect on their approach to the elements of advocacy and equity for ELs and students with disabilities that Principle 1 embodies.

Chapter 5. Principle 2: Preparing to Support Diverse Learners: The chapter focuses on Principle 2, beginning with the need for teachers to have dispositions that position them to effectively teach ELs and students with disabilities. Principle 2 is then examined in light of how it can affect the education of ELs and students with disabilities as well as the processes necessary for establishing the principle in the evaluation of educators working with these populations of students. The chapter places an emphasis on what evaluators can expect to see in classes where all students are included, centering on the need for active and language-rich classrooms as well as the development of student-centered strategies. A sample rubric from Rhode Island sheds light on how one state has incorporated some understandings of Principle 2 into its teacher evaluation system. Principle 2 look-fors and sample teacher/evaluator scenarios follow that contribute to support how Principle 2 can be operationalized in the school setting.

Chapter 6. Principle 3: Reflective Teaching Using Evidence-Based Strategies: This chapter focuses on Principle 3 and teachers' levels of skill in using effective strategies with ELs and students with disabilities. The chapter highlights types of classroom strategies for ELs and students with disabilities that might be present and observable by evaluators, including an emphasis on universal design for learning. A series of identifiable look-fors is provided that pertains to teachers of ELs, teachers of students with disabilities, and both groups of students that evaluators can witness in inclusive classrooms. A sample rubric from New York State exemplifies how elements of Principle 3 can be incorporated into an authentic teacher evaluation rubric. Scenarios at the end of the chapter highlight how explicit evidence for Principle 3 can be found in the evaluation process. Reflective questions at the end of the chapter allow evaluators and teachers space to consider the extent to which they incorporate Principle 3 into their teacher evaluation systems.

Chapter 7. Principle 4: Building a Culture of Collaboration and Community: This chapter describes Principle 4 and the need for developing the means to cultivate close connections between all the individuals who know and serve diverse students. The chapter also includes a focus on acquiring greater understanding of professional, collaborative, and community relationships. Regular connections with families of these populations of students are examined as well as the means to full, equitable, and culturally and individually responsive collaboration that includes advocacy for diverse learners. The chapter follows with a set of look-fors that teachers and evaluators can use as evidence when creating strong collaboration and a sense of community in schools to support diverse learners. The chapter then includes a sample rubric from New York State that incorporates tenets of Principle 4. It also contains sample conversations between evaluators and teachers of ELs and students with disabilities to illustrate how Principle 4 can be embodied during evaluation as well as culminating reflective questions.

Chapter 8. Empowering Educators Through Coaching: The final chapter sets the four principles examined in this book in the practical context of implementing, through coaching, teacher evaluation protocols that are inclusive of all learners. The chapter first provides a definition of coaching for teachers of diverse learners as well as the circumstances under which coaching through teacher evaluation protocols can most likely succeed. The chapter then discusses why coaching is needed as a construct within schools and how evaluators can successfully help create higher-performing teachers and more effective classrooms for ELs and students with disabilities. The implications of well-designed and thoughtfully developed coaching strategies for improved student outcomes for ELs and students with disabilities are discussed next. Finally, a series of considerations for evaluators and teachers as part of establishing coaching relationships is provided.

1 Need for an Inclusive Teacher Evaluation Framework

When we look closer at teacher evaluation's impact on English learners, students with disabilities, and students from low socioeconomic backgrounds, it's a dicey state of affairs. These children are usually placed in classrooms with teachers who have the least amount of years in the profession and/or resources.

Mr. C. Martin, Principal

Administrators in PreK–12 public school face daily decisions that directly affect their school communities. The teachers they work with rely on their administrators for leadership and support. The demands of standards, assessments, and curricular needs for diverse learners can be overwhelming for both administrators and teachers. Administrators' knowledge of students in their schools, the needs of those students, and the needs of those responsible to teach them are necessary for students to be academically and socially successful. Evaluators of teachers of diverse learners have the responsibility of not only recognizing the unique needs of diverse learners but also recognizing the strengths and knowledge that the teachers demonstrate in their classrooms. As noted in the opening quotation, if administrators lack this knowledge, then ultimately two of the most vulnerable populations in U.S. schools today—English learners (ELs) and students with disabilities—are most likely not being afforded learning opportunities by teachers who teach them. Teacher evaluation systems must be inclusive of and responsive to the needs of educators who are being evaluated by them. That is, the evaluations must capture the authenticity of diverse learners and their academic needs. This book will call attention to this need to include diverse learners in teacher evaluation systems and include insight as well as considerations for practitioners who work in school communities with diverse learners.

CONTENT OF THIS CHAPTER

This chapter begins with an overview of the phases of teacher evaluation that are referenced throughout the book as well as a definition of "look-fors." It then outlines the areas that provide the sense of urgency that undergirds the book, drawing on diverse student demographics, research, and recent events that support the argument that educators must consider supplementing teacher evaluation systems so that the systems are inclusive of diverse students, especially English learners and students with disabilities.

PHASES OF TEACHER EVALUATION

The focus of inclusive teacher evaluation systems includes a transparent evaluation process. It is necessary for each phase of the evaluation process to be understood by both teacher and evaluator. While student test scores often compose one element of teacher evaluation, the focus of this book is on the process described below. Figure 1.1 outlines the iterative nature of the teacher evaluation process that this book esposes.

The primary goal that frames the evaluation process is for all students to be supported and experience academic as well as social success. For this support of diverse learners to occur, it is just as important that this evaluation process be practiced both formally and informally. If the only time teachers engage in conversations about instruction is during their formal observation, then an important step, building trust, is absent. Without establishing this professional relationship first, formal evaluations will continue to be viewed as stale and scripted teaching for the sake of completing required evaluations versus as learning experiences for both teacher and evaluator. This understanding is imperative if an objective observation is to take place and if both the pre- and post-observation conferences are productive and focused on supporting student achievement for all learners, especially ELs and students with disabilities.

It is important that the teacher feel comfortable and confident during the observation so that questions, suggestions, and feedback during the

Figure 1.1 Teacher Evaluation Process

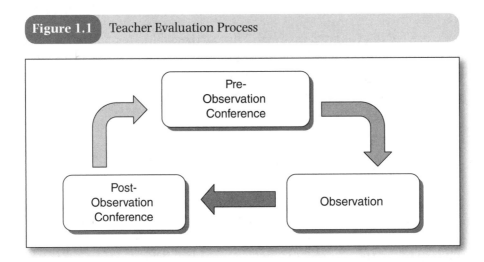

pre- and post-observations can be received. The level of comfort and trust established may manifest themselves during the pre- and post-observation conference, in which evaluators must be viewed as instructional coaches instead of solely as administrators. In addition, teachers and evaluators must be committed to the overall goal of student achievement as the focus of the process of inclusive teacher evaluation. Each phase of evaluation is unique in nature due to its specific purposes and roles of its stakeholders. Table 1.1 outlines each phase of teacher evaluation referenced in this book and the purpose for each phase.

Look-Fors

One crucial element of the teacher evaluation process highlighted in this book is the concept of "look-fors." Look-fors assist teachers and evaluators by providing specific, practical, observable criteria for evaluators to use in the evaluation process so that they can recognize effective teaching. They also give teachers insight into the criteria by which they will be evaluated so that teachers have a deeper understanding of their evaluator's expectations. These examples of effective practice are given so that evaluators have a clearer picture of what types of evidence support the effective instruction of diverse students (Staehr Fenner, Kozik, & Cooper, 2014, p. 8). Look-fors that describe effective teaching of English learners and students will disabilities will differ from look-fors that have been created for other teacher evaluation systems without considering the rich diversity of learners.

In Chapters 4 through 7, tables of look-fors are provided through checklists for evaluators as well as teachers. While sample look-fors are given to support each of the four principles of inclusive teacher evaluation in this book, teachers and evaluators are also encouraged to design

Table 1.1 Phases of Teacher Evaluation and Purpose of Each Phase

Phase of Teacher Evaluation	Purpose of Phase
Pre-observation conference	Goals of the observation are set and agreed upon
	Teacher/evaluator rapport is built
	Students, including their unique strengths and needs, are discussed
	Expectations and questions regarding the observation are discussed
	The evaluation instrument is reviewed together
	Data, as needed, are provided to establish a context for the content, student strengths, and student needs
	The lesson planned to be taught in the formal observation is discussed
Observation	Practitioner-based delivery of instruction occurs
	Evaluator observes and documents teaching performance based on pre-established teacher evaluation criteria or look-fors
	Evaluator collects evidence of teaching practices, including classroom management
	Evaluator documents collaboration, if applicable, with other teachers and/or support personnel
Post-observation conference	Teacher and evaluator discuss and summarize overall evaluation
	Teacher and evaluator ask and answer clarifying questions from observation
	Notes from evaluation, if available, are shared and discussed
	Formal write-up of observation may be signed by both parties
	Additional observations, if necessary or requested, are scheduled

their own-look fors that capture what effective teaching looks like for diverse students in their specific context.

NATIONWIDE DIVERSE STUDENT POPULATIONS

As U.S. schools increase in their diversity, teacher evaluation systems must recognize the unique strengths as well as considerable challenges such student populations bring with them. To adapt teacher evaluation systems so that they take diverse learners into consideration, it is first necessary to place the numbers of the nation's diverse populations into context. Table 1.2 provides pertinent demographic information about ELs

Table 1.2 Diverse Student Populations

Diverse Student Populations	
English Learners	**Students With Disabilities**
• ELs make up 9% of all preK–12 students enrolled in U.S. schools.[a] • States with the largest EL populations are California, Texas, Florida, New York, and Illinois. • The majority of ELs were born in the United States. • Spanish is the predominant language spoken by ELs in the United States, followed by Chinese, Vietnamese, Arabic, and Hmong.	• There are almost 6.5 million students with disabilities in the United States, a 26% increase since 1990. • Since 2001, there has been a 77% increase in the number of students with autism. • Nationwide in 2011, 80% of students in all disability categories were educated for more than half the school day in general education classrooms. • Some ELs are also students with disabilities

Source: Adapted from Staehr Fenner, Kozik, and Cooper (2014).

a. See EDFacts Consolidated State Performance Report, 2011–12 at www2.ed.gov/ad mins/lead/account/consolidated/index.html.

and students with disabilities populations. This information is helpful about educators to have a better understanding of the landscape of diverse learners. The information presented is at the nationwide level, but districts and states may differ in terms of their diverse student populations.

CALL FOR AN INCLUSIVE TEACHER EVALUATION FRAMEWORK

This book will lead to the better understanding of all students, not only ELs and students with disabilities. The rhetoric of the book is really about changing the entire dynamic in classrooms; there is not a classroom in the country that is not diverse in some way. This book will help make leadership programs, evaluation programs, and teacher preparation programs think about the teacher evaluation process differently. When teachers and evaluators are held accountable for all students, they will be more likely to change their practices. They will also be more in touch for how to make their classrooms and schools better places for all learners.

Teacher evaluation has been given a high priority in federal policy. For example, the Race to the Top program demands multiple ways of measuring teacher performance, with an emphasis on student academic growth (U.S. Department of Education, 2009). In addition, states had to demonstrate a federally approved plan for teacher evaluation as one criterion to receive a waiver from No Child Left Behind provisions. Eighteen states and the District of Columbia received Race to the Top funding, and 43 states and the District of Columbia were approved for No Child Left Behind waivers; these states are in different phases of implementing their teacher evaluation systems (Whitehurst, Chingos, & Lindquist, 2014). Currently, teacher observations and student test scores comprise the primary tools for measuring teacher quality (Jones, Buzick, & Turkan, 2013). Further, while the impact of teacher evaluation on teachers' careers is of great significance, schools, districts, and states are in need of professional development necessary to integrate teacher evaluations into educators' professional growth (Culver & Hayes, 2014).

Teacher evaluation systems vary from state to state and place varying priorities and weight on different measures such as student growth on state assessments (or value-added scores) and/or student test scores and classroom observations of teachers. While recognizing that there are other components to teacher evaluation, this book focuses solely on the teacher observation component of teacher evaluation systems. The book aims to increase the validity of classroom observations for those educators who work with those diverse learners who are often left out of policy decisions—namely, ELs and students with disabilities. The book is not prescriptive in telling readers how to word their teacher observation rubrics to make them more inclusive of all learners. Instead, the book provides considerations for those interested in equity for diverse learners to use as conversation starters in order to make changes that will benefit students as well as their teachers.

BIAS IN TEACHER EVALUATION OF DIVERSE LEARNERS

The need for more inclusive teacher evaluation practices has recently come to the forefront. For example, a new study (Whitehurst et al., 2014) found that bias in teacher observation surfaces when teachers are assigned more diverse students—such as ELs, students with disabilities, and/or students living in poverty. Under current teacher observation system rubrics that have not taken ELs' and students with disabilities' unique characteristics into consideration, those teachers who were not working with top-performing students tended to receive lower ratings than teachers who were working with students who were higher academic achievers. The researchers concluded that bias in the observation system significantly affects evaluators' decisions on teachers' performance. When evaluators witness a teacher working with higher-achieving students, they tend to judge the teacher as more effective than that same teacher would be with lower-achieving students. Nine percent of teachers working with lowest-achieving students were identified as top performing in contrast with 37% of teachers with highest-achieving students who were evaluated as top performers.

Because of the way in which the most popular teacher observation rubrics are constructed, the unique strategies teachers must use to support diverse learners are not specified. For example, the Danielson (2011) and Marzano (2011) frameworks are research based, move the field of teacher evaluation forward, and have been adopted by numerous states and districts. Despite the traction these frameworks have gained, these frameworks fall short in one noteworthy area: The ability of all teachers to effectively teach diverse student populations of ELs and students with disabilities receives minimal focus (Jones et al., 2013). The limited extent to which current teacher evaluation systems address ELs and students with disabilities is a concern for the validity of evaluation systems, failing to present a complete picture of instruction and of student equity. In addition, the Whitehurst et al., study (2014) would contend that teachers not working with high-achieving students (who are typically not ELs or students with disabilities) who are observed through these frameworks would tend to be rated lower than teachers working with high achievers. If teacher evaluation frameworks become more inclusive of diverse learners, teachers might be better positioned to be recognized for their skills in working with these students.

Teacher evaluation protocols should reflect the rich variety of students that teachers encounter in classrooms throughout the country on a daily basis. However, the language of most evaluation instruments fails to acknowledge the efforts of teachers to reach and teach diverse learners such as ELs and students with disabilities, let alone the growth and contributions that these students can make to their classrooms. This book focuses on trying to ensure that teachers are acknowledged and evaluated for these valiant efforts through teacher evaluation systems that are inclusive of all learners.

The framework presented in this book provides an additional resource that can be used in those districts and states who have already committed to such teacher evaluation frameworks (or adaptations thereof) as the Danielson or Marzano frameworks. The four principles for inclusive teacher evaluation of *all* students, defined and explained later in this chapter, complement the domains of the two preexisting frameworks as described in the crosswalk in Table 1.3.

RECOGNIZING DIVERSE STUDENTS' STRENGTHS AND CHANGING EDUCATORS' DISPOSITIONS

There are many truisms about teaching that carry varying degrees of validity. One truism by which policymakers seem currently to abide

Table 1.3	Four Principles for Inclusive Teacher Evaluation's Crosswalk With Danielson and Marzano Domains

Principle Number	Principle for Inclusive Teacher Evaluation	Danielson Domain	Marzano Domain
1	Committing to equal access for all learners	Planning and preparation	Classroom practices and strategies
2	Preparing to support diverse learners	The classroom environment	Planning and preparing
3	Reflective teaching using evidence-based strategies	Instruction	Reflecting on teaching
4	Building a culture of collaboration and community	Professional responsibilities	Collegiality and professionalism

is this: Change the test and you change the teaching. This observation holds true in the efforts to implement College- and Career-Ready Standards (including the Common Core State Standards) and the series of changes underway to the standardized tests that are being implemented across the nation. The same holds true for teacher evaluation systems. If teachers—general educators, special educators, and English for speakers of other languages (ESOL) teachers alike—are evaluated using similar detailed means that challenge them to the highest levels of differentiation using evidence-based practice in the planning, implementation, and evaluation of their lessons, their teaching and student achievement results can likely improve. At the same time, teacher performance can be seen at different moments and from different angles designed to capture both a teacher's strengths and areas of needed improvement (Kane, 2012; Kane & Cantrell, 2012; Marshall, 2012; Stronge, Ward, Tucker, & Hindman, 2007).

As is true for every important change, the prospect of evaluating teachers of *all* students begins with a change in outlook and in dispositions. The first step to ensuring this important change of dedicating the system to teaching all students needs to be taken by administrators and evaluators of teaching. Of all potential variables in schools, fundamentally sound teaching has been shown to affect student success the most significantly (Kane, 2012; Kane, Taylor, Tyler, & Wooten, 2011). Setting the tone to create an environment in which sound teaching can flourish in different classrooms is the role of the administrator as instructional leader. Knowing, recognizing, acknowledging, and celebrating sound teaching practice in the service of all students is paramount if ELs and students with disabilities[1] are finally to find a place at society's table.

For example, the mind-set cultivated in some schools of burying or obviating the testing results for students with disabilities in an effort to generate more favorable consequences must stop. Policymakers can assist by continuing to lift the consequences associated with adequate yearly progress (AYP). At the same time, teachers who are challenged by the diversity that ELs and students with disabilities represent in their classrooms need to be completely supported in their efforts by knowledgeable and forthright administrators who can clearly recognize the strengths that these students bring as well as focus on the challenges that also come with teaching them. This administrative focus can serve as a springboard to conversations about how ELs and students with disabilities can achieve and prosper within every single school.

VULNERABLE POPULATIONS AND TEACHER EVALUATION

The great sense of urgency to create a supplement to teacher evaluation frameworks that acknowledges the strengths and challenges presented by ELs and students with disabilities comes at a critical time. Not only do these students face cultural obstacles to becoming fully privileged and participating members of society, but the prognosis for their success in much of the American educational system remains dim if changes aren't made. These two populations of students are often considered an afterthought—if they are considered at all—when important policy decisions such as teacher evaluations are being made and are therefore two of the most vulnerable student populations whose voices often remain unheard. This book seeks to give these students a stronger voice by considering how their unique circumstances play out in teacher evaluation.

The increasing number of ELs belie the amount of sway they have in U.S. classrooms. In 2011–2012, there were an estimated 4.1 million ELs or 9.1% of the PreK–12 population across the United States (National Center for Education Statistics, 2014). After 2014, ELs constitute a growing presence across the United States. Between 2002 and 2003 and 2011 and 2012, the percentage of ELs in public schools increased in all but 10 states. For example, seven states experienced more than 100% growth in their PreK–12 EL populations between the 2004 and 2005 and 2011 and 2012 school years. Although ELs' numbers are growing, their unique challenges are often not considered in policy decisions. Also, ELs and their families often face discrimination due to their growing English skills and their race or ethnicity. Further, some ELs face acute challenges due to their immigration status.

In U.S. culture, people with disabilities tend to be among the least visible of any subpopulation of individuals. That is to say, they tend to have less privilege in society and garner the least amount of social capital compared with other groups, even some historically underrepresented and critically vulnerable populations. The voices of people with disabilities are routinely either unsought or ignored (Mooney, 2007). To complicate their status, people with disabilities are often misunderstood, placated, pitied, or disparaged. The very language of the culture—that is, questions such as, "Are you blind?" and derogations such as *imbecile* and *retard*—reinforces negative connotations of disability (Valle & Connor, 2011).

While ELs and students with disabilities are regarded as two distinct groups of students in this book, there is also a third category of students who should also be considered. Dually identified ELs are ELs who have been identified as needing special education services. According to Watkins and Liu (2013), more than 11% of ELs were identified as also receiving some type of special education services. Within that national average, great variations exist depending on the demographics of school districts in terms of the number of dually identified ELs as well as the ethnic origin of the students. For example, in 2003, in districts that educated more than 100 ELs, an average of 9% of students were dually identified. However, in districts with fewer than 99 ELs, nearly 16% of ELs were dually identified (Zehler et al., 2003).

ESOL AS A SERVICE

In addition to being aware of the numbers and diversity of ELs and students with disabilities, it is also important to recognize that instruction for ELs and students with disabilities represents a service, not a "placement." The education of ELs has typically operated from a deficit model, focusing primarily on these students' lack of English and absence of knowledge of U.S. culture. ELs are a heterogeneous mix of students with different literacies, knowledge bases, school experiences, and levels of English proficiency. Sometimes parents of ELs sense a stigma with their children being eligible for ESOL support and consequently opt out of their children receiving ESOL services. In essence, these parents see ESOL support as a placement, not an enriching service to support their children's academic success. Many ELs are taught by being pulled out of content classes to receive ESOL instruction, missing out on opportunities to have access to rich content experiences that their fluent English peers take part in. Many schools have not yet embraced coteaching, dual-language instruction, or sheltered instruction for varying reasons as a way to teach ELs content and academic language simultaneously.

Further, the classes into which an EL is placed serve as a greater predictor of the student's academic outcomes than that student's level of English language proficiency (Callahan, 2005). This finding underscores the need to provide ELs access to challenging academic content while supporting their linguistic development. Although the type of classes they take tends to predict ELs' academic outcome, high schools tend to track ELs into remedial literacy and mathematics courses and lower-level academic courses (Gándara, Rumberger, Maxwell-Jolly, & Callahan, 2003; Parrish et al., 2006). This tracking of ELs takes place despite numerous research findings that point to the deleterious effects of such practices for this population of students (Callahan, 2005; Swail, Cabrera, Lee, & Williams, 2005).

Along with primarily being seen for what they lack and tracked into lower-level courses, researchers acknowledge that EL students' achievement scores tend to be lower than those of non-EL students (Abedi, 2002; Fry, 2008). An EL's achievement and solid academic background in the first language is the strongest predictor of future success in English (Thomas & Collier, 2002). In addition, there is also a gap between EL and non-EL high school completion rates as well as attainment of postsecondary degrees (Kao & Thompson, 2003; National Center for Public Policy and Higher Education, 2005; Reardon & Galindo, 2009).

Many theories exist to explain these gaps and in turn the EL deficit model. One reason is the perceived lack of EL parental involvement in their children's education. Research shows that parental involvement positively affects student achievement (Ferguson, 2008). However, parents, families, and caregivers of ELs tend to participate in their children's education in less obvious and visible ways than parents of non-ELs. While it may appear that EL families and caregivers participate in fewer school events, factors that tend to inhibit more visible EL familial involvement include English language proficiency of families, parents' educational level, differences between school culture and parents' home culture, and logistical challenges such as securing child care, finding transportation, and taking time off from work (Arias & Morillo-Campbell, 2008; Tinkler, 2002). In fact, although EL parents tend to place a high value on their children's education, they might find it very difficult to relate to their children's U.S. school experience or understand how to help their children succeed in the U.S. school environment (Suarez-Orozco, Suarez-Orozco, & Doucet, 2004).

SPECIAL EDUCATION AS A SERVICE

In the case of special education, educators have learned to think of this service as a geographic location, dating back to the era of institutionalization and completely segregated classrooms within schools when in fact it has always been defined as a series of services. Although it is the special education services themselves for which parents advocate, sometimes to the point of exhaustion, the system of schooling often leaves few options for families but to undertake the provision of those services in separate settings. Educators neglect at their peril and our students' peril the findings of *PARC v. Commonwealth of Pennsylvania* (1972), a precursor to the Individuals with Disabilities Education Act, which stated unequivocally that general education classrooms were the environments of choice for students with disabilities. It seems all special educators might begin every committee on special education (CSE) meeting, no matter the educational history or previous placement, assuming that general education is the environment of choice for the student with disabilities. The mobility of services, the ubiquity of assistive technology, the practice of coteaching, and the incorporation of *universal design for learning*, or UDL (see Chapter 3; also see Rose & Meyer, 2002) mean that students with disabilities can be more likely educated alongside their nondisabled peers in the same classrooms.

ASSESSMENT OF DIVERSE LEARNERS

Student test scores often form one prominent component of teacher evaluation systems. Yet ELs and students with disabilities tend to score at lower levels on content assessments than their English-proficient or nondisabled peers. Even though most ELs are required to take part in summative content assessments, research suggests that ELs' scores on summative academic content assessments in English are not always representative of these students' true content skills and knowledge. Research has clearly and consistently demonstrated that content assessments designed primarily with native English speakers in mind may not yield valid and reliable results for ELs (Abedi, 2006). Because of this lack of reliability and validity, many experts caution that practitioners and policymakers interpret ELs' content assessment scores carefully, especially when using these content scores to make language support placement or EL redesignation/exit decisions (Linquanti, 2001; Ragan & Lesaux, 2006). For these reasons, Abedi and Dietel (2004) claim that the use of multiple assessment measures is the only way to combat issues that surround accountability of ELs. In short, educators should not use one sole assessment measure to make high-stakes decisions that affect ELs' instruction and ultimately ability to graduate.

Students with disabilities, as part of an educational system that has tilted further and further toward standardized measures of achievement and success, have continued to find themselves disenfranchised from the system. Historically, standardized tests have been designed without the population of students with disabilities in mind (Lai & Berkeley, 2012; Thurlow, Lazarus, Thompson, & Morse, 2005). The development of the Common Core State Standards and the rollout of norm-referenced tests for these standards have, by and large, failed to acknowledge and take into account the uniqueness that the population of students with disabilities represents. Although proposed computerized access for these examinations may make the use of certain accommodations more dependable, the connection between what is taught and what is tested can remain tenuous at best. Since the Common Core only represents a set of standards, the guesswork for teachers of providing a curriculum that will, in actuality, be the basis for commercial test specifications makes successful outcomes for students with disabilities practically impossible.

The situation is confused by the fact that norm-referenced tests compare students in the aggregate. The students compared have drastically different access to quality educational opportunities depending on any school's geographic location, its levels of poverty, the values and attitudes of its teachers and administrators, and the backgrounds of its students (Adamson & Darling-Hammond, 2012; Kenyatta, 2012; Madrid, 2011). The high-stakes decisions that depend on norm-referenced tests, in some states up to 50% of a teachers' professional profile, make it less likely that the students who face barriers to learning will be represented in any aggregate. In 2009, 70% of all schools that failed to make AYP failed because of the performance of students with disabilities. Because of high-stakes testing, administrators may ensure that students with disabilities are more often excluded from what is taught and tested in schools (Bacon & Ferri, 2013). Against this backdrop of system intransigence, many schools in the United States have opted not to include students with disabilities in their aggregate scores. It is no wonder that our country may be seeing substantial backsliding in the education of students with disabilities.

ACHIEVEMENT AND GRADUATION GAP

Both ELs and students with disabilities continue to significantly lag behind their non-EL and nondisabled peers when it comes to academic achievement and graduation rates. As the U.S. population ages, immigrants and their children will compose much of the U.S. labor force growth during the next few decades. According to Batalova, Gelatt, and Lowell (2006), nearly one in five U.S. workers will be an immigrant by the year 2030. For the United States to be a serious contender in such a global economy, the country will need highly skilled workers. Creating highly skilled workers begins with providing all the nation's students—including ELs—a solid educational foundation in grades PreK–12. Beyond creating a highly skilled workforce, it is our nation's legal as well as moral obligation to educate all learners, regardless of their or their parents' county of origin.

Data from the 2011–2012 academic year paint a stark disparity between states' graduation rates of ELs and those of non-ELs. Preliminary data released by the U.S. Department of Education (2014) showed that 58% of ELs graduated in Texas, compared to 86% of non-ELs. California's ELs graduated at a rate of 62%, compared with 78% of non-ELs. In Florida, 57% of ELs graduated as compared to 75% of all students. In New York State, 44% of ELs graduated while 77% of all students completed their high school education. Finally, Arizona reported the lowest EL graduation rate of all the states, with 24% of ELs in Arizona graduating from high school in 4 years as compared with 76% of all students.

Some researchers believe ELs' low graduation rates and low rates of academic achievement overall are in place because the U.S. educational system was designed for the mainstream, middle-class native-English-speaking students and education policies have not been appropriately adapted (Bowman-Perrott, Herrera, & Murry, 2010; Houseman & Martinez, 2002). Such conceptualization that excludes ELs also seems to be the case for teacher evaluation policies.

Although in some states, students with disabilities have made gains, generally they lag behind their nondisabled peers in completion rates and in the quality of their educational outcomes overall (National Drop-Out Prevention Center for Students with Disabilities, 2013). In fact, for high school graduation rates, 26 of 47 states reporting (81%) experienced "slippage" from the year before (2010) in the percentage of students with disabilities graduating high school (National Drop-Out Prevention Center for Students with Disabilities, 2013). The mean completion rate for those states reporting reveals an overall national graduation rate for students with disabilities of 56.6%. In analyzing the dropout rates of students with disabilities, 28 of 43 states reporting (65%) documented "slippage" compared to the previous year (2010), and 22 states reported an actual increase in dropout rates for the period. The overall dropout rate for students with disabilities, depending on the calculation method used, ranged anywhere from a mean of 10.8% to a mean of 22% (National Drop-Out Prevention Center for Students with Disabilities, 2013).

COLLEGE AND CAREERS FOR
ELs AND STUDENTS WITH DISABILITIES

To a country focused on competing successfully in a global economy, the tendency toward underrepresentation of ELs and students with disabilities in college and careers represents a dire loss of human capital that cannot be overlooked. In the case of ELs, these students are frequently the first in their family to attend college (American Youth Policy Forum, 2009). A report by the Pew Research Center (Fry & Taylor, 2013) shows that in 2012 69% of Latino[2] high school graduates pursued higher education compared with 67% of White graduates. However, while those figures are encouraging, Latinos are still less likely than Whites to actually complete a bachelor's degree. These statistics point to the need for ELs to have access to rigorous coursework provided by teachers who are adept at modifying instruction based on ELs' strengths and needs, academic support throughout their PreK–12 careers, guidance in the college application process, support with academic assessments, and information about college financial aid opportunities (Robertson & Lafond, 2008). These extra supports are necessary to help level the playing field for ELs who are first-generation college applicants and for their families, who are most likely unfamiliar with the U.S. college application process. Beyond these supports at the PreK–12 level, assistance is also needed to help ELs obtain a college degree once they have begun a postsecondary program.

Similarly, low high school completion rates affect workers with disabilities, who are often "older, work fewer hours, and are more likely to be single and less likely to have a college degree. They are still disproportionately represented in low-growth, low-wage occupations" (Wonacott, 2003, p. 3). Studies have also shown that people with disabilities are disproportionately represented among prison populations (Harlow, 2003). In addition, the disproportional representation of people of color and people in poverty in prisons reflects their disproportionate numbers in special education programs (Berliner, 2006; Sherwin & Schmidt, 2003; Winters, 1997). As much as these realities exist, an increasing number of students with disabilities, particularly intellectual disabilities, avail themselves of postsecondary education opportunities. Martinez, Conroy, and Cerreto (2012) report that parents of these students who have been schooled in inclusive settings are more likely to desire college for their children.

IMPACT OF TEACHER EVALUATION ON TEACHER PREPARATION

ELs as well as students with disabilities are often taught by general education and content teachers who have not been afforded the type and amount of training to properly prepare them to effectively teach these unique populations. In addition, widely adopted teacher evaluation systems seem to have been designed with White, middle-class, nondisabled, native-English-speaking students in mind. If teacher evaluation systems are not inclusive of ELs and students with disabilities, then there is no immediate impetus for teacher preparation programs to also consider and prepare teachers for the unique nature of educating these students.

The disconnect between the realities of today's classrooms and antiquated teacher evaluation systems ensures that general education teachers are not held accountable for teaching to today's diverse student populations. In turn, general education teachers are not often provided the training they need to engage effectively with these diverse learners to support their academic growth and potential. As a result, ELs and students with disabilities will remain on the sidelines until teacher evaluation systems thoughtfully ensure that they are included.

Teacher Preparedness for Diverse Learners

The field of teacher education has been criticized for not preparing teachers for the needs of diverse learners. Although the methodology of the study has been critiqued, the National Council on Teacher Quality (NCTQ) (2014) teacher preparation review affirmed the need to increase teacher capacity to serve ELs and students with disabilities. The report ranked teacher preparation programs by 19 standards, which were used to evaluate teacher preparation programs within institutions. One standard addressed the preparation of elementary teacher candidates to teach reading to ELs. This standard noted whether elementary teacher candidates are taught any strategies for teaching reading to students for whom English is an additional language. Another standard addressed the degree to which special education programs' content preparation aligned with state student learning standards in the grades candidates became certified (NCTQ, 2014).

From the 665 elementary programs reviewed for English learner content, the study found that 76% of the programs did not have literacy coursework that adequately addressed strategies to prepare teacher for English language learners (NCTQ, 2014, p. 38). Subsequently, the 45 programs offering special education at the elementary or secondary level showed 78% required little or no coverage of the content spanning the curriculum for which the candidate would be certified to teach. Programs offering PreK–12 special education showed 98% of the programs required little or no coverage of the content spanning the curriculum for which the candidate would be certified to teach. These data substantiate the need for more high-quality preservice teacher preparation for both teachers of ELs and teachers of students with disabilities.

The most recent national policy review shows that only 20 states require that all teachers have some type of training in working with ELs. Furthermore, the breadth, depth, and quality of this training varies widely both across and within states (Ballantyne, Sanderman, & Levy, 2008). The growing linguistically and culturally diverse student population in PreK–12 U.S. schools is taught by a mostly monolingual English-speaking teaching staff (de Jong & Harper, 2008). Despite the necessity for all teachers to teach challenging academic content and academic language simultaneously to ELs, most ELs still spend the majority of their school days with content area teachers who are not properly trained in working with them (Ballantyne et al., 2008). However, some states are beginning to see the value in training all teachers to work with ELs. For example, in Massachusetts, the state Board of Elementary and Secondary Education adopted new regulations[3] in June 2012 that include a requirement that all incumbent core academic teachers of ELs earn a Sheltered English Immersion (SEI) Teacher Endorsement by July 1, 2016.

In addition, school administrators also often find themselves unprepared to lead their teachers to teach ELs. The principal's role is critical in strengthening a positive school culture, which includes espousing the values, beliefs, and norms that characterize the school (Deal & Peterson, 2009). In strengthening a school culture that supports high achievement for all ELs, shared beliefs at the school level include the benefits of multilingualism, an appreciation of ELs' culture, and the need to overcome stereotypes and a deficit paradigm in order to see the strengths that ELs bring. The principal influences this culture in serving as a key spokesperson for the school's embrace of ELs, as an evaluator of effective practices that are inclusive of ELs, and as a model of commitment to student success (Alford & Niño, 2011).

Teacher preparedness to instruct students with disabilities also has an effect on decisions these students' parents make in terms of the best setting available for their children. Some parents of students with disabilities decide that segregated settings are preferable for their children (Palmer, Fuller, Aurora, & Nelson, 2001). This is not because they love their children or yearn for their children's success any less. It is often because they recognize that the culture, where disabilities are invisible and belittled, and the system, where individual uniqueness is often a liability and cause for concern, may not offer the care and supports necessary for their children to thrive. Some parents of students with disabilities do not feel as though their children are understood or welcome in school settings (Bulgren, 2002; Palmer et al., 2001). Also, parents recognize that their students may fare better in their education with the individualized and closely supported environment that a segregated setting can represent.

The promise offered by fully inclusive classrooms—well designed, implemented, and supported—seems as though it may point in a direction where all students can be given the opportunity to work to a fuller potential (Rea, McLaughlin, & Walther-Thomas, 2002). Unfortunately, *inclusion* has many definitions and takes many forms in the culture of schooling. For the purposes of this book, inclusion is defined as an educational philosophy for structuring schools so that all students are educated together in general education classrooms (Salend, 2011).

In spite of this straightforward definition, inconsistencies in definition and of implementation can reify a two-tier system where students with disabilities fail to advance because of the perception of their own lack of ability or effort. This results in their continued segregation from the mainstream for all or part of their school day. Many teachers look to their own practice first when their students struggle to succeed; however, some teachers find plenty to blame outside their classrooms, including administrators, parents, and physical, emotional, or social circumstances of their students over which they have little or no control. Tragically, inclusion has often been implemented in schools in a haphazard fashion without the professional development and administrative support necessary to ensure a quality program. Once the implementation of inclusion goes poorly, teachers and administrators tend to cling to the notion that full inclusion is an impossibility and may never be attained.[4]

GENESIS OF THE FOUR PRINCIPLES FOR INCLUSIVE TEACHER EVALUATION

Given the complexity of the issues involved in educating ELs and students with disabilities, a new conversation regarding teacher evaluation is needed that gives voice to diverse student populations and presents a framework for the skills necessary to teach them as well as be evaluated on these skills. To address the need to include *all* students in teacher evaluation systems, we developed our first version of the four principles for inclusive teacher evaluation framework through our partnership with American Federation of Teachers (AFT). In this project, we collaborated with five school districts each in New York and Rhode Island to develop and pilot inclusive teacher evaluation practices. This work was guided by the first version of four evidence-based principles in the evaluation of teachers focused on the inclusion of all learners in general education classrooms (August, Salend, Staehr Fenner, & Kozik, 2012).

We have further refined the four principles to support successful inclusive practice: (1) committing to equal access for all learners, (2) preparing to support diverse learners, (3) reflective teaching using evidence-based strategies, and (4) building a culture of collaboration and community (Staehr Fenner, Kozik, & Cooper, 2014). For each principle, we explain the principle and provide a rationale for its inclusion for ELs and students with disabilities.

DEFINING THE FOUR PRINCIPLES
FOR INCLUSIVE TEACHER EVALUATION

The four principles that create the framework for this book represent essential understandings, beginning with educator dispositions, with which all educators can better address the needs of *all* students. The principles are applicable in separate as well as inclusive settings, although their purpose is to promote equal and powerful access for all students, including ELs and students with disabilities, to the general education curriculum. Table 1.4 provides a definition of each principle.

PRINCIPLE 1: COMMITTING
TO EQUAL ACCESS FOR ALL LEARNERS

The first principle, *committing to equal access for all learners*, provides the foundation for the three other principles. It represents an acknowledgment and an understanding that the laws governing ELs and students with disabilities in educational settings favors the individual over the institution.

Principle 1 maintains the importance of all teachers (e.g., general educators, special educators, paraprofessionals, and related service providers, as well as ESOL or bilingual teachers) adhering to the laws and to the precedents set in numerous court decisions regarding full and equal access to public education for all students. (See Chapter 2 for more information on laws and court decisions affecting ELs.) Pre-observation conferences with classroom teachers should include conversations about full access and the adaptations for unique learners an observer can expect to see. The teacher should be able to clearly articulate the needs of his or her students and how those needs are being met in the classroom. Conversations should also include the theoretical and evidence-based practices for including all students that are part of the lesson's plan.

The process for evaluating teachers' preparation for classrooms that include ELs and students with disabilities focuses on teacher planning and practices as the primary evidence of a distinguished performance. During pre-observation conferences, in addition to explanations of content knowledge and the ability to integrate subject areas in meaningful ways, evaluators can expect teachers to articulate plans to meet the needs of each individual student, particularly ELs and students with disabilities. As teachers describe the lesson that evaluators will observe, evaluators can gauge the degree to which student engagement, multiple means of representation of skills and content through scaffolds and supports, and varied assessment strategies are present within the lesson.

| Table 1.4 | Four Inclusive Teacher Evaluation Principles and Definitions |

Principle Number	Inclusive Teacher Evaluation Principle	Definition of Principle
1	Committing to equal access for all learners	Educators are aware of and adhere to the laws and to the precedents set in numerous court decisions regarding full and equal access to public education for all students. Educators describe diverse learners' full access to the curriculum and the adaptations for unique learners an observer can expect to see so that all students are included in learning.
2	Preparing to support diverse learners	Educators demonstrate their knowledge of individual student backgrounds as well as the strengths and advantages student diversity brings. They articulate rationales for using appropriate instructional strategies to support diverse learners so that every student will be treated as a valued individual capable of learning.
3	Reflective teaching using evidence-based strategies	Educators' classroom instruction embodies the tenets of universal design for learning. Instruction is individualized, student centered, varied, appropriately challenging, standards based, and grounded in evidence-based practice. Educators build instruction with their diverse students' unique strengths, challenges, backgrounds, experiences, and needs in mind.
4	Building a culture of collaboration and community	Educators focus on professional relationships and connections to culture and community in the service of all students. They work toward establishing a community that is based on collaboration among educators, students, caregivers, families, neighbors, and other relevant groups. They work cooperatively, communicate regularly, and share resources, responsibilities, skills, decisions, and advocacy.

Teachers of ELs must plan and prepare for their students based upon each student's unique background. *All* teachers must be simultaneous teachers of content as well as academic language in order for ELs to succeed academically. All teachers must demonstrate understanding of content as well as English language development standards, the curriculum, and assessments for content and language standards. Knowing information such as whether a student is literate in his or her first language, prior schooling information, and his or her current level of English language proficiency is fundamental to being an effective teacher of ELs. During pre-observation meetings, teachers can articulate which teaching strategies and resources are most appropriate for their ELs and indicate these strategies to the evaluators who will be observing them. To articulate this information to the observer, the teacher must have in-depth knowledge of language development, standards, and assessments. It is equally as important for the evaluator to have knowledge of the same topics— language development, standards, and assessments for ELs—in order to recognize effective teaching of ELs.

For students with disabilities, a multifactored and unbiased identification protocol, the development of an individualized education plan (IEP), and the reassertion of due process rights for the individual and for the family clearly direct schools and school systems to consider the individual student first and above all else when making educational decisions (Heyward, 2009). Within the context of these other tenets, the notion of least restrictive environment (LRE) in the Individuals with Disabilities Education Act and subsequent clarifications becomes less about the appropriateness of the setting from an institutional perspective and more about the delivery of appropriate services for the individual.

Therefore, the first principle of inclusive teacher evaluation hinges on adequate services and supports being provided for students with disabilities for them to succeed in any classroom. This may require subtle yet powerful shifts in how teachers plan, implement, and assess instruction and how evaluators understand and interpret these shifts. Clearly understanding teachers' perspectives on the inclusion of students with disabilities and on their knowledge of the law and how the law translates into classroom practice is critical for the evaluator under this principle.

The task for evaluators under this first principle becomes discerning how and how much students with disabilities are provided meaningful access to the general education classroom. Decisions regarding whether or not some students with disabilities are educated alongside their nondisabled peers are made by a CSE composed of representatives from the school community. However, once a decision is reached to educate a student through access to the general education curriculum and through full inclusion with his or her nondisabled peers, the evaluation protocol used by the school needs to reflect the circumstances of educating the student with those services.

In the same way, the evaluator must engage in the process fully cognizant of the levels and the types of support that the school and the school district are able and willing to provide students with disabilities in general education classrooms. The circumstances under which students are educated need to be explicitly addressed during the evaluation process, ideally within pre- and post-observation conversations. Evaluators can do much to build trust in themselves and in the school and district process by being fully aware of the circumstances and levels and types of support afforded by their institution. For example, teachers cannot be evaluated on how well they educate students with certain low incidence disabilities if those students do not have access to the most current assistive technologies as prescribed by the CSE. Further, evaluators should be conversant in the evidence-based practices on which their teachers may depend for educating students with disabilities. This book provides support for both these strands of evaluator understanding.

By the same measure, evaluators need to be clear about the level and types of support provided by their institutions to teachers, both general and special educators, in the service of students with disabilities. If, for example, all adult partners in a classroom are not given access to student IEPs as part of a recognized school protocol, the ability to fully include students with disabilities and have them achieve is hindered. Likewise, the quality and timeliness of professional development opportunities should be part of the conversations teachers and evaluators have regarding educating these students. Therefore, the evaluation process becomes truly educative, capitalizing on the thinking generated during pre- and post-observation conferences and through the observations about improving practice. This book supports these understandings.

PRINCIPLE 2: PREPARING TO SUPPORT DIVERSE LEARNERS

The second principle, *preparing to support diverse learners*, builds on the foundation of access to ground teacher evaluation in a thorough understanding of the students for whom teachers are responsible. This principle is designed to help evaluators and teachers view teacher performance through several lenses, focusing on both an understanding of individual students and the development and implementation of supportive classroom environments. In assessing teachers' ability to manage these considerations, evaluators focus on the variety of indicators to comprehend how well teachers recognize and use the strengths of their diverse students. At the same time, evaluators appraise the quality of the classroom in regard to its inclusiveness from the perspectives of its social connectedness and communication, its clarity of expectation, its routine and procedures, and the value it apportions to its individuals.

This principle focuses educators' attention on the individualization of instruction and on planning teaching strategies that reflect the tenets of UDL (Rose & Meyer, 2002). The foci of the observation as well as the pre- and post-observation conferences should be on teachers' articulating and exhibiting the multiple ways that different students will be engaged in the lesson, how the information provided during the lesson will be represented, and how students will express the learning that they have achieved.

The design of physical space and its impact on student comfort and responsibility as well as on student interaction (peer to peer and student to professional) are also components of this principle. This principle also focuses on pre- and post-observation conferences and *look-fors* during observation. The look-fors may include students' support for one another, flexible and variable grouping schemes, a culture of warmth and respect, and a classroom that is language rich, thought provoking, and comfortably stimulating. Teachers of diverse students should explain how their classroom's physical space enhances, not limits, students' opportunities to participate in the classroom.

For ELs, it is important that their teachers be able to articulate how their ELs' culture and previous educational experiences, if applicable, can affect how they interact with students and teachers. Teachers of ELs should describe high expectations for their students that demonstrate an understanding of how ELs' English language proficiency level and other background variables determine the type of instructional scaffolding they need in order to access content. Teachers should describe how they model expectations of classroom routines for ELs who are not familiar with American cultural expectations.

Conversations between evaluators and teachers can focus on individual students who will be part of the classroom during the observation. Under Principle 2, teachers, general and special educators alike, should be encouraged to describe the characteristics of the students with disabilities whom they teach. Inventories of strengths and challenges can be opened for these conversations, as can a review of annual goals, assessment levels, accommodations, and curricular modifications. A thorough understanding of learning styles, intelligences, and preferred modalities may become apparent in these conversations. Also important to the evaluation process, behavior management analysis and plans should be described and discussed as appropriate, as well as idiosyncratic student behaviors that may have an impact on the evaluation. After the observation protocol in which the considerations described could be documented, the post-observation conversation can connect more deeply to the teacher decision making for the lesson as connected to the diversity of students in the class.

The classroom environment is also important under this principle. Discussions between the teacher and the evaluator may range from how the teacher has developed groups of students according to strengths and challenges and how the disabilities present in the classroom have been woven into the fabric of the environment. Levels of peer interaction can be discussed and anticipated. The comfort levels of students in a classroom environment of respect, responsibility, and motivation may also be considered.

PRINCIPLE 3: REFLECTIVE TEACHING USING EVIDENCE-BASED STRATEGIES

The third principle represented in this book, *reflective teaching using evidence-based strategies*, comprises the range of observable classroom behaviors that evaluators can expect to see when documenting the teaching of ELs and students with disabilities. The observation phase of the evaluation process is generally the focus of this principle. Levels of student engagement, types and quality of content and process representation, and the means and frequency of student expression are included under this principle. Use of available technologies to support learning, the presence of well-designed scaffolds for student understanding, and various formative and cumulative assessment strategies can be both observed and the topic of post-observation conferences.

Principle 3 embodies the tenets of UDL to concentrate on classroom instruction. The emphasis in this principle is on instruction that is individualized, student centered, varied, appropriately challenging, standards based, and grounded in evidence-based practice. These practices become apparent primarily during the teaching observation. A teacher who is in command of content and of instructional strategies enough so that ELs and students with disabilities are able to initiate and actively take responsibility for their learning becomes easier to recognize through Principle 3. However, because inclusive classrooms often make demands of subtler and more nuanced instructional strategies on educators of diverse populations, teachers may demonstrate their command of instructional strategies in ways that may be less obvious, especially to an evaluator who may not be as familiar with specific instructional strategies that are effective for ELs and students with disabilities.

For ELs, look-fors related to the effective instruction of ELs depend on each EL's level of English language proficiency and background. Teachers' use of integrated or separate content and academic language objectives to guide instruction provides evidence that the teacher recognizes his or her students' need to acquire content knowledge and academic language simultaneously. Other scaffolds for ELs include teachers' use of visuals, graphic organizers, home-language materials, and supports. For example, the use of sentence frames provides support for ELs to participate in more discussions in pairs, small groups, and/or with the entire class. Other look-fors include supporting ELs to use academic language and the incorporation of ELs' culture, questions, and interests in instruction.

Evaluators of special educators and general educators in inclusive settings may want to focus on particular students with disabilities during lessons to discern levels of differentiation. Questions for the observation may concentrate on balances between effective and efficient use of time. Discussions in pre- or post-observation conferences may focus on pre- and postteaching strategies for students with disabilities as well as on the active encouragement and responsiveness to student voice and self-advocacy in the classroom. Look-fors in this book are designed to suggest the gamut of evidence-based practices that evaluators can expect to see in classrooms that are responsive to all students and to students with disabilities.

PRINCIPLE 4: BUILDING A CULTURE OF COLLABORATION AND COMMUNITY

The fourth and final principle, *building a culture of collaboration and community*, focuses on how well teachers fulfill professional responsibilities to work within the community to ensure the best education for students with disabilities and ELs. Usually the topic of the post-observation conference, issues of collaboration and professionalism can elicit structures that are in place to support the academic, social, and emotional growth of ELs and students with disabilities. Under the purview of the post-observation conference, evaluators can ascertain the levels of involvement with families and within communities on behalf of children for specialists and for general educators. As part of the discussion, additional documentation such as call logs, e-mail exchanges, and take-home notebooks can be presented and evaluated as evidence. Responsiveness to parental input, person-centered planning techniques, knowledge of opportunities within communities for support of diverse learners, and culturally responsive communication can also be examined as part of a full and rich understanding of a teacher's attention to these responsibilities.

Relationships with support personnel and service providers are also part of this principle. Coteaching can be described as can relationships with paraprofessionals and related service providers. Look-fors may include oral or written documentation of frequent planning conversations between teachers, collaboration on classroom routines and protocols, or sharing of professional development opportunities. These elements are not necessarily observable within one setting but can be demonstrated and documented on an ongoing basis. Memberships and active involvement with professional organizations can serve as evidence of professional development. The post-observation conference can also focus on teacher decision making regarding the kind of coteaching strategies exhibited during the lesson and evidence of regular contact with families. Evidence can also include the regularity and quality of teacher interactions with the larger community since communication with parents and active participation in the community are important to establish.

At the core of professional responsibility for all teachers of ELs is the need to develop themselves professionally to become advocates for their EL students (Staehr Fenner, 2014). Professional responsibility calls for teachers of ELs to reflect on their teaching, maintain required as well as appropriate records to document ELs' language growth, and effectively communicate with EL families as a form of advocating for their students. Teachers may consider joining a local and/or national organization, attending professional conferences, and reading materials that highlight strategies for effectively teaching ELs. Teacher involvement in family literacy events and adult ESOL programs are also examples of ways to build relationships with ELs and their families.

In addition, Principle 4 highlights the levels of cooperation and professional collaboration in which teachers and related service providers engage. Through the observation and post-observation processes, coteaching relationships can be explored and evaluated. Sharing responsibilities and overseeing paraprofessionals within classrooms also falls under this principle in which evaluators may draw attention to the quality and purposefulness of these relationships and the way in which they can benefit students. As is true of each of the four principles, opportunities for professional development for staff are abundant and are based on the full evaluation of educators. This book details models and methods for ensuring that the highest degrees of collaboration with home, with community, and within the school and classroom can be achieved. Table 1.5 highlights the

Table 1.5 Phases of Teacher Evaluation and Principles of Inclusive Teacher Evaluation

Phase of Teacher Evaluation	Which Principles of Inclusive Teacher Evaluation Are Expected
Pre-observation conference	1, 2, (3), (4)
Observation	(1), 2, 3, (4)
Post-observation conference	(1), 2, (3), 4

phases of teacher evaluation and where each of the principles of inclusive teacher evaluation can primarily be found. The principles in parentheses indicate that these principles can be found during this phase but are often not the main focus of the phase.

CONCLUSION

For students learning English as an additional language, the barrier to a quality education can continue to be seen as an individual issue versus a collective one. High-quality educational experiences may continue to be out of reach for some diverse learners. People with disabilities may continue to be misunderstood, placated, pitied, and disparaged so long as they remain invisible. Their visibility depends on their full participation in American PreK–12 education so that they are no longer regarded as somehow different or, worse, somehow less than the nondisabled population.

Ultimately, this book seeks not only to improve teaching and performance evaluation for professionals in school settings, but to ensure that all students enrolled in U.S. public schools secure the right to a free and appropriate public school education that builds upon their strengths while meeting their unique needs. The four principles to support successful inclusive practice—(1) committing to equal access for all learners, (2) preparing to support diverse learners, (3) reflective teaching using evidence-based strategies, and (4) building a culture of collaboration and community—are explicated in this book as a guide for teachers and evaluators (Staehr Fenner et al., 2014). Diverse student populations, teachers, and evaluators will benefit greatly from a more inclusive teacher evaluation system framed around these principles.

NOTES

1. While we refer to ELs and students with disabilities separately, we also recognize that dually identified ELs belong to both groups.

2. We recognize that not all Latinos are English learners.

3. See http://www.doe.mass.edu/retell/.

4. Critical conversations in teacher preparation programs and in school districts that sponsor student teachers are necessary for access to the general education curriculum for students with disabilities to improve.

Foundations of Education of English Learners   2

My concern is that school leaders don't have a clear understanding of the challenges that ELs face in and out of school, as well as the challenges that teachers of ELs and instructional coaches face when designing and implementing curriculum and assessments.

Dr. C. Woods-Washington, ESOL Teacher

This chapter frames basic foundations for English learner (EL) education that undergird each of the four principles for inclusive teacher evaluation. It provides a research-based view of effective practices for educating ELs that all teachers of ELs and their evaluators need to be aware of and demonstrate through their teaching. As quoted above, Dr. Woods-Washington's concern for a clearer understanding of ELs by school leaders is not unique. The chapter addresses some of the challenges noted by including fundamental areas of EL education, organized by each of the four principles of inclusive teacher evaluation that educators must be aware of to equitably support and evaluate all teachers of ELs. These areas support look-fors fine-tuned to the unique strengths and challenges ELs present, which are more fully described in Chapters 4 through 7. These foundations of EL education include the federal definition of ELs, different types of language support programs, the influence of ELs' culture on language acquisition, effective instructional techniques, academic language, collaboration, and advocacy.

INTRODUCTION

While teacher evaluation has not typically focused on evaluating all teachers who work with ELs, more attention has been given to the topic during the past few years. In addition to the American Federation of Teachers' focus on the issue, some other groups have been taking notice as well. For example, the National Comprehensive Center for Teacher Quality convened a forum of national experts in 2011 to discuss efforts to develop evaluation systems designed to assess how well all teachers of ELs are educating these students. Also, the American Institutes for Research (AIR) created a research pocket guide (August, Estrada, & Boyle, 2012) to assist states and districts implement the plans in their No Child Left Behind flexibility waivers. In terms of teacher evaluation, AIR recommends the following:

1. Develop evaluation systems reflecting the special knowledge and skills that teachers require to effectively educate ELs.

2. Develop exemplars of teaching practice at different levels of teaching proficiency to guide evaluators in evaluating effective teaching practices for ELs.

3. Build the capacity of schools and districts to implement teacher evaluation systems that drive improved instruction for ELs.

4. Connect evaluation standards and teacher preparation programs. (pp. 19, 20, 21)

PRINCIPLE 1: COMMITTING TO EQUAL ACCESS FOR ALL LEARNERS

Principle 1 states that all teachers adhere to the laws and precedents set in numerous court decisions regarding full and equal access to public education for ELs. Along those lines, the pre-observation conferences that would take place as part of Principle 1 should include conversations about educators' dispositions about teaching ELs as well as adaptations for unique learners such as ELs that an observer can expect to see and why such adaptations are necessary. The conference should also contain discussions of the theoretical and evidence-based practices for including ELs that are part of the soon-to-be observed lesson's plan. Effective planning for the instruction of ELs requires teachers to be aware of the type of language support their ELs receive as well as each of their ELs' unique background, including the language(s) the student speaks and his or her level of English language proficiency (ELP). In addition, teachers should know the degree to which a student is literate in his or her home language as well as prior schooling information, whether schooling took place inside or outside the United States. Further, all teachers must be simultaneous teachers of content as well as academic language in order for ELs to succeed in school, which can be a new construct for many teachers. Teachers must demonstrate understanding of content standards, the curriculum, English language development (ELD) standards, and assessments for content and language standards. During pre-observation meetings, teachers can articulate which teaching strategies and resources are most appropriate for their diverse ELs and indicate these strategies to the evaluators who will be observing them. The following sections that pertain to Principle 1 outline relevant laws, precedents, and policies that influence how ELs are taught and assessed as well as how the effectiveness of all teachers of ELs is affected.

EL FEDERAL DEFINITION

A good starting point for educators to begin deepening their knowledge of Principle 1 and how it affects educators of ELs is in knowing and understanding the federal definition of an English learner,[1] which is found next. According to Section 25 of Title IX of the Elementary and Secondary Education Act of 1965, as amended by the No Child Left Behind Act of 2001, the term *limited English proficient* is an individual

A. who is aged 3 through 21;

B. who is enrolled or preparing to enroll in an elementary school or secondary school;

C. (i) who was not born in the United States or whose native language is a language other than English;

    1. (i)(I) who is a Native American or Alaska Native, or a native resident of the outlying areas; and

    2. (II) who comes from an environment where a language other than English has had a significant impact on the individual's level of English language proficiency; or

    3. (iii) who is migratory, whose native language is a language other than English, and who comes from an environment where a language other than English is dominant; and

D. whose difficulties in speaking, reading, writing, or understanding the English language may be sufficient to deny the individual—

4. (i) the ability to meet the State's proficient level of achievement on State assessments described in section 1111(b)(3)

5. (ii) the ability to successfully achieve in classrooms where the language of instruction is English; or

6. (iii) the opportunity to participate fully in society.

Although there is a federal definition of limited English proficient students, no single operational definition of the term is used at the state level. Each State uses different identification and assessment measures and makes its own decision regarding ELP assessment cutoff scores for both entering and exiting programs designed for English learners.

One salient point from the definition is that ELs can be educated in U.S. schools through the age of 21, even if they are older than their grade-level peers at the high school level. What the definition does not detail is the multifaceted process for ELs to be identified and placed in language support services. To begin the identification process, students' parents or caregivers typically fill out a "home language survey" upon their enrollment in U.S. schools. After students' parents or caregivers indicate that a language other than English is spoken, students are given an ELD "screener" assessment to determine their level of proficiency in the four domains—speaking, listening, reading, and writing—and their need for English language support services. As part of the Elementary and Secondary Education Act of 2001 (also known as No Child Left Behind), English learners in districts receiving Title III funds must be assessed annually for their level of proficiency in English. After they have reached proficiency in reading, writing, speaking, and listening, as determined by their state department of education and/or local school board, they exit from language support. At that point, their progress on content academic achievement standards is monitored for two additional years.

FEDERAL REGULATIONS, MANDATES, AND COURT DECISIONS GOVERNING THE EDUCATION OF ELs

Numerous regulations, mandates, and court decisions support the way in which ELs are educated; teachers and evaluators need to be aware of these policies and mandates that support an equitable education for ELs. Table 2.1 outlines highlights of major legal influences on equitable education for ELs. While the table is not an exhaustive review of legislation, it

Table 2.1 Court Cases and Impact on EL Education

Legal Influences	Year	Impact on EL Education
Brown v. Board of Education	1954	Segregation is ruled unconstitutional.
Title VI, Civil Rights Act	1964	Prohibits discrimination based on race, color, or national origin.
Lau v. Nichols, U.S. Supreme Court	1974	School systems must provide assistance to help ELs attain proficiency in English.
Castañeda v. Pickard	1981	A bilingual education program must satisfy three specific criteria: 1. It must be based on sound educational theory. 2. The education system/agency implementing the program must do so to the full effect. 3. If the program fails to overcome linguistic barriers for students after enough time to be considered a fair trial period, it should be discontinued in favor of another theory.
Plyler v. Doe, U.S. Supreme Court	1982	Persons without legal status are still constitutionally protected. States are obligated to provide free public education services to all children within their jurisdiction, regardless of their citizenship status.
OCR (Office of Civil Rights) policy memorandum	1990	Defined ESOL teacher qualifications as consonant with program requirements.
OCR policy memorandum	1991	Obligated well-trained staff for ELs in order to avoid relegating ELs to second-class status.
Elementary and Secondary Education Act (NCLB)	2002	Defined teacher qualifications, tracked EL subgroup test achievement in content, mandated EL parent notification, mandated annual administration of language development assessment and reporting of scores, prescribed EL family outreach and communication in a language and form that parents can understand.

serves as a starting point for all teachers and evaluators of ELs' knowledge base related to ELs' educational rights.

THE OFFICE FOR CIVIL RIGHTS AND ENGLISH LEARNERS

In addition to the legislation noted in Table 2.1, the Office for Civil Rights provides guidance for school districts to develop and maintain effective lanuage support programs for ELs. The recommendations include eight sections:

- Selecting the educational approach and setting goals
- Identification of potential ELs
- Assessment of EL status
- Program of services provided for ELs
- Staffing and resouces
- A transition plan for students who reach proficency and monitoring performance
- ELs and other distirct programs (e.g., special education, gifted and talented)
- Program evaluation, review, and improvement

Teachers and evaluators must have an understanding of how their district's language support program is structured and how they are an active part of that structure. Knowledge of these components is reflected throughout the four principles of inclusive teacher evaluation.

LANGUAGE SUPPORT PROGRAM MODELS

Many types of language support program models are used to provide ELs language support, ranging from dual language, in which both English and the home language are developed simultaneously, to pull-out ESOL, in which ESOL services are provided to groups of ELs separately from their content or grade-level classroom instruction. Table 2.2 presents information on some different types of language support programs. These are all factors that affect how a teacher works with ELs and how teachers are evaluated. Subsequently, all teachers and evaluators need to have a firm understanding of the type of program implemented at their school through which their ELs receive language support.

ELEMENTARY AND SECONDARY EDUCATION ACT WAIVERS AND IMPLICATIONS FOR THE TEACHING OF ELs

Within the U.S. Department of Education's new flexibility initiative, there are three key and fundamental principles:

1. State Education Agencies (SEAs) must adopt and implement college- and career-ready (CCR) standards for all students.

2. SEAs must develop and implement differentiated recognition, accountability, and support to ensure that all students are taught by effective teachers and receive an education that will allow them to be successful in college and/or careers.

3. SEAs must develop and implement systems of determining and supporting effective instruction and leadership within schools.

The impact of these three Elementary and Secondary Education Act (ESEA) waiver principles can be seen through the considerations for ELs that all teachers and evaluators should be aware of as described next.

Table 2.2 Language Support Programs, Goals, and Delivery of Instruction

Language Support Program	Language Support Goal	How Instruction Is Delivered
Dual language or two-way immersion	To develop proficiency in both languages	Learning in both languages with native speakers of both languages
Developmental bilingual	To develop proficiency in both languages	Learning is for ELs in their home language as well as in English
Transitional bilingual	To develop proficiency in English as early as possible	Instruction for ELs begins in their home language and moves into English as quickly as possible
Structured English immersion	To develop English proficiency and content knowledge	Instruction is provided solely in English
Plug-in or push-in ESOL	To develop English proficiency and content knowledge	ELs are provided instruction in general education classrooms; ESOL teacher either coteaches or works with small groups of ELs
Pull-out ESOL	To develop English proficiency	ESOL teachers remove ELs from general education classes to provide them specialized ESOL instruction

Source: This table is adapted from Forte and Faulkner-Bond (2010).

COLLEGE- AND CAREER-READY STANDARDS FOR ELs

College- and Career-Ready Standards (CCRS) define the level of preparation and achievement in English language arts and mathematics that a student needs to enroll and succeed—without remediation—in credit-bearing first-year postsecondary courses at a two-year or four-year institution, trade school, or technical school. The standards must be "based on evidence regarding what students must know and be able to do . . . to be on track to graduate from high school college- and career-ready" (U.S. Department of Education, 2010, p. 2). To receive Race to the Top funds and ESEA flexibility waivers, states had to agree to adopt CCRS. If a state has adopted CCRS, all teachers and administrators must ensure that ELs are given the type and amount of support necessary for these students to access the content standards. Common Core State Standard (CCSS) fall under the umbrella of CCRS.

The CCSS are aligned with college and career expectations. The CCSS outline what students should know and be able to do at the end of each grade and were created to ensure that all students who graduate from high school have the knowledge and skills necessary to succeed in college or career (see www.corestandards.org/about-the-standards/).

In addition to using CCRS or CCSS for content, teachers of ELs should first be knowledgeable about which ELD standards their state uses and how these standards are structured. ELD standards are designed to be aligned with CCRS and define the type of academic language at each English proficiency level that is necessary for ELs to access those content standards. Teachers should draw from their state's ELD standards to design and implement simultaneous instruction of content and academic language.

COMMON CORE FOR ELs EQUITY AUDIT TABLE

There are multiple considerations for implementing the CCSS for ELs at the classroom, district, state, and national levels. Educators need to first reflect on how these facets play out in their own context before they can channel their energy into making sure ELs are represented and fully considered in their classroom, school, or district policies. Table 2.3, the CCSS for ELs Equity Audit Table, is a collaborative tool designed to foster conversations and brainstorm actions for educators as they consider the degrees to which ELs are included in policy decisions at the school level.

Table 2.3 CCSS for ELs Equity Audit Table

CCSS Implementation Consideration	Questions to Ask: To What Degree . . .	Response	Action Items
Role of ESOL teacher	Are ESOL teachers working as experts and consultants and collaborating with general education teachers in implementing the CCSS?	Not at all Somewhat Extensively	
Instructional materials and curriculum	Are CCSS-based instructional materials and curriculum appropriate for ELs?	Not at all Somewhat Extensively	
Professional development	Does professional development focus on preparing *all* teachers to implement the CCSS for ELs?	Not at all Somewhat Extensively	
Assessment	Are teachers aware of demands of CCSS assessments for ELs and adjust instruction?	Not at all Somewhat Extensively	
EL parent outreach	Are parents of ELs aware of the implications of CCSS and their assessments?	Not at all Somewhat Extensively	
Teacher evaluation	Is teacher evaluation for all teachers inclusive of ELs accessing the CCSS?	Not at all Somewhat Extensively	

Source: Staehr Fenner (2013c).

LEVELS OF ENGLISH LANGUAGE PROFICIENCY

To effectively educate ELs, all teachers need to be aware of their ELs' level of ELP on a case-by-case basis, and evaluators will need to recognize what effective teaching looks like and how instructional strategies must be mapped to ELs at different levels of ELP. Beyond knowing the ELP levels of their students, teachers will need to know what these levels actually mean in terms of expectations for language use and instructional supports needed to teach content. Students' level of ELP directly affects the amount and type of support they need, so teachers need to know the ELP level for each of their students as well as which strategies work best for ELs at different ELP levels. ELP levels are determined each year through an ELP assessment that yields a score in each domain of language—speaking, listening, reading, and writing. Also, a composite score across language domains is provided that is used to place the EL in appropriate language support programs or exit the EL from language support services.

Each state determines which ELD standards and annual assessment will be administered. For example, to date, 35 states and U.S. territories belong to the World-Class Instructional Design and Assessment (WIDA) consortium. WIDA was formed in 2003 through an Enhanced Assessment Grant from the U.S. Department of Education. These states and territories use the same ELD standards and assessments. The Assessing Comprehension and Communication in English State-to-State for English Language Learners or ACCESS for ELLs is administered annually by WIDA consortia members to determine the amount of language growth and the number of students who reach English proficiency. In turn, these scores are used to determine which students can "exit" from needing language support services. The English Language Proficiency Assessment for the 21st Century (ELPA21) consortium is the other ELD standards and assessment consortium with ten member states. ELPA21 was formed in 2012 through an Enhanced Assessment Grant from the U.S. Department of Education. In addition to states that are part of WIDA or ELPA21, other states, such as Arizona, California, New York, and Texas, use their own ELD standards and assessments.

Knowing ELs' ELP levels is crucial for several reasons, including being able to provide appropriate adaptations to classroom instruction as well as accommodations on annual content assessments. It is important for all teachers of ELs to know not only the students who are identified as ELs but also to understand their state's ELP exam exit criteria and to know which students are monitored for two years after exiting from a language support program. This knowledge base is established through Principle 1: Committing to Equal Access for All Learners.

PRINCIPLE 2: PREPARING TO SUPPORT DIVERSE LEARNERS

Principle 2 is designed to focus educators' attention on the individualization of instruction and on teaching strategies that reflect the tenets of universal design for learning[2] (Rose & Meyer, 2002). During the pre-observation conference (as well as during the teaching observation and in the post-observation conference), teachers should exhibit the multiple ways in which they will plan for ELs to be engaged in the lesson and how they will adapt instruction based on their unique ELs' strengths and needs. For educators to address Principle 2, they need to be knowledgeable about the connections between culture and language, the diversity of EL backgrounds, second language acquisition, developmentally and linguistically appropriate scaffolds, and accommodations for ELs and to have an understanding of how to include ELs thoughtfully in instruction.

Principle 2 also involves educators' ability to create a welcoming environment for ELs. This open atmosphere includes learning to pronounce students' names correctly; learning about students' home cultures, including resources in instruction that are representative of the students' cultures; and making ELs feel at ease. This principle also focuses on the design of physical space, on student comfort and responsibility, and on student interactions, both peer to peer and student to professional. Teachers of ELs should be able to describe how their ELs' culture and previous educational experiences can affect how they interact with students and teachers.

HOW CULTURE IS CONNECTED TO LANGUAGE

Culture and language are intricately intertwined and cannot be separated. When teaching ELs, the teacher's understanding of a student's culture should be taken into consideration. Although EL students are part of the U.S. school culture, their home culture is equally important. ELs tend to live in two worlds—the culture of school and the culture of home—and must learn to effectively navigate both cultures. The iceberg concept of culture shown in Figure 2.1 illustrates aspects of culture that teachers of ELs must be aware of that can easily be seen "above the surface." One's style of dress, diet, language and religious affiliations, for example, are more easily identifiable compared to cultural aspects that are unseen or below the surface. More complex aspects of culture such as gender roles, nonverbal communication, tone, word choice, and concepts of time are just a few cultural considerations that are not easily communicated or readily understood compared to U.S. cultural norms. All teachers of ELs will need to include ELs' culture and thoughtfully build upon it in instruction (Staehr Fenner, 2014). Teachers may initially be unaware of cultural norms of a student's culture and how those norms may affect teaching and understanding student needs. However, Principle 2: Preparing to Support Diverse Learners encourages all teachers of ELs to learn more about aspects of ELs' culture that lie below the surface, respect ELs' culture, and integrate culture into instruction.

Figure 2.1   Iceberg Concept of Culture

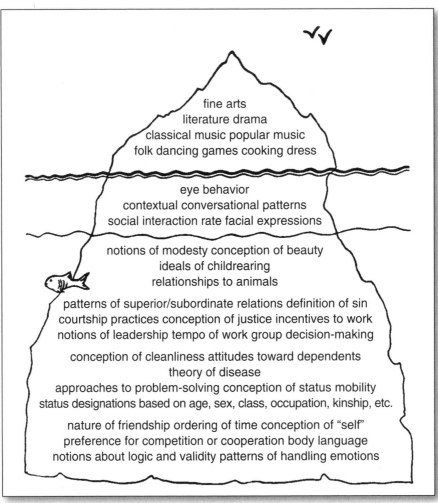

Source: Hamayan (2006).

STAGES OF SECOND LANGUAGE ACQUISITION

Another aspect of EL education that teachers of ELs and these teachers' evaluators must be knowledgeable of is second language acquisition (SLA). Researchers often define language acquisition into two categories—first language acquisition and second language acquisition.[3] Where first language acquisition, or how babies and children acquire their first language, tends to be universal, second language acquisition is much more nuanced. SLA is predicated upon knowledge in the first language and addresses the process a person goes through as he or she acquires the elements of a new language, which include vocabulary, phonology, grammar, and writing (Robertson & Ford, 2008).

Four main approaches to SLA have influenced language teaching—formal, cognitive, functional, and sociocultural. Valdés, Kibler, and Walqui (2014) state that the field of SLA has often debated the focus of the field because of different conceptualizations of what language is and how SLA works. ELs can typically learn a relatively high level of conversational or social English within two to three years, but it typically takes six years or more of effective instruction for ELs to acquire proficiency in the more complex academic English they need to be successful in school (Genesee, Lindholm-Leary, Saunders, & Christian, 2006). While teachers of ELs do not need to be linguists, they do need to understand and recognize the different stages ELs progress through as they acquire English, be aware of the time it takes ELs to learn English, and adjust their teaching in response. Table 2.4 highlights typical stages of SLA and common behaviors of ELs

Table 2.4 SLA Stage and Common EL Student Behaviors

SLA Stage	Common EL Student Behaviors
Preproduction	This is also known as the "silent period" in which ELs take in the new language but often do not speak it. This stage can last six weeks or longer, depending on the individual student.
Early production	The student begins speaking using short words and sentences, but the student still spends more time listening (receptive language). The student's spoken or written (expressive) language contains many errors.
Speech emergence	Students produce more expressive language, but the student still relies heavily on context clues and familiar topics. Vocabulary increases and errors begin to decrease in common or repeated interactions.
Beginning fluency	Expressive language becomes more fluent in social situations. Academic language and new contexts remain challenging; in these situations students struggle to express themselves because of gaps in academic language.
Intermediate fluency	Communication becomes fluent in social language situations. In new or academic situations, there are gaps in academic language.
Advanced fluency	The student communicates fluently in all contexts and can maneuver successfully in new contexts and when exposed to new academic information. The student may still have an accent (which may remain forever) and use idiomatic expressions incorrectly at times.

Source: Adapted from Robertson and Ford (2008).

who are passing through those stages. Each EL is different and will pass through the stages at different rates of speed depending on his or her background factors.

FACTORS THAT INFLUENCE SLA

When students progress through different stages of language acquisition, unique student background variables can influence the rate at which they acquire a second or additional language. Walqui (2000) describes several factors that affect the way students learn English:

- **Home language proficiency:** The more academically sophisticated the student's first language abilities, the easier it will be for that student to learn an additional language (i.e., skills such as decoding in the first language transfer to the second language).
- **Language attitudes:** The attitudes of the learner, peer group, school, community, and society toward the home and additional language can have an enormous effect. ELs and teachers must understand that learning a second language does not mean giving up one's first language or dialect.
- **Role models:** ELs need to have role models who demonstrate the value of being proficient in more than one language.
- **Home support:** Families should value both the home language(s) and English and communicate with their children in whichever language is most comfortable. Parents should be encouraged to speak, read, and write with their children in the first language at home.
- **Learning style:** Students vary greatly in the ways they learn language, with some analyzing words and sentences, some needing to experience language within meaningful contexts, some being more visually oriented, and some more geared toward sounds.
- **Motivation:** ELs may have different levels of intrinsic motivation to acquire an additional language.
- **Classroom interaction:** ELs need to experience meaningful interaction with others in the second language.

SAME LANGUAGE, DIFFERENT EXPERIENCE

ELs who speak the same language are not a monolithic group. For example, French speakers from Paris may have had different experiences before coming to the United States than French speakers from Côte d'Ivoire. Therefore, understanding that ELs' experiences, status as U.S. citizens or not, prior schooling, cultural considerations, English language program model, and teacher preparedness are some factors that contribute to a student's academic success. Besides being identified as ELs, students may have very different experiences learning and becoming proficient in English. Even students who come from the same country or region may bring experiences that are worlds apart. Consider the distinct experiences of Marie and Jean.

Marie: Grew up in a single-family household in the countryside in Côte d'Ivoire, was raised by an aunt, and attended public school sporadically since the civil war. She was sent to the United States to live with relatives. Her school offers a multilevel English language class for one hour per day. Her teacher does not allow her to use any resources in her home language and encourages students to work independently at their own pace. Marie is possibly a student with interrupted formal education (SIFE) and has fewer supports in place. She tries hard, behaves well, and is quiet, but it is difficult for her to keep up with her coursework. She is resilient and dedicated to school, although she doesn't always know how to ask for help or where to get support.

Jean: Grew up in the capital of Côte d'Ivoire in a literacy-rich household with well-educated parents. He attended private school before coming to the United States, receiving extensive instruction in English, without missing any school in his home country. His family moved to the United States together by choice. He is literate in his home language and has access at home to reading materials in French and English. Jean's school offers advanced ESOL classes across various subject areas. He is allowed and encouraged to use resources in French to assist him with assignments and assessments. Jean is well liked by his peers and actively participates in group projects. He is interested in a career in international business communication and volunteers after school at the Boys & Girls Club as a tutor.

Although these two students may speak the same language and share the same ethnicity, they present very different experiences as English learners in U.S. public schools. The language support program model, their teachers' preparedness to teach them, the school's instructional practices, their ability to get the holistic type of support they need, their learning styles, and their teachers' expectations for achievement all contribute to each of their academic successes.

SCAFFOLDS TO SUPPORT
SECOND LANGUAGE ACQUISITION

In Principle 2, teachers need to demonstrate their ability to plan instruction using scaffolds.[4] The concept of scaffolding goes hand in hand with Vygotsky's (1978) concept of the zone of proximal development in which students collaborate with others who are more expert in order to reach higher levels of attainment. Wood, Bruner, and Ross (1976) coined the term *scaffolding* to describe temporary instructional supports for students. These supports are gradually removed as students become better versed in working independently. When it comes to ELs, scaffolding provides an appropriate level of support for students who must access content material in a language in which they are developing proficiency. To effectively scaffold instruction for ELs, teachers must know their ELs' backgrounds, including their linguistic, cultural, and socioemotional strengths as well as areas of need in order to use the most effective scaffolds and also appropriately remove scaffolds as students gain proficiency in English (Staehr Fenner, 2014). In addition to providing support for ELs, many scaffolds have the added benefit of also providing assistance to learners who are non-ELs.

In a synthesis of research, Goldenberg (2008) suggests scaffolds for ELs at beginning proficiency levels, such as teachers speaking slowly and deliberately, using clear diction and purposeful vocabulary, and using pictures, objects, and movements to help illustrate the content being taught. Teachers can also provide such supports as graphic organizers; word banks; glossaries, either English to English or bilingual; succinct background knowledge; and home language support when using complex vocabulary and sentence structures during the instruction of ELs at the beginning and intermediate levels (August, Staehr Fenner, & Snyder, 2014). ELs at a more advanced level of English proficiency may also need some adaptations when working on new or particularly difficult topics. One goal of teaching ELs is to support students to a point at which they require minimal scaffolding, although ELs may require additional support during instruction for much of their school careers (Goldenberg, 2008). Further, the amount of scaffolding needed may vary from one student to the next, even if they are at the same proficiency level. Goldenberg (2008) outlines several scaffolds that can be used for ELs in Table 2.5.

While it is important to have an understanding of what scaffolds are and how they can be used with ELs, it is equally important to know when and how to gradually remove scaffolds so that ELs can work with fewer scaffolds as their levels of proficiency increase. Table 2.6 outlines sample scaffolds for ELs that are recommended for ELs varying proficiency levels.

Table 2.5	Scaffolds and Explanations

Scaffold	Explanation
Graphic organizers	To make content and the relationships between concepts and different lesson elements visually explicit
Predictable and consistent classroom routines	Should be supported by diagrams, lists, and easy-to-read schedules
Purposeful instruction of vocabulary	To identify, highlight, and clarify difficult words and phrases/passages within texts
Summarization and paraphrasing	To help students consolidate text knowledge
Identifying, highlighting, and clarifying difficult words and passages	To facilitate comprehension and emphasize vocabulary development
Adjusting instruction	For vocabulary used, rate of speech, sentence complexity
Content and language objectives	For targeting both types of objectives in every lesson

ACCOMMODATIONS FOR ELs

Teachers' awareness of what accommodations are will affect their use of accommodations in the classroom. Thompson, Johnstone, and Thurlow (2002) define accommodations as student-focused options to level the playing field on large-scale tests. Willner, Rivera, and Acosta (2008) further categorize two types of accommodations. The first type is direct linguistic support accommodations, which are adjustments to the text of the assessment with the intent of reducing the linguistic load necessary for ELs to access the content of the test. Some examples of direct linguistic support include simplified text (or "plain English"), bilingual glossaries, and translated test questions. Indirect linguistic support accommodations involve adjustments to the conditions under which a test is taken to allow ELs to more efficiently use their linguistic resources. Unlike direct linguistic support accommodations, indirect linguistic support accommodations do not focus on the language of the test. Instead, their focus is on adjustments to the test environment and test schedule. Some examples of indirect linguistic support accommodations include allowing ELs extended time and a separate location to take their tests.[5]

Each state specifies the allowable accommodations for statewide content area assessments. While multiple accommodations exist for ELs to use on content assessments, teachers must exercise caution in assigning

Table 2.6 Scaffolds for ELs at Different Levels of English Proficiency

Level of Proficiency[a]	Scaffolds for Instruction by Level	Scaffolds for All Levels
Beginning	• Access to text, video, and/or instructions in home language as well as in English • Sentence frames to help ELs respond to text-dependent questions posed throughout the lesson • Word banks	Scaffolds that provide multiple means of representation, expression, and engagement Concise background knowledge Text in home language as appropriate Graphic organizers Vocabulary instruction
Intermediate	• Sentence starters • Word banks	Predictable and consistent classroom routines Summarizing and paraphrasing
Advanced	• Word banks	
Proficient	• See "Scaffolds for All Levels" Column	Identifying, highlighting, and clarifying difficult words and passages Adjusting instruction Content and language objectives

Source: This table is adapted from August, Staehr Fenner, and Snyder, 2014.

a. The terms *beginning, intermediate, advanced,* and *proficient* describe levels of English proficiency that can be mapped to any state's proficiency level descriptors.

them. Research on accommodations for ELs suggests that assigning inappropriate accommodations for ELs may even hinder their performance on assessments (Rivera & Collum, 2004; Willner et al., 2008). In terms of the states that are members of Smarter Balanced Assessment Consortium (SBAC) and Partnership for Assessment of Readiness for College and Career (PARCC) to assess students' progress on the Common Core, there are differences in these consortia's approach to accommodations for ELs on annual state content assessments. For example, SBAC offers a full Spanish translation on its mathematics exam as well as computer-based glossaries in ten languages. PARCC provides a Spanish translation of its mathematics exam if requested by the state. PARCC also allows ELs to use paper glossaries (Maxwell, 2014).

Teachers of ELs should be knowledgeable about their state policy in regard to accommodations, understand when and how accommodations can be used, and know which types of accommodations are best for students at different levels of ELP. They should make sure they regularly integrate accommodations into classroom instruction to the extent possible so that ELs do not encounter an accommodation for the first time on a high-stakes content assessment. To hone these skills, all teachers of ELs should consult frequently with ESOL teachers.

PRINCIPLE 3: REFLECTIVE TEACHING USING EVIDENCE-BASED STRATEGIES

Principle 3 concentrates on classroom instruction and usually becomes apparent during the classroom observation. The emphasis in this principle is on instruction that is individualized, student centered, varied, appropriately challenging, standards based, and grounded in evidence-based practice. Look-fors related to the effective instruction of ELs as part of Principle 3 depend on the EL's level of ELP and background and build upon the dispositions, awareness, understandings, and skills teachers of ELs develop through Principles 1 and 2. To provide evidence for Principle 3, teachers should use either integrated or separate content and academic language objectives to guide instruction as evidence that the teacher recognizes ELs' need to acquire content and language simultaneously. Teachers of ELs should also use scaffolds that are appropriate to the ELs' strengths, backgrounds, and needs. Instruction should incorporate students' cultures to the extent possible. All teachers of ELs must teach academic language as well as support ELs in using rich academic language during the instruction of content. Teachers of ELs should adapt instruction so that ELs can participate in discussions in pairs, small groups, and/or with the entire class. They should also consider using ELs' home language as a support and build on as well as develop ELs' background knowledge during instruction.

FACTORS TO CONSIDER WHEN TEACHING ELs

The Institutes of Education Science's practice guide for the instruction of ELs in Grades K–8 makes four overarching research-based recommendations: (1) Teach a set of academic vocabulary words intensively across several days using a variety of instructional activities; (2) integrate oral and written English language instruction into content-area teaching; (3) provide regular, structured opportunities to develop written language skills; and (4) provide small-group instructional intervention to students struggling in areas of literacy and ELD (Baker et al., 2014, p. 3). These recommendations should be embodied in instruction and visible via Principle 3.

ACADEMIC LANGUAGE

While ELs bring many strengths to the classroom, all teachers of ELs face the task of teaching academic language and challenging content simultaneously to ELs, often without enough training to do so effectively. One cornerstone of providing effective instruction to ELs involves teaching ELs the academic language they will need to be an active participant in accessing challenging content in school. Honoring ELs' home language while developing their command of academic language in English—which extends beyond vocabulary alone—is crucial to supporting ELs' academic success. In short, all teachers must share the responsibility to teach ELs academic language so that students are provided frequent opportunities throughout the school day to increase their proficiency and be positioned for success in the content areas (Staehr Fenner, 2014).

To be able to teach academic language, teachers will first need to have an understanding of what it is. While many definitions of academic language exist today, several researchers have defined academic language as being distinguished from nonacademic language on several levels: lexical/vocabulary, grammatical/syntactical, and discourse/organizational (Bailey, 2010; Gottlieb & Ernst-Slavit, 2014; Gottlieb, Katz, & Ernst-Slavit, 2009; Scarcella, 2003, 2008).

Further, preliminary descriptive research indicates that ELs must be proficient in academic language in order to meet grade-level standards in content areas and on content assessments (Bailey, Butler, & Sato, 2007; Bailey, Butler, Stevens, & Lord, 2007). To learn the academic language necessary for success in school, all teachers of ELs need to work with them on several levels that go beyond vocabulary. Table 2.7 outlines features of academic language, what ELs need to know and be able to do with academic language, and examples of ways in which ELs use features of academic language.

CREATING CONTENT AND LANGUAGE OBJECTIVES

In addition to defining content objectives that guide their instruction, teachers also need to define the academic language ELs need to meet the content objectives. While teachers can use separate content and language objectives, Stanford University's Understanding Language initiative (http://ell.stanford.edu) argues for integrated content and language learning objectives to be used as "ways of engaging in academic practices, communicating, doing, and being by using language for different audiences and purposes" (Understanding Language, 2012, p. 2). Whether

Table 2.7	Academic Language: Features, What ELs Need to Do With It, and Examples

Feature of Academic Language	What ELs Need to Know and Be Able to Do With This Feature of Academic Language	Examples of Ways in Which ELs Use This Feature of Academic Language
Lexical/ vocabulary	Know and use the meanings of many words and phrases, including multiple meaning words and multiple words for the same or related concepts	• The word *table* is used differently in social English (I eat at a table), math (multiplication table), and science (water table) • The word *analyze* is used across multiple content areas
Grammar/ syntax	Understand and use complex sentence structures and syntax (or principles by which sentences are constructed)	• ELs must be able to comprehend and analyze complex sentences, such as these: "But, in a larger sense, we can not dedicate—we can not consecrate—we can not hallow—this ground. The brave men, living and dead, who struggled here, have consecrated it, far above our poor power to add or detract."[a]
Discourse/ organization	Understand how language is used for different purposes and create appropriate linguistic and organizational structures for different purposes	• Appropriately explain the answer to a word problem • Successfully create a written chemistry lab report • Take part in a Socratic discussion

Source: Adapted from Staehr Fenner (2014).

a. From the Gettysburg Address: www.abrahamlincolnonline.org/lincoln/speeches/gettysburg.htm.

they choose integrated or separate content and language objectives, teachers should consider the language functions of the lesson being planned that will support content. For example, content teachers can collaborate with ESOL teachers to brainstorm the language functions, or what students have to accomplish with language in order to access the content. For example, teachers can consider whether students need to name, describe, classify, compare, explain, predict, infer, suggest, or evaluate, which are all language functions. They can then determine linguistic supports to allow ELs to be successful with the language functions necessary to meet content objectives.

Teachers should also consider the language structure in terms of what expressions and phrases are needed for the lesson. For example, teachers can consider whether there are any key content-specific or academic vocabulary words or phrases that students must know to be successful with the lesson. Also, teachers should reflect on what type of grammar or syntax support might be needed for ELs to be successful with this lesson (e.g., the past tense, subjunctive, the structure of interrogatives). Once they are aware of the academic language necessary for ELs in any given lesson or text, they will need to then teach these academic language structures through mini-lessons as well as building these structures into their scaffolding of instruction.

USING THE HOME LANGUAGE AS A SUPPORT

Assuming content instruction takes place in English, students' home languages can and should also be used as a support even in an English setting. Encouraging students to summarize information in their home language and define words in their home language is a type of support that can be provided ELs as a part of classroom instruction, even if the teacher does not speak the students' home language.[6] ELs can also be encouraged to use cognates (or words descended from a common ancestor—that is, words having the same linguistic family or derivation such as *prediction/predicción*) to help them figure out the meaning of unfamiliar words in English. In addition, teachers can supplement complex English texts with texts on similar topics in the home language to build ELs' knowledge of concepts. Students should also be encouraged to use their home language when working in pairs or small groups to check for understanding of topics.

SUPPORTING EL ENGAGEMENT

Putting ELs in pairs or small groups will certainly help foster their engagement, but merely placing them together does not ensure they will have the support they need to contribute to discussions and engage in classwork. Some ways to encourage ELs' engagement is to provide sentence frames to support their academic language use, such as, "I agree with _____ because _____." Teachers can also integrate sentence stems for ELs at higher levels of proficiency, such as, "I predict that _____." Word banks could be provided for ELs at beginning to intermediate levels of proficiency as a support for sentence frames. Teachers can also give ELs time to think and/or write about a topic before engaging in a discussion. They can also do a think-pair-share exercise in which students are provided the opportunity to think about a topic, share with a partner, and then share with whole group.

JUDICIOUSLY SUPPLYING BACKGROUND KNOWLEDGE

Another area in which teaching ELs differs from teaching non-ELs is in providing background knowledge. Shanahan (2013) describes considerations in teaching background knowledge to all students (not ELs in particular) as part of their close reading[7] of texts that plays an increased role with college-and career-ready standards. When trying to decide how much background knowledge to teach ELs as they focus intensely on a text to make meaning of it, it is important to consider how critical background knowledge is in terms of ELs' understanding of the text. In addition, teachers must also determine how they will teach ELs the background knowledge the students will need to make meaning from texts. Table 2.8 can be used to help teachers decide whether to teach certain pieces of background knowledge they are considering to ELs prior to or as part of a close reading of text.

PRINCIPLE 4: BUILDING A CULTURE OF COLLABORATION AND COMMUNITY

Principle 4 focuses on professional relationships and connections to culture and community in the service of ELs. Usually the topic of the post-observation conference, issues of collaboration and professionalism can elicit structures that are in place to support the academic, social, and emotional growth of ELs. In addition, communication with ELs' parents, caregivers, and families and active participation in the community are important to establish. At the core of professional relationships for all teachers of ELs is the need to share the responsibility to teach ELs and move into roles as advocates for EL students (Staehr Fenner, 2014). In addition, professional responsibility calls for teachers of ELs to reflect on their teaching, maintain required as well as other appropriate records to document ELs' language growth, and effectively communicate with EL families. Principle 4 also embodies collaboration between content and ESOL or bilingual teachers as well as other teachers and specialists who have an impact on the education of ELs.

Table 2.8 EL Background Knowledge Considerations and Comments

EL Background Knowledge Consideration	Comments
Do non-ELs have background knowledge on the topic?	Teachers must ensure that ELs approach the text with comparable levels of background knowledge that non-ELs already have. If non-ELs already approach the text with certain background knowledge, teachers should make sure ELs have the same information. However, non-ELs (as well as ELs) will also need background knowledge to comprehend some texts.
Does the background provide information in place of what the author is going to provide in the text?	The background information provided can't give away the text. (No spoilers!) Students must gather information from the text itself instead of learning it from background knowledge the teacher provides. ELs will still need support and scaffolding to gather information from the text itself. The next two considerations can help both groups of students.
Is the background knowledge about big issues that will help students make sense of the text?	Teachers must focus instruction only on the background knowledge that is critical to ELs' comprehending the text. ELs don't need to know everything possible related to the topic. For example, ELs don't need to be pretaught *all* the vocabulary they will encounter in a text but will need to know *key* vocabulary that will help them unlock the meaning of the text.
Is the background knowledge you'd like to provide concise?	The more concise the background information is, the better (e.g., you may wish to reconsider taking an entire class period to build ELs' background knowledge). For example, teachers could provide some background knowledge via homework that students complete prior to class time and briefly discuss the background the next day of class.

Source: Staehr Fenner (2013a).

SHARING THE RESPONSIBILITY AND JOY OF TEACHING ELs

The topic of sharing the responsibility of teaching ELs has started to gain traction lately. For example, Lewis-Moreno (2007) argues that general education classroom teachers are just as responsible for the success of EL students as administrators and EL specialists. She believes that all teachers have a moral responsibility to ensure the success of ELs. In addition, every teacher, regardless of role or specific job description, must incorporate strategies that develop the language acquisition of ELs.

Staehr Fenner's framework (2014) for sharing the responsibility and joy of teaching ELs deepens the conversation about advocating for ELs, highlighting four areas that educators need to explore or develop so that ELs' success becomes everyone's charge. In addition, educators should not only focus on the responsibility of teaching ELs but should move toward finding the joy in teaching these students that comes with adequate preparation to work with them. Figure 2.2 outlines the four factors necessary to explore or develop so as to share the responsibility as well as find the joy in teaching ELs.

To shift educators' thinking to create inclusive classrooms for ELs, educators should examine each of the factors included in the framework, ideally in the following order: (1) First they examine their beliefs and expectations about working with ELs. (2) Next, they reflect on their own culture and its impact on their teaching. (3) Then educators need to build empathy for ELs and their families. (4) Finally, they collaborate more effectively with various stakeholders involved in ELs' education. The process is iterative and requires continually moving through the

Figure 2.2 Sharing the Responsibility and the Joy of Teaching ELs

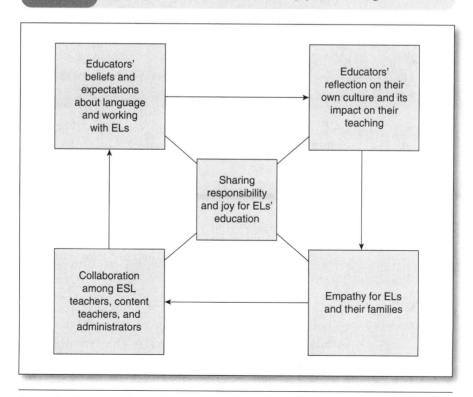

Source: Staehr Fenner (2014).

sequence so that shared responsibility for ELs changes in response to different ELs and their families as well as to new issues that arise with current ELs.

COLLABORATION

Honigsfeld and Dove (2010) highlight several factors that indicate the need for collaboration in schools so that ELs can succeed. They point out that sociocultural, socioeconomic, affective, linguistic, and academic factors can affect an EL's success. In addition, the new demands of College- and Career-Ready Standards (such as the Common Core State Standards) for ELs call for a reconceptualized framework for collaboration among EL and general education teachers as well as administrators. Teachers must have a structure in place so that sustained collaboration on teaching ELs the new content standards can occur regularly and teachers can share their expertise with each other. Some key pieces of this new framework include ensuring that ESOL teachers and content teachers are both involved in policy decisions that affect ELs in the school, regularly planning for the instruction of ELs, and using professional learning community time to focus on ELs (Staehr Fenner, 2013b).

Honigsfeld and Dove (2013) outline six instructional conversations and activities that concentrate on ELs meeting the Common Core:

1. Joint planning: ESL and general education teachers contribute to lesson planning collaboratively guided by the CCSS.

2. Curriculum mapping and alignment: ESL and general education curricula are mapped and aligned to follow shared CCSS goals.

3. Parallel teaching: During a pull-out ESL program, the ESL teacher focuses on the same or similar instructional outcomes as the general education teacher.

4. Codeveloping instructional materials: ESL and general education teachers create multilevel, differentiated instructional resources that help all students make steps toward meeting the CCSS.

5. Collaborative assessment of student work: ESL and general education teachers analyze the same student product and offer their unique perspectives to each other on areas of student needs.

6. Coteaching: ESL and general education teachers share the classroom to deliver instruction together that is driven by the expectations of the CCSS. (p. 4)

COMMUNICATING WITH DIVERSE FAMILIES

It is not only a good idea to communicate effectively with EL families; it is also a federal requirement for school districts receiving Title I or Title III funds. Portions of Title III, Part A, and Title I, Part A, contain "to the extent practicable" language with reference to communicating with EL families. This requirement appears in most instances as follows: "in an understandable and uniform format and, to the extent practicable, in a language that the parent can understand." In other words, schools must adequately notify EL parents, caregivers, or families of any school activities that non-EL parents are made aware of. To be considered adequate, such communication may (and most likely will) have to be provided in a language other than English. EL parents, caregivers, or families may not always be literate in their home language, so educators must ensure that EL parents fully understand written communication by following up in person or on the phone as necessary.

Beyond fostering effective communication with EL families, schools must also be make EL families feel welcome in school. Teachers and evaluators can discuss ways in which they establish trust with EL families during a pre- and post-observation conference. Breiseth (2011) describes several ways educators can create a welcoming environment by conveying to EL families and the community that their school places value on ELs' languages:

- Posting information in school in the EL families' languages
- Discussing with families the value of their children's strong home language skills and being bilingual and biliterate
- Encouraging families to read or tell stories to their children in their home language
- Offering parents sessions, workshops, and classes in their home languages
- Including books in EL students' home languages in the school and classroom libraries and letting EL families know that these books are available
- Making resources (e.g., texts, video clips) available to students in their home languages to support content learning in English
- Considering the possibility of adding academic coursework (such as Spanish for Spanish speakers) in students' home languages
- Hiring bilingual staff and recruiting bilingual volunteers to the extent possible
- Providing training to all staff about the importance of maintaining and developing students' home language and on how to support students' bilingual development

- Offering high school foreign language credits if students can demonstrate proficiency in their home language

CONCLUSION

This chapter examined foundations of EL education that all educators—both teachers being evaluated as well as administrators conducting teacher evaluations—need to be aware of. It mapped each of the four shared values principles to aspects of EL education that are relevant for each principle. While all facets of EL education that are necessary to effectively educate ELs cannot be contained in one chapter, this chapter provides the beginning of a much-needed conversation in order to more equitably educate ELs in all classrooms in which these students are present.

NOTES

1. While the federal term used for English learners is *limited English proficient*, we use the term *English learner.*

2. For a deeper explanation of universal design for learning, please refer to Chapter 3.

3. Even though the field is called second-language acquisition, ELs may be acquiring an additional language beyond their second (e.g., their third or fourth language).

4. To provide evidence for Principle 3, teachers will need to then effectively integrate those scaffolds into instruction.

5. While all ELs are allowed certain accommodations on content assessments, ELs with disabilities are allowed accommodations on ELP assessments as well.

6. In multilingual classrooms, it is nearly impossible to expect teachers to speak all students' home languages.

7. Close reading of texts—or focusing on the text itself to make meaning from it—is one of the major shifts in the Common Core State Standards.

Foundations of   3
Education of
Students With
Disabilities

Teachers of students with disabilities are concerned about the component of their evaluation that rests solely on academic test scores. Students with disabilities often times have disabilities that can impede the expected academic progress. Some of their academic needs manifest in behaviors that make it challenging to gauge student improvements concretely.

Ms. L. Jackson, Third-Grade Teacher

The goal of any teacher evaluation system should be the continual improvement of student social and academic achievement in schools. As Ms. Jackson noted above, it can be challenging for evaluators to evaluate teachers of students with disabilities for multiple reasons. This chapter frames the basic foundations for the education of students with disabilities that undergird each of the four shared values principles. It provides a research-based overview of current practices for educating students with disabilities that all teachers and their evaluators need to consider and see demonstrated through teaching. The chapter begins with a discussion of the Individuals with Disabilities Education Act (IDEA), its fundamental principles and renewals of the law, and the translation of these principles into educational practice. The chapter continues by describing the types of programs available for students with disabilities and their differences when evaluating teaching, the effects of inclusion, effective instructional techniques based on universal design for learning (UDL), literacy and academic language, collaboration, and advocacy.

INTRODUCTION

Students with disabilities and hence teachers of students with disabilities can often find themselves as afterthoughts in school systems. The American Institutes for Research (AIR) describes how students with disabilities have been historically left out of efforts at accountability in schools (AIR, 2012). Among the recommendations made by AIR regarding the education of students with disabilities, priority is given to their inclusion in school district accountability models, their being held to consistently high expectations, and the alignment of special education and general education teacher requirements.

By the same token, special education teachers of these children have received similar short shrift in the system's valuation of their efforts and the equity of their evaluation process. Of the 75 models of teacher evaluation provided by the National Comprehensive Center for Teacher Quality (2014), only four deal in any way with the evaluation of special education teachers. One of those models is designed for speech pathologists; one is designed as an evaluation protocol for special populations; one is designed to understand classroom ecology and interactions, including interactions with teachers; and one is designed to gauge student behaviors and teacher impact in inclusion classrooms (Measures of Effective Teaching Project, 2014). None of these instruments target teacher evaluation as the primary outcome.

Although researchers counsel care in embracing full inclusion for students with disabilities (Blecker & Boakes, 2010), full inclusion of students with disabilities is recognized as an effective means to provide equitable education as well as equality in the society (Downing & Peckham-Hardin, 2007). Full inclusion means that rather than providing a separate placement for a student with disabilities, the full range of services recommended by the student's individualized education plan (IEP) are provided within the general education classroom. In fact, the single variable that most significantly affects the performance of students with disabilities on statewide assessments is the performance of their general education peers on the same tests (Malgram, Mclaughlin, & Nolet, 2005). This finding may well indicate, as the truism goes, that "good teaching is good teaching." However, working with students with disabilities may, inadvertently or otherwise, create an untoward impact on how the teachers of these students are evaluated. Without knowing students with disabilities and the evidence-based strategies that best support and promote their learning, it becomes less likely that teacher evaluations will remain valid, let alone fair (Blanton, Sindelar, & Correa, 2006).

Lack of administrative support, lack of preparation and training, and poorly conceived and implemented transitions to inclusion are often cited as the reasons for the inclusion reform's failure (Praisner, 2003; Shippen et al., 2011). Attitudes regarding inclusion and the potential of students with disabilities on the part of teachers and administrators (Parrish & Stodden, 2009; Tankersley, Niesz, Cook, & Woods, 2007) and systems (Martinez, Conroy, & Cerreto, 2012) can also create barriers to successful implementation. Invariably, the literature points to the need for improved teacher education both through more robust teacher preparation programs and through more targeted professional development opportunities in order for inclusive practice to be implemented and to flourish. However, the diversity of today's classrooms is a reality that needs immediate attention, and the conversations between teachers and the administrators who evaluate them about the means to providing equal access to the general curriculum for all learners may provide a purchase on full inclusion. It should be remembered also that the IDEA remains a *civil rights* law, meaning that it affords rights and protection to students and their parents for a free and appropriate public school education in a least restrictive environment and makes schools accountable to those standards in the statute (Turnbull, 2005).

PRINCIPLE 1: COMMITTING TO EQUAL ACCESS FOR ALL LEARNERS

Principle 1 addresses the need for all teachers to adhere to federal laws governing persons with disabilities (American with Disabilities Act, 1990) and students with disabilities (IDEA, 1975, known originally as the Education for All Handicapped Children Act, 2004) and includes an understanding of applicable court decisions and of full inclusion. Given that, conversations between evaluators and teachers can focus on the six principles of IDEA (P.L. 94-142) because they represent the foundation for all subsequent legislation governing the education of students with disabilities. These principles include the following:

1. *Zero reject*: No student, no matter the disability, can be denied an education.

2. *Nondiscriminatory identification and evaluation*: The identification of any disability must take place through a multifactored process of evaluation and cannot be limited to potentially biased tests like IQ tests (Heyward, 2009).

3. *Free and appropriate public education*: An education must be provided at no cost to the caregivers by implementing an individualized education plan (IEP) that is collaboratively developed.

4. *Least restrictive environment*: A student with a disability can be removed to a segregated classroom only when the nature and severity of his or her disability is such that the student cannot receive an appropriate education in the general education classroom with the use of adequate supplementary aids and services.

5. *Due process safeguards*: Student and parental rights must be protected through consent for evaluations and placement decisions, confidentiality must be upheld, and processes must be in place to resolve conflicts.

6. *Parent and student participation in shared decision making*: Student and parent input and wishes must be considered in determining the development and implementation of the IEP and its related service.

The conversation between evaluators and teachers should also focus on the theoretical and evidence-based practices for including students with disabilities in the academic and social aspects of the teacher's classroom. As such, effective planning for the instruction of students with disabilities requires teachers to be aware of each student's classification and, within that classification, the unique characteristics of the learner. These characteristics include the student's strengths and preferences, any barriers to learning the student might experience, his or her levels of academic functioning (with particular regard to literacy and mathematics), and how the particular disability might influence classroom behavior.

Both general and special education teachers should have a clear understanding of the student's background, the connections and aspirations of the student's family, as well as the accommodations and modifications that will be in play for the observed lesson. Both teachers should be able to review and discuss the planning process for lessons, and evaluators should be open to the need for improvements in service delivery and adjustments to planning time. The nature and frequency of continual assessment and progress monitoring should also be included in pre- and post-observation conferences. Finally, both general education and special education teachers should have a clear understanding of the timing and nature of the related services being provided to the student in the classroom as well as the support being provided the student by paraprofessionals.

Just as all teachers of ELs must be simultaneous teachers of language and content, all teachers of students with disabilities must be simultaneous teachers of skills as well as content in order for students with disabilities to succeed in school. With the CCRS or Common Core (or state adaptations thereof) in place in most states of the country, the side-by-side emphasis on skills and content can be easier to negotiate into lesson planning and delivery. Given the Common Core, the emphasis on distinct skill development should be evident at the secondary grade levels in addition to the elementary grades where this focus has commonly resided. Therefore, teachers of students with disabilities should demonstrate their understanding of content standards, the curriculum, standard and academic language proficiency and development, and assessments for content and skill standards. During pre-observation meetings, teachers can articulate which teaching strategies and resources are most appropriate for their students with disabilities and articulate these strategies to the evaluators who will be observing them.

FEDERAL LAWS AND COURT DECISIONS GOVERNING THE EDUCATION OF STUDENTS WITH DISABILITIES

Federal Law defines a student qualifying for special education as being between the ages of three and 21 and as having an *identified disability* that makes the student unable to access the general curriculum without specially designed instruction or related services (Heyward, 2009). Teachers, in conversations with their evaluators, should be cognizant of the implications of this definition, which emphasizes that the disability must be "identified," ruling out overspeculation on any student's barriers to learning. It also emphasizes the student's inability "to access the general curriculum," indicating that students with disabilities must be given the opportunity afforded their nondisabled peers to engage with the same skills and content. Finally, as the definition states, access must be provided through strategic "instruction or related services," both of which can be offered in any general education classroom at any time throughout the school day.

In fact, federal law and state regulation are predicated on the fact that special education can be defined in at least three ways: (1) as an intervention, acknowledging different stages to a learner's development; (2) as instruction provided within the classroom environment; and (3) as a process whereby a child is considered, evaluated, determined eligible for services, planned for, and continually assessed through progress monitoring (Heyward, 2009). All teachers should be versed in all three definitions by expressing their expertise in intervention strategies, be they behavioral or academic; evidence-based instructional strategies that benefit students with disabilities and all students; and understanding of the IEP process and the IEP itself. Evaluators should make sure that teachers, particularly those whose primary responsibility is communicating content, have access to the IEPs for the students for whom they are responsible. Table 3.1 identifies

Table 3.1 Court Cases and Federal Laws' Impact on the Education of Students With Disabilities

Court Case\Law	Year	Implications for the Education of Students With Disabilities
Brown v. Board of Education	1954	Segregation is ruled unconstitutional. In overturning *Plessy v. Ferguson* (1896), the Court rules that all children have the right to an equal opportunity for education.
Title VI, Civil Rights Act	1964	This act codified equal participation for all.
Mills v. the District of Columbia	1972	The court ruled that school districts were equally liable for paying for the education of students with and without disabilities.
Pennsylvania Association for Retarded Citizens v. Commonwealth of Pennsylvania	1972	The court upheld the right for a free and appropriate public school education (FAPE) for children with mental retardation.
Section 504 of the Rehabilitation Act of 1973	1973	This law defined a disability as a physical or mental impairment that substantially limits major life activities. The Office of Civil Rights (OCR) has used this statute to enforce provision of the education of children with handicapping conditions. The broad definition allows for students with disabilities not protected under IDEA to be given accommodations for equal access.
Education for All Handicapped Children Act (EAHCA) (PL.94-142)	1975	The federal government mandated free and appropriate public school education for all children with disabilities ages six to 21, protected the rights of families and care givers, defined parameters for testing for disabilities, required the development of IEPs for students with disabilities, and stated that students with disabilities must receive their education within the least restrictive environment.

Court Case\Law	Year	Implications for the Education of Students With Disabilities
Amendments to the Education of the Handicapped Act	1983	These amendments required that states keep data on students with disabilities exiting their systems, addressed the needs of students transitioning to adulthood, and provided incentives for states to support programs for infants and preschool children with disabilities.
Education for the Handicapped Act Amendments	1986	This act mandated states to provide education to three- to five-year-olds with disabilities who are eligible for federal funding and encouraged states to provide comprehensive service delivery to children from birth through age two.
Americans with Disabilities Act	1990	Employers are required to make reasonable accommodations in workplaces for persons with disabilities. The act outlawed discrimination against people with disabilities in private sector employment and provided access to all public services, public accommodations, transportation, and telecommunication.
Individuals with Disabilities Education Act (IDEA) Amendments of 1990	1990	This act required IEPs to include a statement of transition services no later than age 16.
Individuals with Disabilities Education Act (IDEA) Amendments of 1997	1997	This act provided for regular education teacher's attendance as an IEP team member and for access to the general education curriculum.
Elementary and Secondary Education Act (No Child Left Behind)	2001	This act sought to ensure that all students were taught by highly qualified teachers and that curriculum and instruction methods were validated by rigorous scientific research; all subgroups, including students with disabilities, were expected to make adequate yearly progress.
Individuals with Disabilities Improvement Act	2004	"Responsiveness to intervention" may be used to identify learning disabilities; highly qualified special education teachers are defined; the act combines with . . . NCLB to develop greater inclusion.

court cases and federal laws that have an impact on the education of students with disabilities.

COLLEGE- AND CAREER-READINESS STANDARDS

As they are written, IEPs in many states are forward-thinking documents. In other words, the IEPs have been developed with the future of the student in mind, shaped by the person's strengths and preferences and by the aspirations of the student and his or her family included in the plan.

The advent of the Common Core, based as it is on the standards of College and Career Readiness, can provide greater access than historically inflexible curricula with its forward-thinking emphasis. With their broader focus on creativity and innovation, on critical thinking and problem solving, on communication and collaboration as well as on information, media and technology skills, and life and career skills, the College- and Career-Readiness skills can afford greater access to students with disabilities.

Conversations between teachers and their evaluators, therefore, can range from the ways in which College- and Career-Readiness skills are developed through the grade-level curriculum and through individual lessons. Evidence of self-direction, independence, decision making, managing time and resources effectively, interacting with peers helpfully and responsibly, and active and reliable participation for students with disabilities as well as their nondisabled peers can be accumulated during classroom observations. In the process, evaluators can expect to see varied student grouping, multiple means of instructional delivery and multiple means of assessment as well as an emphasis on relevance and the use of background information in the teaching.

CURRICULAR AND INSTRUCTIONAL ADJUSTMENTS FOR STUDENTS WITH DISABILITIES: ACCOMMODATIONS AND MODIFICATIONS

Both general education and special education teachers should be knowledgeable about implementing appropriate accommodations and modifications for students with disabilities. Evaluators should be well versed in the kinds of accommodations allowed state by state, for what students they are deemed appropriate, and for what situations they are recommended. Accommodations should be developed based on the annual goals designed for each particular learner and reflected in the conditions expressed, and they should be employed on a regular basis during instruction as well as during testing to acclimate the learner to their use.

Modifications—changes not only to the circumstances of the learning but to the curriculum being learned to reduce thinking or processing (reading) loads—should be carefully designed through lesson objectives and lesson adaptations.

PRINCIPLE 2: PREPARING TO SUPPORT DIVERSE LEARNERS

Principle 2 focuses on the preparation of the design, development, and implementation of differentiated instruction and on the use of UDL and its principles of engagement, representation, and expression. At the same time, this principle anticipates the use of varied and evidence-based teaching strategies articulated in Principle 3, all of which are based on these important elements finding expression through lesson delivery during observations. For Principle 2 to be fully realized, teachers' classrooms should be welcoming places where the diversity of learners is acknowledged and celebrated.

Conversations should focus in the pre- and post-observation conferences on individual learners and in particular, their strengths, preferences, and challenges as well as how varied grouping contributes to effective teaching and learning. Pre-observation conferences can also focus on the means by which students have been integrated into the classroom through activities such as "morning meeting," the use of cooperative learning groups, the assignment of classroom responsibilities, and students' active engagement in decisions about the life of the classroom. Principle 2 demands that all students be held to high expectations and that the classroom goals and objectives be posted for the teaching to be transparent. Ideally, the plans developed and the resources used, such as books and videos, can express the full range of diversity in the culture, including the active and fruitful participation of persons with disabilities. Models of people with disabilities who have succeeded in the culture can be provided and their examples described and discussed. Finally, evaluators can be made aware of how students in the class help each other and promote a culture of inclusivity and friendship.

DISABILITY CATEGORIES

Principle 2 emphasizes knowledge on the part of general and special educators about the various disability categories distinguished under regulations for P.L. 94-142 and its several amendments and subsequent revisions of the law. At the same time, educators need to be able to articulate the range of behaviors that may be manifest in these individual categories. During preconferences, educators can provide background about their students and help the evaluator anticipate what kinds of behaviors to expect during the observation and the kinds of responses to these behaviors that have been developed and will be used.

In addition, teaching is made more complicated because students can often be described by more than one category, in which case the behaviors of the student may require deeper analysis and more refined understanding on the part of evaluators and teachers. Critical to understanding the academic performance and behaviors of students with disabilities is that no category completely captures the uniqueness of the person. Although at times more pronounced, the behaviors of students with disabilities reflect student moods, attitudes, and experiences both historical and immediate. Who they are is as different as it would be for any student, and no categorization can completely capture either their characteristics or their potential. Table 3.2 provides information about behaviors that evaluators might see with children in these different disability categories. The more engaged students are within the observed classroom, the less likely for these kinds of behaviors to occur. Evaluators should be well versed in functional behavioral assessments to call upon their use when necessary and to ensure that positive behavior intervention plans are in place for all students and especially for those with disabilities. Table 3.2 outlines the wide diversity within disability categories.

PROGRAM MODELS FOR EDUCATING STUDENTS WITH DISABILITIES

Although this book is designed to describe and discuss teacher evaluation within the context of an inclusive classroom, students with disabilities may find themselves in many kinds of learning environments throughout the day and throughout their school careers. The same principles of evaluation apply in all learning environments for all teachers of students with disabilities. Evidence in these venues should include observation of the four principles for inclusive teacher evaluation: (1) the planning and implementation of instructional delivery and assessment based on law and regulation, (2) acknowledging and understanding individual strengths and challenges, (3) using reflective and evidenced-based practice to provide instruction, and (4) collaborating with families, other professionals, and the community.

At the same time, it is important to remember that, although it shares these qualities with general education practice, special education

Table 3.2 Diversity Within Disability Categories

Disability Category	Characteristics and Challenges	Range of Student Behaviors
Autism	Limited communication, sensory sensitivities, social interactions, minimal skill transference	Student may be engaged in repetitive behaviors, may show irritation or frustration, may appear disconnected or unresponsive to the lesson, may be up and moving through the classroom, may speak at random and inappropriate points in the lesson, may be disruptive through tantrums, aggression, noncompliance, and self-injury.
Deaf-blindness	No or minimal sight and/or hearing; darkness and silence, minimal social interactions, understanding at the level of comprehension	Student may appear withdrawn or unresponsive or may become aggressive or self-destructive.
Deafness	Limited vocabulary, isolation and lack of social contacts, missing all or most verbal interactions	Student may exhibit signs of distraction or irritability, may miss academic or social cues during a lesson or become withdrawn.
Developmental disabilities	Becoming independent, easily distracted, unwanted behaviors, difficult social interactions	Student may fall off task, be up in the classroom and moving, may connect inappropriately with peers or at inappropriate times in the lesson, may touch, hug, or try to connect with peers during the lesson.
Emotional and behavioral disabilities	Following directions, maintaining boundaries, appropriate self-expression, recovery from an upsetting event, awaiting turns, satisfying interactions	Student may appear isolated and withdrawn or angry and aggressive.
Intellectual disabilities	Adaptive behaviors and flexibility, independence, perseverance, processing speed and acuity, skill transference	Student may appear lost or off task, may need additional prompting to complete tasks, may be passive or appear uninvolved.

(Continued)

71

Table 3.2 (Continued)

Disability Category	Characteristics and Challenges	Range of Student Behaviors
Multiple disabilities	Limited experience, limited communication, forgetting skills through disuse, skill transference, abstract thinking, social interactions	Student may appear unresponsive or lost, may need additional cues or prompting, may face interventions by multiple providers.
Orthopedic impairments	Pacing and speed, mobility, balance, handwriting, fatigue	Student may appear uncomfortable or unable to focus, may seek assistance from peers or from professionals in the classroom, may appear awkward or clumsy or movements may momentarily distract.
Other health impaired	Distractibility, overactivity, restlessness, fidgeting, careless or incomplete work, impulsive behavior, blurting out answers, wide ranges of mood swings	Student may appear to be daydreaming or unable to focus or continually moving during the lesson, may appear bored and uninvolved, may speak inappropriate comments out loud, may be unable to remember short term.
Learning disabilities	Basic skill acquisition, processing speed, dyslexia, dysgraphia, memory, attention and focus, organization	Student may appear frustrated, angry and off task, may have difficulty following along in class, may not respond or may respond incorrectly to questions needing long-term memory, may appear unsure or passive in response to directions or activities.
Speech and language impairments	Articulation, fluency, voice	Student may remain silent or answer quietly and may appear reticent.
Traumatic brain injury	Compromised ability to communicate, compromised ability to use and store information, memory, ineffective learning, physical, academic, social consequences	Student may appear confused, disoriented and slow to respond to questions or prompts or may appear to move with difficulty or be unable to respond and appear to be in pain.
Blindness and visual impairments	Receives information auditorily, pictures, print, and visual representation are of limited or no value	Student may engage in repetitive or stereotyped behaviors, may appear isolated or withdrawn or gravitate toward the teacher instead of interacting with peers.

Sources: Gadow, DeVincent, Pomeroy, and Azizian (2004); LeCalvalier (2006).

is seen as unique because it provides instruction that is individualized, systematic, goal directed, evidence based, and dictated by and responsive to student progress through the curriculum. Observers of teacher behavior can focus on the close and coordinated planning of lesson experiences that skillfully consider where students are in their learning, where they need to be, and what they will look like, sound like, and be able to know and do at relevant benchmarks and endpoints in their education. Likewise, just as in general education practice, special education planning and instruction should be clear, precise, detailed, and reinforced with individual practice and sound assessment. Teachers should be privy to the evidence base from which they plan and implement lessons and articulate these sources for understanding teaching and learning. Monitoring of student growth can and should be documented and discussed. Table 3.3 describes types of education programs, the goals of those programs, and how instruction is delivered by program.

PRINCIPLE 3: REFLECTIVE TEACHING USING EVIDENCE-BASED STRATEGIES

Principle 3 emphasizes not only the range of expertise of instructional strategies that teachers must have in order to help today's students with disabilities succeed, but also the ongoing pursuit of greater wisdom about teaching. First of all, this principle directs the evaluator and the teacher's attention to the need to have clear and well-reasoned social and academic goals in place for students with disabilities and for all learners. From these goals, developed in collaboration with families, their students, and related service providers, the design of the learning experiences can be expressed as taking shape.

Evaluators can ask, "What do you want these students to look like, sound like, and be able to do when they graduate from school? What do you want these students to look like, sound like, and be able to do when they leave your classroom at the end of the school year?" These questions aim to cultivate teacher thinking as "backward design"—namely, developing overall goals first and then designing learning experiences so that those goals are eventually met (Wiggins & McTighe, 2005a, 2005b). Teachers should be able to articulate how every strategy employed during an observed lesson contributes to the learning objectives for the lesson and to the overall goals that are in place for the students in the class. By the same token, a process of assessment for the learning objectives and goals should be in place day to day so that the teacher, whether a general educator or special educator, can articulate the academic progress students

Table 3.3 Program, Goal, and How Instruction Is Delivered

Program	Goal	How Instruction Is Delivered
General education classroom	To provide full access to the general education curriculum for the whole school day	Student receives instruction provided by the general education teacher who is responsible for the students and is the teacher of record.[2]
General education with consultation	To provide full access to the general education curriculum for the whole school day	Student receives a prescribed program under the direction of the general education teacher, supported by ongoing consultation from a special educator.
General education classroom supplementary instruction and services	To provide full access to the general education curriculum for the whole school day	Student receives a prescribed program under the direction of a general education teacher and also receives instruction and related services within the general education classroom from the special educator and the para-educator.
Resource room	To provide academic support for the student outside the general education classroom where there may be more individualized delivery of content and fewer distractions for the student	Student is in the general education classroom for a majority of the school day but goes to a special education resource room for specialized instruction for part of each school day.
Separate classroom	To provide specialized instruction with a curriculum that may or may not resemble the general education curriculum	Student attends a special class for most or part of the school day and receives special education in the form of specialized instruction and related services under the direction of a special education teacher.
Separate school	To provide specialized instruction away from the home school due to the inability of the school to educate the individual and the need to provide greater supervision	Student receives special education and related services under the direction of a specially trained staff in a specially designed facility (day program).

Program	Goal	How Instruction Is Delivered
Residential school	To provide specialized instruction away from the home school due to the inability of the school to educate the individual and the need to provide greater supervision or care	Student receives special education and related services from a specially trained staff in a residential facility in which children receive care or services 24 hours a day.
Homebound or hospital	Due to circumstances, to provide specialized instruction at home or in a hospital that may or may not reflect the general education curriculum	Student receives special education or related services at home or in a hospital program.

Source: Adapted from Heyward (2009).

are making. In addition, fidelity with evidence-based practices in place for students with disabilities during study halls and during periods in resource rooms to supplement and extend instruction can be discussed and described in pre- and post-observation conferences.

Principle 3 also focuses on the tenets of UDL and how they are managed and find expression in the classroom experience for students. UDL's brain-based and straightforward framework of engagement, representation, and expression for instructional strategies forms the succinct basis of lesson planning for the delivery of skills and content (Rose & Meyer, 2002). Evaluators should look for evidence of these three supports in the framework to be articulated by teachers during pre- and post-observation conferences and during classroom observations. Combinations of approaches and teacher creativity in delivering instruction and in designing and implementing activities can be highlighted in conversations and evaluated during observations (Allor, Mathes, Jones, Champlin, & Cheatham, 2010).

Finally, Principle 3's foundation rests on the model of the reflective practitioner (Schöen, 1984). Teachers should engage with evaluators in conversations about the relative success of lesson strategies and attempts at differentiation and implementing UDL. Connections between classroom learning, local evaluation data, student work, and student achievement on state assessments can also be described and discussed. Teachers should also remain curious about the effects of these strategies and about the means to improve their efficacy through action research.

FACTORS TO CONSIDER WHEN TEACHING STUDENTS WITH DISABILITIES AND OBSERVING TEACHERS

Value-added models are being developed in an attempt to capture the work teachers do in achieving academic progress with students with disabilities. Although these models focus school district evaluators on standardized test results, they do so in a way that acknowledges the differences in how and when students with disabilities learn. Unique student behaviors and how they fit into the larger context of a classroom environment of high expectations and welcome for all students need to be part of the conversations between evaluator and teachers early in the evaluation process. Clear understandings of special adaptations and more intensive teaching techniques that may be required from time to time need to be part of the overall accountability that teachers undergo. Evaluators need to be cognizant of evidence-based special education practice. Finally, general education teachers who welcome diversity into their classrooms and working with students with disabilities who may challenge them to teach their best need to be rewarded with knowledgeable and attentive evaluators and fair and reasonable evaluation protocols.

SUPPORTING STUDENTS WITH DISABILITIES THROUGH UNIVERSAL DESIGN FOR LEARNING

UDL[1] offers a practical and evidence-based approach to teaching all students. Developed from the architectural design model of providing people with disabilities access to buildings and urban spaces such as ramps, curb cuts, and mechanical doors necessitated by the American with Disabilities Act of 1990, UDL extends these principles to classroom learning. Just as curb cuts provide functional access for people in wheelchairs so, too, do they provide ease of movement for caregivers with strollers and for the elderly. David Rose and Anne Meyer (2002) and a team of educators and technologists at the Center for Applied Special Technology in Waltham, Massachusetts (cast.org), expanded the use of assistive technologies originally designed for children with severe and profound disabilities into principles to ensure better learning for all students. These principles include providing students with well-designed lessons focused on engagement, representation, and expression by encouraging student affective, strategic, and recognition neuropathways. Table 3.4 highlights each UDL principle, its strategies, and some examples of how to implement these strategies into lesson design and implementation.

Universal Design for Learning Principle	Potential Strategies to Undertake Using UDL	Examples of Cow UDL Strategies Can Be Incorporated Into Lesson Design and Implementation
Engagement	Setting clear goals and expectations for classroom performance; articulating a well-detailed task analysis; offering choice of context, rewards, and tools; adjusting levels of challenge; mixing novelty and routine; connecting with each student and displaying an awareness of the affective domain	• Displaying clear goals, objectives, and essential questions in the classroom • Using modified curricular materials • Allowing for time for students to make decisions; keeping track of student choices • Articulating student strengths and challenge
Representation	Supporting student learning from multiple perspectives; using multimedia options and diverse tools to access the curriculum	• Providing multiple examples and examples in different media • Providing clear directions • Providing direct instruction • Highlighting critical features • Implementing and supporting background knowledge and schema development • Varying the pace and level of difficulty for lessons • Providing opportunities to practice with supports
Expression\action	Analyzing and managing individual learning differences, media constraints, appropriate supports for learning, and the relevance and integration of the curriculum	• Displaying and celebrating student progress and achievement • Frequent use of informal and formative evaluation techniques • Using varied and flexible assessment techniques • Providing and discussing multiple examples of skilled performance • Offering choices of assessment options based on strengths, preferences, and appropriate levels of challenge • Providing frequent and timely feedback

Source: Adapted from Rose and Meyer (2002).

UDL provides an easy-to-understand framework for describing and explaining teaching strategies and the rationales for their use. Evaluators should consider thinking through lesson planning during pre-observation conferences and post-observation conversations with teachers focused on the principles of UDL. Teachers should be able to articulate how various students will be engaged in the lesson and that engagement kept strong throughout the lesson, how the skills and content provided during the lesson will be represented using several means and various media, and how outcomes will be gathered and the success of the learning determined using varied forms of action and expression.

SUPPORTING THE ENGAGEMENT OF STUDENTS WITH DISABILITIES

Teachers can display their use of powerful engagement practices for all students in various ways. Engagement begins with careful planning, so the conversations in pre-observation conferences can focus on the goals and essential questions for the unit and the objectives and learning outcomes for the lesson. Likewise, the teaching in the classroom should be as transparent as possible, so evaluators should see evidence during the observation of the goals and objectives being made clear to students, displayed prominently, and revisited through repeated focus. Teachers should be able to describe the various tasks in which the diverse learners in their classrooms will be engaged and break those tasks down into sub-tasks to ensure that students are able to achieve understanding.

Choice is a critical factor in student engagement, so the deliberate design of choice for students participating in the lesson should be part of the discussion between evaluators and teacher. The regular implementation of student choice will become evident in how students connect with one another and with their teacher and in the levels of participation students experience during the lesson. The most effective teachers have created environments for learning where student input is highly valued and where students help one another and help the teacher gain understanding through design and development. For many reasons, students with disabilities may or may not exhibit what teachers and evaluators may think of as typical behaviors to show their engagement with these levels of understanding. However, particularly during pre-observation conferences, teachers can describe the levels of participation in the lesson that evaluators can expect to see from students in various disability categories as well as articulate the expectations that they have for each student.

USING POWERFUL REPRESENTATION STRATEGIES

Representing the skills and content of a unit and of a lesson requires teachers to establish a clear understanding of the tasks to be undertaken by students and putting in place scaffolds to ensure that the outcomes to which these tasks build are met. In the planning and implementation of lessons, teachers should consider all available resources, including electronic and other technologies to enhance learning. Given that UDL is designed to create powerful learning for all students and not just those with disabilities, teachers may also consider how these technologies can be used with or without adaptations to make the learning experience truly "universal." For example, Julie Causton, an inclusion advocate and professor of teacher preparation at Syracuse University, tells the story of a cotaught fifth-grade classroom that was reading *Where the Red Fern Grows*. The special educator for the classroom described how students with learning disabilities and other health impairments could access the text with an e-reader during the read-aloud of a chapter from the book. She and the general educator decided to project the text through the e-reader onto the SMART Board so the entire class could supplement access to the book that all students had at their desks if they chose to read that way. By the same token, the special educator had determined that to help keep her students with attention deficit hyperactivity disorder focused, she would provide them with small plastic facsimiles of one of the main characters, the dog in the novel. She and the general educator ended up distributing facsimiles of all the major characters to the entire class and used them as teaching tools in addition to stress relievers and attention getters.

SCAFFOLDS THAT SUPPORT STUDENTS WITH DISABILITIES

The process of scaffolding learning begins with analyzing the tasks necessary for a student to be successful at the skills and content of a given lesson. These tasks may include connecting new ideas to prior knowledge, developing background knowledge for the content, reading, writing, speaking, and listening, problem solving, or engaging in group work. Each of these tasks can be broken down further, depending on the needs of the students and the complexity of the tasks in the process. If the lesson requires comprehending text after partners read to one another, for example, then this task may be analyzed further to determine if fluency will be an issue and for whom, and if so, preteaching and practicing the vocabulary in the text passage may be a necessary prerequisite skill and a separate task (Causton, 2011). Table 3.5 highlights examples of scaffolds that can be used with students with disabilities.

ENSURING FULFILLING STRATEGIES FOR ACTION, EXPRESSION, AND ASSESSMENT

The point of UDL as applied to action and expression is to ensure that students are able to display what they have learned using multiple means and measures. These include methods that incorporate student strengths and preferences and use multimedia resources for presentations, portfolios, and performance assessments. Rather than take pencil-and-paper tests or write timed essays, students are encouraged to stage dramas, develop films, create ad campaigns, or display their understanding of content through posters and PowerPoint presentations. Models for the process involved and the products created are provided early in the unit so that students can understand the evaluation criteria. Likewise, feedback on how well students achieved is delivered constructively, clearly, and quickly so that students can continue to shape exemplary performance.

Table 3.5 Examples of Scaffolds to Be Used for Students With Disabilities and Their Purposes

Scaffold	Purpose
Visual aids	Use charts, graphs, pictures, and videos to make content and the relationships among concepts and different lesson elements explicit and memorable.
Preteach lesson vocabulary	Cull new or challenging words and phrases from a lesson or text prior to teaching it and then spend time presenting and explaining the vocabulary in context to students who may need this reinforcement to be sure students can keep pace with the lesson.
Think-alouds	Talk students through the process of thinking about and understanding a piece of text, solving a problem, or designing a project so that they can see, hear, and repeat the process themselves.
Summarize and paraphrase	Have students transpose and translate ideas from lectures, notes, reading text, and group work into their own idiom to capture the important understanding and to remember the content.
Questions, prompts, and cues	Regularly assessing students' understanding of concepts for misconceptions, reviewing student background knowledge and the procedures for solving problems, and shifting students' attention to potential resources for learning can help guide learning so that students can begin to think critically and understand more keenly.

Conversations between evaluators and teachers can focus on how all students will provide evidence of understanding and on the various means that will be made available for students to be assessed.

PRINCIPLE 4: BUILDING A CULTURE OF COLLABORATION AND COMMUNITY

Special education by its nature can be a complex process and may require especially high degrees of communication skill and collaboration among the community, the family, and school professionals and among the professionals themselves within the school setting. The craft of educating students with disabilities, therefore, also depends on a high degree of understanding of adult learning and adult processes and professional needs. Pre- and post-observation conversations may include discussions about the coteaching models being implemented in classrooms and the rationales for using these models applied to the particular lesson being observed. Special education teachers and general educators in inclusive classrooms are responsible for close coordination of coteaching activities as well as the smooth and effective delivery of related services and paraprofessional support. In addition, teachers should provide evaluators with evidence of ongoing and effective communication with caregivers and the families of students with disabilities. Finally, educators working with students with disabilities should create and help manage connections to the larger community in anticipation of the transition needs of their students.

Although federal legislation mandates that the conversation about transition begin for the student no later than by the age of 16, keeping life goals firmly and continually in the minds of educators at every level can ensure greater continuity and a likelihood of success. Ideally, therefore, the best transition practice is an ongoing enterprise, undertaken from the point when a student is either identified with a disability or when a student enters a school system with a disability. In the same vein as lesson design, transition design should begin with a clear understanding of the expectations and aspirations of the child and of the child's caregivers for life beyond graduation—that is, the goals for what the child will look like, sound like, and be able to do.

Related services are those provided under IDEA in order to support the education of students with disabilities. Conversations between evaluators and teachers, particularly post-observation, can highlight the relationships among these various providers and their impact on the lesson and on the learning of students with disabilities in the class. Although inclusive classrooms should allow for the seamless delivery of these related services within the physical confines of the classroom itself, sometimes pull-out

Table 3.6 Service Providers and Interface With Classroom Teachers and Shared Responsibilities

Related Service Providers	Interface With Classroom Teachers and Shared Responsibilities
Audiology	Audiological services are provided primarily on a consultative basis with students, parents, and teachers. These services extend to testing and diagnosis and to providing education on hearing loss and on strategies for hearing loss, including amplification.
Counseling services	Services can be provided to any student with a disability by a qualified social worker, psychologist, school counselor, or other qualified service provider.
Interpreting services	These services include supports for persons who are deaf and hard of hearing and electronic translation and transcription services as well as special services for students who are deaf-blind.
Medical services	Evaluation and diagnostic services are provided by a licensed physician relating to the identification of a child's medically related disability.
Occupational therapy	Services are provided by a qualified occupational therapist to improve, develop, or restore functions impaired lost through illness, injury, or deprivation or to perform tasks necessary for independent functioning or to prevent further impairment.
Orientation and mobility services	Services are provided to students who are blind or visually impaired to enable them to become systematically oriented to and safely move within their environments at school, at home, and within the community.
Parent counseling and training	Qualified personnel may provide counseling and training services to assist caregivers in understanding their child's IEP, obtaining information on a child's development, and acquiring the skills to help support implementation of the IEP.
Physical therapy	This refers to any therapies provided by a qualified physical therapist.

Related Service Providers	Interface With Classroom Teachers and Shared Responsibilities
Psychological services	Services allowed include administering tests and other assessment procedures; obtaining, integrating, and interpreting information on a student's behaviors and conditions related to learning; consulting with school personnel and planning school programs to meet the needs of students with disabilities; planning and managing psychological and counseling services; assisting in the implementation of positive behavioral support strategies.
Recreation	These services may include assessments of leisure functioning, therapeutic recreation services, recreation programs in schools and in the community, and leisure education.
Rehabilitation counseling services	Qualified personnel may provide individual or group sessions.
School health services and school nurse services	A school nurse or other qualified person can provide services to a child with a disability to ensure free and appropriate public education as documented in the student's IEP.
Social work services in schools	These services include preparing a social history, group and individual counseling with the student and family, troubleshooting the student's living situation for anything that may affect school adjustment, mobilizing and integrating school and community resources, and helping develop positive behavior intervention strategies (PBIS).
Speech-language services	Services may include identification of a student with a speech or language impairment, diagnosis of specific speech or language impairments, referrals for further medical interventions to habilitate speech or language impairments, provision of services for speech and language habilitation or the prevention of communication disorders, and guidance to students, teachers, and parents regarding speech and language impairments.
Transportation	School personnel provide travel to and from school, between school, in and around school buildings, knowing how to use specialized equipment if required.

Source: IDEA regulations 34 C.F.R 300.34; Authority: 20 U.S.C 1401 (26).

services for students with disabilities can be the better option. The number of adults present at any given time in the classroom should be discussed. If pull-out services are implemented, conversations can also focus on the smooth transition during instruction for these services and minimizing disruption as much as possible. Table 3.6 provides information on related service providers for students with disabilities and their connection to classroom teachers.

The range of potential service providers can seem overwhelming; however, clear communication as well as organized collaboration and planned follow-through can go a long way toward implementing a student's IEP and ITP (individualized transition plan) with consideration of all the professionals involved.

SHARING THE RESPONSIBILITY AND FULFILLMENT OF TEACHING STUDENTS WITH DISABILITIES

To shift their thinking to create inclusive classrooms for students with disabilities, educators should examine each of the factors included in the framework, ideally in the following order: (1) First they examine their beliefs and expectations about working with students with disabilities; (2) then they reflect on diversity and the strength that comes from integrating diverse learners; (3) next, educators need to build the professional capacity to connect all students to powerful learning experiences; (4) finally, they need to collaborate thoughtfully with various stakeholders involved in the education of students with disabilities. The process demands that educators be fully committed to the notion that all children can learn and to becoming the best teachers they can possibly be.

NOTE

1. While described in this chapter that focuses on students with disabilities, UDL is also applicable to English learners.

2. In rare but successful inclusive programs, the general educator and the special educator are both teachers of record." Kozik, P., Osroff, P., Lee, S., Marr, W. (2010). Listening first: Designing and implementing middle school inclusion. *Duets and Dialogue: Voices on Inclusive Practices in Our Schools*. [Monograph] Cianca, M., & Freytag, C.C. (Eds.)

Principle 1: Committing to Equal Access for All Learners

4

Teachers in my school district received a brief training at our opening faculty meeting in September 2012. At the training, the rubric was introduced and reviewed during a PowerPoint presentation given by the school principal. Each staff member was given a hard copy. Staff members were told that this would be used for all future announced and unannounced observations. No teaching scenarios were provided.

Ms. J. Carroll, Third-Grade Teacher

CONTENT OF THE CHAPTER

This chapter introduces educators to Principle 1, committing to equal access for all learners; the chapter is grounded in teaching scenarios with ELs and students with disabilities. The chapter begins by citing the need for this principle, which provides the foundation for inclusive teacher evaluation, both in terms of all diverse students and also specifically for English learners (ELs) and students with disabilities. It then explores the process of using Principle 1 as a starting point for teacher evaluation, describing how and when to incorporate it into an inclusive teacher evaluation system. Chapter 4 then explores look-fors to support the use of Principle 1, including specific examples of look-fors that apply only to teachers of ELs, look-fors that apply only to students with disabilities, and look-fors that apply to teachers of both groups of students. The chapter continues with a sample teacher evaluation rubric from Rhode Island as well as scenarios highlighting dialogues between teachers and evaluators that exemplify how Principle 1 could play out when in use. The chapter ends with questions that educators can use as part of their own professional development to determine their approach to the elements of advocacy and equity for ELs and students with disabilities that Principle 1 embodies.

FOCUS OF PRINCIPLE 1: COMMITTING TO EQUAL ACCESS FOR ALL LEARNERS

Principle 1 definition: Educators are aware of and adhere to the laws and to the precedents set in numerous court decisions regarding full and equal access to public education for all students. Educators describe diverse learners' full access to the curriculum and the adaptations for unique learners an observer can expect to see so that all students are included in learning.

Principle 1 describes the importance of all teachers (e.g., general educators, special educators, and English for speakers of other languages [ESOL] teachers) adhering to the laws and to the precedents set in numerous court decisions regarding full and equal access to public education for all students.[1] Evaluators and teachers should be aware of the impact of these laws and court decisions on the design and implementation of lessons that are observed by making sure that competent, qualified personnel are delivering instruction. Educators should also guarantee that efforts are being made to ensure least restrictive environment for students with disabilities and consistent opportunities for the most effective means of instruction for both groups of students. In sum, Principle 1 calls for educators to voice their commitment to provide an equitable education for diverse learners.

WHY PRINCIPLE 1 IS NEEDED FOR DIVERSE LEARNERS

English learners and students with disabilities are at high risk for not graduating from high school and have historically found themselves disenfranchised from many classrooms and from schools as a whole. A recent study conducted by the National Center for Educational Statistics (NCES) on adjusted cohort graduation rates found that English learners and special education students had below-average rates of 59% and 61% in 2011–12 (NCES, 2014) in the nation as a whole.[2] In comparison, the estimated adjusted cohort graduation rate for public high school students in 2011–12 was 80%. When teachers are not held accountable for integrating effective practices for these students into instruction or given the support to do so, it becomes easier to overlook these students, who are often seen as presenting more challenges than bringing strengths to the classroom. In spite of federal law, state regulations, and court decisions at a level so far beyond the classroom, equal access for all learners can sometimes be ignored. Historically, educators have tended to shy away from the commitment of effort required to educate these populations of students or may have focused on these students' challenges as an excuse to not effectively teach them. Therefore, a commitment on the part of teachers and evaluators to becoming and remaining knowledgeable and to upholding the spirit and the letter of the law may improve outcomes for these populations of students.

NEED FOR PRINCIPLE 1 FOR TEACHERS OF ELs

There are some issues particular to ELs that warrant the use of Principle 1 in inclusive teacher evaluation systems. The Elementary and Secondary Education Act (ESEA), commonly referred to as the No Child Left Behind Act of 2001, allocates funds for school districts that have students identified as limited English proficient,[3] including immigrant children. These funds are used to help students develop academic achievement in English and to help them meet the same state academic content and student academic achievement that is expected for all children (No Child Left Behind, Section 3102[1]). School districts must maintain that they are in compliance in order to be allocated Title III funding. Initial identification of students; an English language proficiency screening assessment; placement into an appropriate language support program, if eligible; and informing parents of this process are some of the requirements of Title III. Families and caregivers are also required to be informed of their child's level of English proficiency and how the level was assessed. In addition, the district must inform parents of the methods of instruction and how the program will meet the educational needs of the student. Graduation requirements, ESOL exit requirements, English language programs, and information about special education services (if necessary) are all requirements of Title III.

Families and caregivers have the right to remove their children from English language programs or refuse language support services. Since this is the case, it is especially important for all teachers and administrators to have knowledge of Title III requirements. Additional requirements of Title III require school districts and state departments of education to report their three annual measurable achievement objectives, or AMAOs. Title III, Section 3122(a) assists states in monitoring and measuring student language development and state academic achievement standards. Table 4.1 outlines what each AMAO entails.

The AMAO that most educators are familiar with is AMAO 3 since it directly affects the school and district's adequate yearly progress, or AYP status. Educators often question whether or not their school or district made AYP. This status is also shared publically, usually in local newspapers and websites. Very rarely are educators aware of how ELs' language development is measured or how proficiency is determined. These two factors are an important part of an EL's school experience, supporting the need for educators who are part of that learning experience to be aware of AMAOs. Important information for educators to be aware of specifically related to AMAO 1 and AMAO 2 includes knowing the information displayed in Figure 4.1.

School, district, and state educational agencies need to engage in discussions about Title III requirements as part of teacher evaluation systems since these systems will require a shared understanding of how AMAOs affect a sense of shared responsibility for English learners. Administrators, content teachers, ESOL or bilingual teachers, and special education teachers must all be engaged in dialogues about how to most effectively educate ELs within their own contexts.

PROGRAM MODELS FOR ELs

Another area to consider in terms of Principle 1's effect on EL education is the type of program model and its impact on the instruction of ELs and,

Table 4.1 AMAOs for English learners

AMAO Number	What the AMAO Means
AMAO 1	Annual increases in the number or percentage of children making progress in learning English
AMAO 2	Annual increases in the number or percentage of children attaining English proficiency
AMAO 3	Making adequate yearly progress (AYP) for limited English proficient children as described in Title I, Section 1111(b)(2)(B), of ESEA

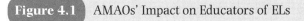

Figure 4.1 AMAOs' Impact on Educators of ELs

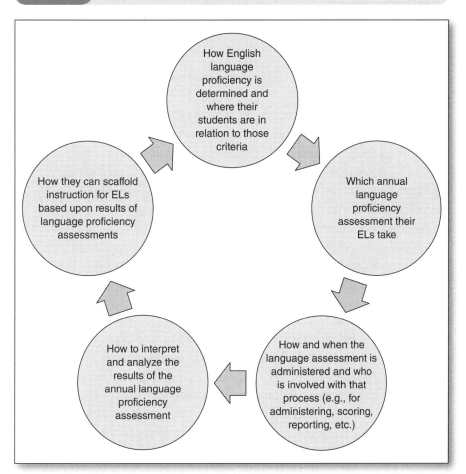

in turn, the evaluation of teachers who serve these students. Although several models of English instruction are used across the country, knowledge of the specific type of program or programs used within the district and individual schools is an important part of building and sustaining a shared responsibility for English learners. In the Title III Biennial Report to Congress, School Years 2008–10, the models of EL instruction reported were as follows:[4]

- Two-way immersion or two-way bilingual
- Sheltered English immersion
- Specially designed academic instruction in English (SDAIE)
- Content-based ESOL

- Pull-out ESOL
- Dual language
- Transitional bilingual, late-exit transitional, or maintenance education
- Developmental bilingual
- Heritage or Indigenous language programs

Each model brings with it benefits and challenges for educators, students, and their families. English language program models are as unique as the population of students they serve, and program variations may exist. For any English language program model to be successful, the district must take on the responsibility of program implementation and support. Depending on the population of ELs and highly qualified staff, a district may choose one program model over another or a combination of several models to serve its unique students. Also, the language program model implemented at the primary level may not be the language model implemented at the secondary level.

What is important in terms of Principle 1 for inclusive teacher evaluation is for all educators to be aware of the model(s) in place in their school and district as well as expected outcomes for ELs. For example, if a school has implemented a pull-out ESOL program model, attention to scheduling and content taught must be carefully examined. EL students who are removed from one learning environment to receive specialized instruction in English are missing the instruction they would have received if they had stayed in their general education classes. A student's level of English proficiency cannot exclude him or her from receiving content-based instruction. Program design must be carefully planned, staffed accordingly and must be thorough and responsive to district cultures, practices, procedures, and policies. Teachers and evaluators need to have candid conversations about English language program models and clear expectations for a collaborative approach to teaching students content and language simultaneously.

NEED FOR PRINCIPLE 1
FOR STUDENTS WITH DISABILITIES

The need for Principle 1 can be most strongly seen in terms of providing students with disabilities a sound education in the least restrictive environment. A comparison of several dozen studies on providing students with disabilities full access to the general education curriculum in the least restrictive environment—that is, the full inclusion classroom—has proven inconclusive and often contradictory (Berman, 2000; Carlburg & Kavale, 1980; Demchuk, 2000; Elbaum, 2002; Wang & Baker, 1985–1986). A wide range of appropriate comparisons, differing research methodologies, numerous confounding variables, and varying disability types makes determining the academic and social benefits of full inclusion for students with disabilities seem problematic (Wiener & Tardif, 2004). However, efforts to pinpoint the differences for students with learning disabilities among their parents, teachers, and the students themselves between resource room and segregated settings on the one hand and inclusive and cotaught classrooms on the other teased out results in favor of inclusion (Causton-Theoharis, Theoharis, Orsati, & Cosier, 2011; Wiener & Tardif, 2004).

Federal legislation and the courts have made clear that discrimination based on disability (Americans with Disabilities Act, 1990) is a violation of the law, and that education is a basic human right (see P.L. 94-142; *Board of Education of the Hendrick Hudson Central School District v. Rowley* [1982]; *Department of Education of Hawaii v. Katherine* [1984]; *Timothy W. v. Rochester School District* [1989]). Why then do segregated settings continue? In some cases, educators can agonize over this ethical dilemma when, for example, they are balancing a potential segregated placement for a child with emotional and behavioral disabilities against the safety of other children (Bon & Bigbee, 2011). Decisions about special education placement have an immediate and lasting impact on the educational opportunity of some students with disabilities (Bon & Bigbee, 2011). Ironically, sometimes the very personnel who serve as evaluators of teaching performance, school administrators, may be in some part responsible for perpetuating fewer inclusive opportunities for students with disabilities.

Principal attitudes about inclusion have been shown to influence the effectiveness of teachers in inclusive classrooms (Stanovich & Jordan, 1998). As Bell et al. (2012) report, biased teacher evaluations by some observers can be a significant threat to the validity of performance protocols. Any bias by an evaluator against the inclusion of all students in general education classrooms can therefore undermine the evaluation process as well restrict access for students with disabilities. Biases against inclusion aside, under Principle 1, the structure of the school should enhance the coordination of general education with special education services, provide for sufficient planning time together for general and special educators, and encourage a culture that values students with disabilities as full and contributing community members (Otis-Wilborn, Winn, Griffin, & Kilgore, 2005).

DEVELOPING AND IMPLEMENTING TEACHER EVALUATION PROTOCOLS FOR INCLUSIVE CLASSROOMS

Educators should be mindful of two pitfalls when developing and implementing teacher evaluation protocols for inclusive classrooms to ensure quality general education curriculum access for all students. The first issue focuses on the translation of compliance as it is understood in public policy when designing programs and services for students with disabilities. Administrators, particularly those who may also be evaluators of teacher performance in inclusive classrooms, must be mindful of creating opportunities for the successful inclusion of students with disabilities by, at the very least, not undermining a fair and equitable system of providing these students with a quality education.

For example, compliance with the law can sometimes mean creating conditions under which inclusion is not optimally operationalized. Although under No Child Left Behind, the composition of the individualized education plan (IEP) team can be altered by excusing a team member whose area is unaffected by modifications to the curriculum or to the related service, the result can mean that the student's general education teacher is not present at the IEP meeting (Etscheidt, 2007). This is clearly a missed opportunity to bring together all the educators who touch the life of a particular student. Administrators should be vigilant about not allowing the quality of the educational program offered to all students and especially those with disabilities to deteriorate because compliance can sometimes justify expedience. At whatever level, policy should only enhance the delivery of instruction to children or else that policy should be questioned. In addition, policies should be designed that make inclusion not only preferable but likely. Ideally, particularly in cotaught classrooms, the general educator and the special educator should both be teachers of record because this acknowledges their individual as well as their shared expertise and effort (Kozik, Osroff, Lee, & Marr, 2010).

Administrators need to dedicate themselves to the full and appropriate education of all students. This means always putting the child first. So an administrator, particularly one who is an evaluator, needs to bolster high expectations for all students among his or her staff. This can also mean recognizing and questioning teacher discourse ideas and phrases that may indicate low expectations for students. For example, although modifications to the curriculum and to classroom resources may be important, they should be provided sparingly. Better, using the principles of UDL, teachers should be designing instruction that engages students at as a high a level of thinking as possible and managing learning that incorporates student strengths, preferences, and intelligences.

Educators should carefully apply the notion of developmentally appropriate practice to any students with disabilities. The term *developmentally appropriate practice* (DAP) derives its origins from early childhood research where it is a hallmark of learning design and implementation. It depends on three principles to be applied by educators: (1) knowledge of typical development at each age and stage of a child's life before kindergarten; (2) knowledge of the child as an individual based on close observation of the child's interests, abilities, and progress; and (3) knowledge of the values, expectations, and factors that shape a child's cultural experiences (National Association for the Education of Young Children, 2014). As might be evident, DAP is based on the educational philosophy of Jean Piaget who postulated age-based boundaries to student cognitive development (Piaget, 2003). However, the application of these age-based boundaries and stages of development, and therefore commensurate learning strategies and curricular modifications to students with disabilities, is tenuous as best (Willingham, 2008). Certainly, knowing the student as an individual and connecting teaching and learning to the student's culture can result in improved engagement and increased student performance.

Lower age and grade equivalents on standardized and psychometric tests indicate two qualities of a student's performance: it will take longer for that student to complete work assigned than the mean at a given level, and the student will make more mistakes (Gronlund & Waugh, 2009). Although a student with disabilities at the ninth-grade level may be reading at a fourth-grade level, that does not relegate that student to that developmental level over others. Modifying everything that is read in the class to the fourth-grade level is simply not an appropriate strategy nor is segregating that student to a class of fourth-grade readers. Good teaching demands an array of strategies that will allow the student access to access age-appropriate text and reading matter (Shurr & Taber-Doughty, 2012). Grade and age level as applied to any student provides a snapshot of a person's performance or potential. Students with disabilities, even those in identical disability categories, indeed all children, are more unlike one another than they are the same.

Rather than allow for the easiest path and explanation for why a particular student may be receiving instruction that is below either grade-level expectations or the high expectations that necessitate strong student achievement, evaluators should demand instruction in the student's best interest. In fact, student achievement is less a product of DAP and more a product of creative and well-reasoned instructional design. Strides in neuroscience and research in learning and the brain have determined that the nature of the task and how the task is presented by the teacher is more instrumental in student success than the "developmental" level of the student (Willingham, 2008). Evaluators should focus on teacher thinking during pre-observation conferences, requiring evidence-based justification for the types of instructional decisions that are made. Evaluators should strive to understand the purpose, nature, and design of the tasks students will be required to do during observed lessons. For teachers of students with disabilities, clear and appropriate annual goals and well-reasoned benchmark objectives for these students can be starting point for pre-conference conversations. At the same time, clear assessment protocols for a lesson's objectives that use multiple means of expression and action in keeping with universal design for learning (UDL) should be determined by the teacher and communicated to the evaluator. And discussion about developmentally appropriate practice between the evaluator and a teacher should be avoided.

WHAT PRINCIPLE 1 MEANS FOR ELs

To effectively teach ELs, all teachers of ELs need to be knowledgeable of the relevant laws and court cases that define equitable teaching of these students.[5] In addition to knowing the legal mandates, teachers of ELs also need to be aware of federal, state, and district policies that affect these students' education. Specifically, the TESOL P-12 Professional Teaching Standards (2010), the most widely used set of professional teaching standards for ESOL teachers, call for teachers to

> understand legal processes, mandates, and policies that have had an impact on the development of the field of ESOL. They are knowledgeable about the history of legal decisions (e.g., *Lau v. Nichols*) and national legislation (e.g., No Child Left Behind) and their subsequent application to the instruction of ELs. They can explain the impact of state and federal legislation on their classrooms and the school's community. (p. 63)

Figure 4.2 provides a visual of how mandates flow from the federal to the classroom level.

For example, teachers of ELs need to be aware of the ways the No Child Left Behind Act (2001) requires ELs to participate in summative content area assessments. Beyond their participation, teachers must know the accommodations their state allows for content area assessments. In addition, teachers of ELs should follow their district's policy in terms of how to provide accommodations on content assessments. At the classroom level, teachers of ELs must know how to provide the same accommodations ELs will use on summative assessments in classroom instruction.

Figure 4.2 Impact of Mandates on Classrooms

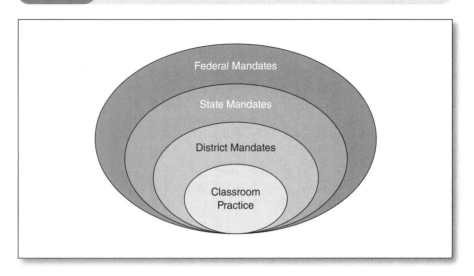

Beyond their awareness of legal and policy mandates, and even as importantly, Principle 1 calls for all teachers of ELs to exhibit dispositions that pave the way for them to teach ELs from a holistic perspective that intertwines students' academic success with support of their personal development. The Council for the Accreditation of Educator Preparation (CAEP, n.d.) glossary defines *dispositions* as "the habits of professional action and moral commitments that underlie an educator's performance." The CAEP (2013) standards state that teachers "nurture the academic and social development of all students through professional dispositions such as caring, fairness, and the belief that all students can learn" (p. 3). Specifically, for ELs to be instructed effectively as well as equitably, all teachers must have the dispositions to work with these students and hold the belief that ELs can achieve academic success.

Part of teachers' dispositions to teach ELs is based on teachers' shared sense of responsibility to foster their ELs' academic success. The term "shared responsibility" describes "the mind-set that all educators must see themselves as equal stakeholders who must strive to positively influence the education of ELs in the classroom as well as outside of school" (Staehr Fenner, 2014, pp. 28–29). That is, all teachers of ELs—not only the ESOL or bilingual teacher—must realize they are responsible for ELs' academic as well as socioemotional success. In addition, all teachers must desire to work with ELs and realize they will often have to approach these students' education in creative ways to support them as they achieve. Further, teachers' dispositions toward supporting ELs must extend beyond their academic success to foster their students' well-being outside of classroom walls. To develop an awareness of their disposition to teach ELs, teachers should reflect on their level of empathy for their ELs' experiences in and out of school. Teachers can develop their empathy by learning more about what it feels like to be an EL in an English-only school setting and how ELs navigate U.S. American culture.

WHAT PRINCIPLE 1 MEANS FOR STUDENTS WITH DISABILITIES

All teachers need to know the laws and regulations as they apply to students with disabilities. As a necessary first step to evaluating educators in inclusive classrooms, the IEP should be available as a road map for the student's education to every general education teacher and service provider who comes in contact with that student. If and how this necessity is implemented is an important part of the conversations between teachers and evaluators because administrators need to be accountable for this first step in the process so that every student can be well served by the system.

Before the IEP is implemented, however, the students' general education teacher needs to have provided meaningful input as part of the conversation at the IEP meeting (Burns, 2006; Etscheidt, 2007). More than being present at the meeting (or having a representative present from a discipline outside the core curriculum always represent general education), the teacher should know the academic strengths, needs, goals, and program for the student under discussion and provide insight into how these aspects of the IEP can be best used and attained. This knowledge comes from regular and careful coplanning with a special education colleague, the design, implementation, and scoring of various assessment protocols, in addition to the thoughtful observation of all students in the classroom. The extent to which the general educator in the inclusive classroom as well as the special educator have participated in all these different functions should be part of the conversation teachers have with evaluators focused on the IEP document. For a student with disabilities, therefore, implementing Principle 1 requires both the teacher's and the evaluator's full knowledge and understanding of the student's educational program and the process through which that program was determined.

Once the conversation has established the IEP as the means by which access to the general education curriculum has been developed and knowledge of the student is clear, the teacher and the evaluator can focus next on the implementation of this access. This can be carried out in either the pre- or post-observation conference and during the observation itself. The implementation of access can require an emphasis on individual students with disabilities and groups of students with disabilities about whose participation in the lesson the decision has been made to spotlight. Annual goals and benchmark objectives as well as their rationale and development should be the shared understanding of co-teachers and all collaborators. Beyond this understanding, evaluator knowledge of the child or children and the classroom is critical at this point, and the teacher being observed can provide insight as well caveats about the students with disabilities whose participation in general education is being highlighted. Evaluators may want to consider discussing students and the types of disabilities they will observe, behaviors that might be evident, and the ways in which teachers continue to help students overcome any barriers to learning.

Classrooms where all students are fully participating in the educational process are relaxed and aware. Inquiry is abundant and shared by all class members, including the teacher. Variations in grouping strategies for all learners to gain access as well as different means of presentation of content, repetition, and routine to which students are acclimated can also help support students with disabilities. Patience reigns. Students have learned in truly inclusive classrooms to wait for their colleagues, no matter the amount of time it can take for anyone to respond. The teacher's record keeping indicates clear goals, particularly for students with disabilities, and these goals are shared and discussed on a regular basis with students. The objectives for the lesson, the essential question for the unit, and the indicators of student progress for the quarter and for the year, individually and as a class, are acknowledged, displayed, and celebrated. Rules for the classroom are simple and also prominently apparent, and all students are aware of and try to practice the protocols of good behavior. Resources are at levels physically where any student can reach them. Likewise, different versions of the same text may be available. Teacher-designed texts, such as directions for assignments and local tests, have adequate white space and are designed to minimize memory load and reading load so that students can focus on organizing and answering questions. The tasks for the lesson are provided in a logical order. There is continual feedback and use of exemplars, provided in a way that all students can understand. There is a seamless delivery of curricular adaptations. Assistive technologies are provided for students who need them, and some technologies are shared to be used among classmates with and without disabilities. Adequate supports exist in the classroom for different learning abilities; adequate berth is provided to those students with mobility challenges or those people in wheelchairs; and strategies for helping students through problematic behaviors have been rehearsed and routinized.

Finally, understanding access to general education also has to do with understanding the perspectives of all students and of those students with disabilities. Evaluators can make the effort to explore student, parent, and teacher viewpoints on inclusion (Burden, Tinnerman, Lunce, & Runshe, 2010; Swedeen, 2009); strategies for accessing the general education curriculum for students with disabilities (Alquraini & Gut, 2012); and the benefits of thoughtful leadership for enhanced student satisfaction and achievement (Doyle, 2004; Waldron, McCleskey, & Redd, 2011) through the research literature. Evaluators should also know the students firsthand, having interacted with them and understood them as learners.

PROCESS FOR INTEGRATING PRINCIPLE 1

The process for evaluating teachers' preparation for classrooms that include ELs and students with disabilities focuses on teacher thinking as the primary evidence of distinguished performance. Principle 1 can apply most frequently to the pre-observation phase of teacher evaluation. During pre-observation conferences, in addition to explanations of content knowledge and the ability to integrate subject areas in meaningful ways, evaluators can look for teachers to articulate plans to meet the needs of each individual student, particularly ELs and students with disabilities. Pre-observation conferences with classroom personnel should include conversations about full access and the adaptations for unique learners an observer can expect to see. These conversations should also include the theoretical and evidence-based practices for including all students that are part of the plan for the lesson to be observed. Lesson plans should therefore include detailed adaptations for these populations of students so that they can gain full access to the curriculum that is being taught. As teachers describe the lesson that evaluators will witness, evaluators can gauge the degree to which student engagement, multiple means of representation of skills and content through scaffolds and supports, and varied assessment strategies are present within the lesson. Discussions can range to the rationales for these decisions based, as they should be, on the goals and objectives of documents like the IEP.

In addition, there may be some indicators of Principle 1 that educators can see in the observation itself that evaluators may need to be aware of. For example, having full integration of ELs and students with disabilities in the implementing of the lesson may be an indicator of Principle 1 that could be observed. Mixed groupings of students, adapted resources in students' home languages and at different reading levels, use of adaptive technologies, modified pace to the lesson, and clear direct instruction are all indicators of attempts at equal access for all learners.

The process of integrating Principle 1 fully into the fabric of teacher evaluation in a school will likely begin with strong and well-coordinated professional development. The process of evaluation can be made transparent and can help develop trust in teachers through an open conversation between teachers and evaluators about the expectations for general access for students with disabilities. Mindful debate and discussion about the inclusion of students with disabilities can and should be part of this process as well. All the professionals and paraprofessionals, indeed members of the whole school community who do and will realize the impact of inclusion on education, can assist one another in exploring the best path forward.

PRINCIPLE 1 QUESTIONS FOR DIALOGUE

Questions to consider for discussion during faculty meetings and during weekly or quarterly professional development opportunities might include the following:

- Does our school clearly articulate and communicate a vision for and commitment to educating all students in effective classrooms? If so, how? If not, what barriers to full inclusion and equal access for ELs and students with disabilities exist, and how can they be addressed?
- Do our school's classrooms have appropriate class sizes and composition? How can redesigning class size and composition ensure better proportionate representation? How does our school ensure that legal and educationally sound procedures are followed when identifying and placing ELs and students with disabilities in appropriate educational placements?
- Does our school provide ample opportunities for ELs to interact with fluent speakers of English in order to acquire academic and social language, and to support the acculturation of these students into the school and society while maintaining their home language and culture?
- Does our school provide all educators with access to students' IEPs and Section 504 individualized accommodation plans? Does our school inform and support educators in understanding and implementing these individualized programs? How can we ensure that the best plans to meet all students' individual needs are implemented as intended?
- Does our school provide all educators with access to data (e.g., grades, observations, curriculum-based assessments, formative

assessments, records and test scores) related to students' academic achievement and English language development? Does our school provide support to educators in interpreting these data to promote students' academic, social and behavioral success, and to ensure that ELs learn language and content simultaneously?

- Do our school's policies and practices conform to state and federal laws for students with disabilities and ELs? How can we enhance our school's policies and practices to make them more consistent with state and federal laws?
- Are all the teachers in the district, including special education teachers and teachers of English learners, evaluated by a highly skilled and well-prepared evaluator? Are these evaluations based on the state's teaching standards using relevant performance indicators in a performance-based evaluation system that is inclusive of students with disabilities and ELs? (August, Salend, Staehr Fenner, & Kozik, 2012, pp. 2–4)

The keys to integrating Principle 1 for students with disabilities are knowledge and support through personnel, teachers and evaluators alike.

LOOK-FORS FOR COMMITTING TO EQUAL ACCESS FOR ALL LEARNERS

During pre-observation conferences where lessons are discussed and during observations, evaluators can expect to hear and see evidence of inclusive attitudes toward ELs and students with disabilities and knowledge and accountability to the law by teachers. Tables in this section provide educators with tools to capture their general understanding of concepts embodied by Principle 1 for ELs and students with disabilities and to help educators supply evidence to document their commitment to providing equal access for all learners. Each table provides a space for evaluators to indicate whether evidence has been found for each of the look-fors as well as a place for comments related to the look-for. The look-fors provided in this chapter constitute a sample of look-fors that support Principle 1 and are by no way exhaustive of all look-fors. Educators are encouraged to adapt these look-fors so that they reflect educators' unique contexts.

Look-Fors for Teachers of ELs

For ELs, planning and preparing requires teachers to know each of their ELs' unique background. *All* teachers must accept and embrace their role as simultaneous teachers of content as well as academic language in order for ELs to succeed in school. All teachers must demonstrate understanding of content standards, the curriculum, English language development standards, and how assessments for content and language standards intersect to support ELs' acquisition of content and language. For example, teachers must know the degree to which their students are literate in their home languages, be aware of their students' prior schooling information, and be able to articulate their students' current level of English language proficiency to teach them effectively. These sources of information are fundamental look-for evidence that supports Principle 1. To be able to know this background information on each EL on a case-by-case basis, all teachers of ELs will need to collaborate with ESOL or bilingual teachers, who often have a tighter grasp on ELs' background information, including their home languages and up-to-date English language proficiency levels and assessment data in each domain of language.

During pre-observation meetings, teachers can articulate their dispositions related to teaching English learners and can share which teaching strategies and resources they believe are most appropriate for their ELs. They can indicate these EL strategies to the evaluators who will be observing them so that the evaluators will be more aware of the strategies that will be used. Teachers of ELs should be able to articulate in a pre-observation conference which resources or materials they will be using with their ELs to support their students' achievement and why they chose, created, or adapted those materials.

In addition to teachers of ELs being able to share information related to their students' backgrounds that will affect how they are taught in the classroom, teachers should also be able to articulate an understanding of ELs' educational rights, EL policies, and how these rights and policies affect their classroom instruction. They should also be able to describe ways in which ELs receive instruction in ESOL, bilingual, and/or other language support services in their school. For example, all teachers of ELs should know which type of language support their ELs receive (e.g., cotaught, push-in) to be able to effectively collaborate with their students' ESOL or bilingual teachers.

Table 4.2 (see p. 102) provides key components of Principle 1 look-fors as they relate to all teachers of ELs. The sample look-fors are intended to be used to begin conversations between teachers and evaluators about the degree to which Principle 1, committing to equal access for all learners, is integrated into current teacher evaluation systems.

Look-Fors for Teachers of Students With Disabilities

In the case of students with disabilities, all teachers should be able to convey the goals, objectives, and accommodations for students with

Table 4.2 Principle 1 Look-Fors for All Teachers of ELs

Principle 1 Look-For	Evidence Found: Yes or No	Comments
Awareness of what ELs' home language(s) are and their literacy skills in their home language(s)		
Knowledge of ELs' levels of English language proficiency		
Articulates an understanding of ELs' cultures and backgrounds		
Articulates types of language support services ELs receive at the school		
Identifies desired instructional outcomes for ELs based on content standards and English language development standards		
Describes how instructional materials for ELs at different levels of English language proficiency are chosen, created, or adapted		

disabilities in their classrooms as well as the outcomes of the lesson. Also, all teachers should be able to describe adaptations for students with disabilities and the rationale behind their use. Through the planning process, all teachers should be able to express an understanding of each student's strengths and weaknesses, learning preferences, and the effects that a disability may have on the student's classroom performance. Teachers should be invited to describe the behaviors of students with more profound disabilities and their efforts to work with the students in the class in developing an atmosphere that is safe, friendly, respectful, and conducive to learning.

Table 4.3 outlines look-fors applicable to all teachers of the unique population of students with disabilities.

Table 4.4 shares sample look-fors that are applicable to all teachers of both diverse groups of learners (ELs and students with disabilities). These components are applicable to teachers of both groups of students due to the diverse learners' similarities in some key aspects.

SAMPLE FROM RHODE ISLAND TEACHER EVALUATION RUBRICS

As mentioned in the foreword to this book, New York and Rhode Island have implemented teacher evaluation rubrics that are inclusive of ELs and students with disabilities. Pages 105–106 show an example of how Rhode Island educators have designed their teacher evaluation rubrics

Table 4.3 Principle 1 Look-Fors for All Teachers of Students With Disabilities

Principle 1 Look-For	Evidence Found: Yes or No	Comments
Articulates the types of disabilities present in the classroom and about student strengths and weaknesses		
Articulates clear understanding of and commitment to the process and product of IEP development; input at IEP meetings		
Articulates least restrictive environment (LRE), basic human rights, and evidence-based understanding of the advantages and disadvantages of inclusion		
Describes of varied instructional goals in the IEP that are general enough to guide content area and academic skill acquisition		

Table 4.4 Principle 1 Look-Fors for All Teachers of ELs and Students With Disabilities

Principle 1 Look-For	Evidence Found: Yes or No	Comments
Articulates an understanding of the laws and policies regarding students' educational rights and the adherence to these laws and policies in providing appropriate instruction		
Articulates an understanding of the federal definitions that define diverse learners		
Commits to sharing the responsibility for educating ELs and students with disabilities		
Describes of a positive and respectful classroom community that is conducive to diverse students' learning		
Thoughtfully planned groupings of diverse students		
A working knowledge of the accommodations necessary for students to gain access to the general education curriculum		
A working knowledge of each student's learning and modality preferences, multiple intelligences, strengths, backgrounds, and barriers to learning		
Open and honest discussion regarding diversity (including language and disabilities)		

that serve as examples of Principle 1. This sample shows how this state has incorporated committing to equal access for all learners by providing authentic teacher evaluation considerations for each student population that help clarify expectations for both teachers and evaluators.

For this rubric's element, establishing instructional outcomes, the rubric first outlines four levels of performance applicable to teachers of all students. It then highlights considerations specific to all educators of English learners and also considerations specific to all educators of students with disabilities that detail how these diverse populations of students must be included teacher evaluation. These extra considerations describe how ELs and students with disabilities' outcomes may differ from non-ELs and students without special needs. This rubric suggests that teachers can discuss these different outcomes for ELs and students with disabilities during the pre- and/or postconferences that are part of the teacher evaluation process.

PRINCIPLE 1 SCENARIOS

For teachers to be prepared for ELs and students with disabilities, they will need to be aware of their students' strengths and needs and begin to put practices in place that draw from students' strengths while also meeting their needs. Aside from pedagogical teaching strategies, creating access for all students will require a self-assessment of one's belief system about creating and sustaining equity within their classroom communities. Following are scenarios that demonstrate pre- and post-observation conversations between a teacher and her evaluator in the form of a script of what will be seen and heard in the classroom. These scenarios can be used to reflect on what students bring to diverse classrooms and determine how to help teachers articulate how they are addressing the challenges of educating diverse learners. One scenario focuses on teaching English learners and another on teaching students with disabilities.

Elementary EL Scenario

Ms. Predaris's third-grade inclusive elementary class has 23 students. The demographics of this class include 13 females and 10 males; five students are identified as English learners. The English learners are all native Portuguese speakers at various levels of English language proficiency, including two students who have recently arrived from Brazil. The other English learners were born in the United States and have attended public school since kindergarten. The teacher has a paraprofessional,

RHODE ISLAND RUBRIC SAMPLE

Teaching is goal directed and designed to achieve certain well-defined purposes. It is through the articulation of instructional outcomes that the teacher describes these purposes. They should be clear and related to what it is that the students are intended to learn as a consequence of instruction. 21st Century outcomes must be included, as students must also learn the essential skills such as critical thinking, problem solving, communication and collaboration. (Danielson, 2007)

Elements/ Performance Indicators	Ineffective	Developing	Effective	Highly Effective
1.2 Establishing Instructional Outcomes Rhode Island Professional Teaching Standards 1, 2, 3, 4, 5	Outcomes represent low expectations for students and lack rigor. They do not reflect important learning in the discipline, and/or are stated as activities rather than as student learning. Outcomes reflect only one type of learning and are suitable for only some students. Outcomes are not connected to standards.	Outcomes represent moderately high expectations and rigor. Some reflect important learning in the discipline and consist of a combination of outcomes and activities. Outcomes reflect several types of learning and are suitable for most of the students in the class. Outcomes are connected to standards.	Most outcomes represent rigorous and important learning in the discipline. All the instructional outcomes are clear, written in the form of student learning, and suggest viable methods of assessment. Outcomes reflect different types of learning and take into account the varying needs of groups of students. Outcomes are connected to standards.	All outcomes represent rigorous and important learning in the discipline. The outcomes are clear, written in the form of student learning, and permit viable methods of assessment. Outcomes reflect several different types of learning and, where appropriate, represent opportunities for both coordination and integration with other disciplines. Outcomes take into account the varying needs of individual students. Outcomes are connected to standards.

(Continued)

(Continued)

RHODE ISLAND RUBRIC SAMPLE

Considerations for ELLs
• Lack of English language proficiency will affect student outcomes. • Pre-/postconference is the opportunity to explain why outcomes may look different based on students' language needs. • Teachers must receive guidance on how to assess students with low English proficiency when the lesson and assessment are based on grade-level standards. • Teachers will need knowledge of two sets of standards for ELLS—the general education standards and English language proficiency standards (e.g., WIDA standards). It will be important to have an understanding of both and how they go together.
Considerations for Students With Disabilities
• Pre-/postconference is the opportunity to explain why outcomes may look different based on students' disabilities. • Teachers must receive guidance on how to assess students with various disabilities when the lesson and assessment are based on grade-level standards. • Teachers will need to have access to specialists or support personnel knowledgeable about disabilities.

Source: Rhode Island Federation of Teachers and Health Professionals (2012).

Ms. Hamilton, who assists in her class for one hour each day. An ESOL teacher, Mr. Kenmar, coteaches with Ms. Predaris for 90 minutes three times per week. The teacher, the paraprofessional, and the ESOL teacher work collaboratively. Mr. Davis is the assistant principal and will be evaluating Ms. Predaris, who has been teaching for three years.

Pre-Observation Conference Conversation

Mr. Davis: *Tell me about the students in your class, where they are from, and the languages they speak.*

Ms. Predaris: *Sure, my students are doing well this year and have made great progress. The majority of my students are native English speakers but I do have five students who speak Portuguese.*

Mr. Davis: *Yes, I remember we had a number of new students from Brazil that have enrolled this year. How are they adjusting?*

Ms. Predaris: *It was a little tough for them at first. Both of them rarely spoke in class and really relied on the other students who spoke Portuguese to help them. But now they are really beginning to communicate orally in English.*

Mr. Davis: *That's good to hear. Tell me how you are working with the other teachers who provide support to your class.*

Ms. Predaris: *That was been one of the biggest accomplishments this year. Mr. Kenmar and I coplan lessons and provide specific areas that Ms. Hamilton can work on in small groups. All of my ELs are reading below grade level. Mr. Kenmar and I use lower-level nonfiction texts that align with our units of study for them as a supplement. Ms. Hamilton reinforces sight words, simple grammar, and writing with those students.*

For the students who speak Portuguese, we use an English/ Portuguese picture dictionary to help them. I've also provided their families with online resources in Portuguese for them to use at home.

Mr. Davis: *So you communicate their progress with their families? Tell me more about that.*

Ms. Predaris: *Mr. Kenmar has helped me to do a fantastic job involving their families from the very beginning. He has explained the results of the English language proficiency assessment the students took last spring. Since he has helped me to interpret those scores, I know more about how to scaffold my lessons for my English learners. Being able to show their parents specific examples of how their child has progressed this year in English and in content has been very beneficial.*

Mr. Davis: *Is there something specific you'd like me look for when observing in your class next week?*

Ms. Predaris: *Yes, we are working on students being able to answer text-dependent questions. Will you listen closely to the questions I'm asking and note how my students are using academic language when they are responding?*

This scenario demonstrates Ms. Predaris's commitment to equal access for all learners. She has established a collaborative relationship with the paraprofessional and the ESOL teacher. Mr. Kenmar, the ESOL teacher, has worked with the teacher so that she can interpret the results of the annual language proficiency assessment that the students take in order to support differentiated instruction based on language proficiency. A positive relationship with students' families has also been established. The teacher also suggests an area for the evaluator to listen closely for in the classroom observation, allowing for specific feedback from the evaluator related to her use of text-dependent questions.

Secondary Students With Disabilities Scenario

Ms. Vance, the middle school principal, is preparing to visit the inclusive eighth-grade social studies classroom of Ms. Francona, who is in her fourth year of teaching. The class is composed of 25 students, seven of whom have been identified as having disabilities. Five students have various levels of reading disability; one is a student with cerebral palsy who attends school in a wheelchair; one student is a person with autism who also works with a teaching assistant. Ms. Francona coteaches the class with Mr. Sidney, a special education teacher with 10 years of experience, with whom she plans twice a week for an hour during an available period. In addition, she, Mr. Sidney, and the two teaching assistants try to meet three days a week after school when other meetings are not scheduled to reflect on lessons, troubleshoot problems, and review student progress. Mr. Sidney supports the learning of the students with disabilities in daily resource room by previewing lessons and focusing on reading skills and academic vocabulary and by reviewing lessons to reinforce understanding and answer questions.

Pre-Observation Conference Conversation

Ms. Vance:	*Tell me about the class I'll be visiting this morning.*
Ms. Francona:	*We're doing a lesson on America after World War I and in the 1920s. I'll be introducing the lesson using a timeline that the class will complete as a "Do Now" when they enter the classroom. Once they've written and shared at least five events, they'll come up in pairs to the SMART Board and match their events with the years in which they occurred for everyone to see. We'll talk about the trends, and I'll highlight the major events of the time period. After that, I'll present a PowerPoint on how American painting, sculpture, and architecture changed from before the war to 1930 while they answer questions and summarize what they're seeing. I'll collect their summaries as exit tickets. For homework, they'll look at two pictures of striking workers from 1936 on my website and blog while they compare and contrast the messages in each.*
Ms. Vance:	*It sounds like a very rich lesson with a lot going on. I know you have some students with disabilities in the classroom, a couple of whose disabilities are profound. Tell me about their participation.*
Ms. Francona:	*There's a wide range of disabilities to work with this year. With Mr. Sidney's help, he and I have created adaptations to the lesson based on the students' annual goals. We've also tried to make routine any of the accommodations they have. My students with reading disabilities get to participate because a lot of the lesson is visually based with a graphic of the timeline and a series of slides that they'll be watching. They'll need to write responses, but the lesson has a heavier thinking load than anything else. I always read all the directions to tests and activities while the students read along silently. Jake has autism, and we've tried to make this lesson right up his alley. He loves warplanes and military armor, so he's been able to participate with us about World War I and taught us a lot about air battles and technology. For this lesson, I think the visuals*

will help him, although he may be reserved about going to the SMART Board with his partner, in which case he can tell Ms. Fischer or his partner what event he'd like noted and she can write it. There'll be plenty of peer support for everyone, too. Samantha's got CP, and since day one, we've made sure that she has room to travel to and from the SMART Board and my desk and around the perimeter of the classroom so that she can work with different groups of students. She uses an iPad with a print to voice app to communicate, and the lesson plan, timeline, PowerPoint, and homework have all been loaded ahead of time so she can follow along and participate when she'd like.

Ms. Vance: *So you've thought about your students' needs and some of the barriers that may exist for them to be successful. It sounds as if you've applied that thinking about solutions to everyone else in the class as well. Is there anything in particular on which you'd like me to focus in the observation?*

Ms. Francona: *I'm really trying to hone my facilitation skills, and sometimes I wonder if some of the students with disabilities get lost and disengage when we have discussions. If you could listen to my questions and to the discussion and watch and tell me how consistent the engagement seems to be, that would help. If you see room for any strategies to make discussions more meaningful for everyone, I'd appreciate it.*

Principle 1 is in evidence in several ways during this pre-observation conversation between Ms. Vance and Ms. Francona. First, Ms. Francona clearly understands what equal access to the general education curriculum looks like in that she has planned a lesson in which all students are able to participate, based on their goals and accommodations as well as their strengths and challenges. She, Mr. Sidney, and her team have analyzed the needs and barriers to success that students may have by adapting the means of representation during the lesson, by affording students access to important parts of the room, and by providing support for their expression. Also, Ms. Francona and her team provide students choices, here by having Jake choose how he'd like to express his work and by having Samantha choose when she'd like to participate. Similarly, she provides access by differentiating instruction among her students. She provides opportunities for peer-to-peer interaction, represents subject matter in multiple ways, and speaks about her students based on their individual strengths, interests, and styles. Second, access for all learners is clear in the expectations that she has for everyone in the class. Her focus on thinking indicates her understanding of a teacher's critical role in cultivating students' minds, and her willingness to welcome all levels of mental processing while presenting challenging content indicates her dedication to the least restrictive environment for all. Finally, she has an independent idea of implementing access for all learners and speaks confidently about the course of the lesson. Mr. Sidney's input into the design of the lesson is apparent, and Ms. Francona has rehearsed the implementation of the lesson in her mind and can provide a seamless experience for her students.

QUESTIONS

These questions can be used for self-reflection or as part of a professional learning community to determine how to move forward with incorporating elements of Principle 1, committing to access for all learners.

- How would you summarize the essence of Principle 1: committing to access for all learners?
- Which elements of Principle 1, committing to access for all learners, resonated the most with you?
- Which look-fors of Principle 1 are you ready to integrate into your teacher evaluation system to provide equal access to ELs and students with disabilities?
- How will you integrate these look-fors into your teacher evaluation system?

CHAPTER SUMMARY

This chapter explored the tenets of Principle 1, committing to equal access for all learners, for ELs and students with disabilities. The need for this principle was described for both populations of students, and then the process of using Principle 1 as a starting point for teacher evaluation was described. Look-fors for Principle 1 were included for both groups of students. An example of a teacher evaluation rubric that demonstrates use of Principle 1 was shared as well as scenarios that highlight how Principle 1 can be found in dialogues between teachers and evaluators. The chapter ended with questions that educators can use as part of their conversations to determine their approach to the elements of Principle 1.

NOTES

1. These relevant laws and court decisions for ELs and students with disabilities are outlined in Chapters 2 and 3.

2. See Chapter 3 for sample states' graduation rates that fall below these numbers.

3. While the federal government uses the term *limited English proficient*, advocates for ELs tend to use the term *English learners* or *English language learners*. Some are also using the term *emergent bilinguals*.

4. Please see Chapter 2 for a description of most of these models.

5. For more information on laws and court cases related to teaching ELs, please refer to Chapter 2.

Principle 2: Preparing to Support Diverse Learners

5

For the 50% teacher performance portion of our state's evaluation rubric, the training itself does not single out students with disabilities or ELs; however, the rubric does specifically require the educator to have an in-depth knowledge of students and differentiation (as descriptors). These descriptors illustrate the need for an educator to know their students and differentiate instructional methods to support growth for all learners. ELs and students with disabilities are "understood" as part of the rubric. Many teachers are beginning to change practices to best meet students' needs within the new accountability requirements. It's still a work in progress, but we are moving in the right direction.

Dr. E. McNally, Administrator

CONTENT OF THE CHAPTER

This chapter provides more specifics about the differentiation descriptors Dr. McNally describes in the quotation above, which reflects that administrator's approach to addressing the needs of students with disabilities and ELs. The evaluation rubric descriptors provided require teachers to know and understand the needs of their students holistically versus seeing them as separate and isolated populations. Dr. McNally also acknowledges the work as "in progress," which exemplifies the time and effort it takes to effectively change teaching practices to improve student outcomes. In particular, teacher attitudes about inclusion, the mandate for a least restrictive environment for students with disabilities, the coordinated education of ELs, and a classroom where students enjoy equal status and complete belonging are foundational steps necessary to ensuring that student diversity is understood, used, and celebrated.

This chapter focuses on the Principle 2: preparing to support all learners. Many of the same guidelines that accompanied Principle 1 hold true for Principle 2 as well and are expanded upon through Principle 2. The need for Principle 2 is explored by reviewing the advantages of classroom diversity as well as the impact that teaching with diversity in mind can have on the practice of effective teaching. Principle 2 is then examined in light of how it can affect the education of ELs and students with disabilities as well as the processes necessary for establishing Principle 2 in the evaluation of educators working with these populations of students. Included are look-fors, a sample teacher evaluation rubric from Rhode Island, and scenarios developed to contribute a solid understanding of Principle 2 and its application in classrooms for ELs and for students with disabilities.

FOCUS OF PRINCIPLE 2: PREPARING TO SUPPORT ALL LEARNERS

Principle 2 definition: Educators demonstrate their knowledge of individual student backgrounds as well as the strengths and advantages student diversity brings. They articulate rationales for using appropriate instructional strategies to support diverse learners so that every student will be treated as a valued individual capable of learning.

Principle 2 centers on diversity, its value in the classroom, and how teachers can thoughtfully and carefully adjust learning to make it meaningful and engaging for all students through the design, development, and implementation of lessons and units. Understanding diverse student strengths, preferences, and modalities can assist in providing educational opportunities in which all students can participate and grow. In the case of ELs, it is crucial to possess knowledge of each EL's background, as each EL's previous experiences may affect learning of the English language as well as of content. As a result, the teacher will need to adapt instruction accordingly to ensure students' acquisition of language and content. In the case of students with disabilities, knowing the disability categories and recognizing variations within those categories can assist in planning and carrying out lessons where accommodations and modifications, if necessary, are seamless.

Whereas Principle 1 examines the mandates for educating ELs and students with disabilities, Principle 2 continues to connect the issue of accessibility to the day-to-day delivery of instruction. Therefore, pre-observation conferences should focus on teacher knowledge of student diversity and the strengths and advantages such diversity brings. Exploring rationales for various instructional strategies is one key to understanding how diversity fits into teacher planning and instructional delivery. Also, any instructional adaptations that are in place for diverse students need to be reasonable and balanced against opportunities for complete and full access to the grade-level standards.

Principle 2 is also designed to focus educators' attention on the individualization of instruction and on teaching strategies that reflect the tenets of universal design for learning[1] (UDL; Rose & Meyer, 2002). Therefore, the foci of the observation as well as the pre- and post-observation conferences should be on teachers' being able to articulate the multiple ways that diverse learners will be engaged in the lesson, how the information provided during the lesson will be represented, and how students will express the learning that they have achieved.

Making sure that the performance of all students is guided by high expectations and measured against varied and well-designed assessment instruments and experiences administered with appropriate accommodations is also a necessary touch point for this principle. Conversations between teachers and evaluators can also include the theoretical and evidence-based practices for designing lessons specifically with the diversity of the classroom in mind. Finally, the classroom environment (when visited for the observation) can provide insight into how Principle 2 and the need for capitalizing on student diversity are being operationalized in practice. Flexible grouping, mindful design for connecting students, frequent checks for understanding, prominent and rotating displays of student work, and a conscious effort on the teacher's part to structure student engagement deliberately into the lesson may all point to a teacher's ability to work successfully with diverse student populations.

WHY PRINCIPLE 2, PREPARING TO SUPPORT ALL LEARNERS, IS NEEDED

Principle 2 tends to come into play during the planning of instruction. As indicated in Figure 5.1, classroom instruction is a cyclical process in

Figure 5.1 The Cycle of Instruction

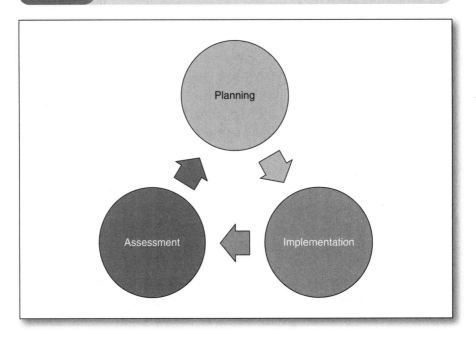

which teachers constantly plan instruction, implement instruction, and assess their students' growth as a result of their instruction. As a result of their analysis of student assessment, they alter their planning for the next cycle of instruction. Effective teachers continually undergo this process of planning, implementing, and assessing their instruction and reflect on all three components.

Principle 2 provides a means by which a teacher can demonstrate knowledge of his or her students, and buoyed with that knowledge, a teacher who adheres to Principle 2 increases the likelihood of a student-centered classroom. In the case of ELs, for diversity to be effectively used and celebrated, the teacher should be aware of his or her students' home language, cultures, and backgrounds. For students with disabilities, the individualized educational plan (IEP) process and product must be sound. For both groups of students, the recommendations developed in Principle 1 should all be in place. While adhering to the blueprint of the student's program on the one hand, a classroom where student diversity finds expression can capitalize on the strengths and strategies noted in designing the EL's language support services or the student with disabilities' IEP.[2] Therefore, students actively participating in the lesson that will be observed and showing themselves to be a valued part of the classroom would be sound indicators of an environment where diversity is seen as a strength and managed for the good of all learners. Peer support within the classroom is critical as part of this process (Alquraini & Gut, 2012).

By focusing on the benefits of diversity while planning for instruction, Principle 2 emphasizes the components necessary to implementing a welcoming classroom environment for all learners. Although movement in states toward implementing College and Career-Ready Standards (including the Common Core State Standards) necessitates concern about increased rigor and maximum exposure to standards-driven content, teachers will still have to create environments of compassion and empathy to help students engage successfully with learning (Morcom & MacCallum, 2012; Staehr Fenner, 2014). Effective classrooms for ELs as well as students with disabilities are marked by a keen and palpable sense of community, which is captured in Principle 2. This sense of community can develop in the school and in the classroom by encouraging and enhancing student views of difference as positive and as strengthening community (Purnell, 2007). Therefore, this sense of belonging in community requires clear effort that can be understood both through the pre-observation meeting and the observation process and should be approached as a shared responsibility of the teacher and the administrator who may be in charge of the evaluation.

Students in such caring classrooms may well have been provided the option to set rules, share perspectives, and regularly find emotional and psychological support (Brock, Nishida, Chiong, Grimm, & Rimm-Kaufman, 2008; McTigue & Rimm-Kaufmann, 2011). In short, all aspects of students' growth, including academic growth, have been accounted for. In particular, ELs may approach instruction with a high "affective filter," or a high level of anxiety, fear, or frustration that they may feel in a learning environment that interferes with the process of acquiring an additional language (Krashen, 1982). All teachers of ELs need to create a comfortable learning environment in which their ELs feel supported in taking risks with the English language in order to acquire it, thereby lowering their students' affective filters. Educators who embody Principle 2 in the planning and implementation of instruction recognize this potential for ELs' detrimental high affective filter and seek to create a caring environment where ELs can feel safe to increase their linguistic proficiency through trying out more complex forms of the language, often making mistakes as they learn about and attempt to use more complicated linguistic structures in English. In the same way, students with disabilities can feel disenfranchised and alienated from the learning process in schools, particularly as they get older, because they recognize the inherent differences present in the challenges they face to learn (Brown, Higgins, Pierce, Hong, & Thoma, 2003).

Students with disabilities in classrooms that embody Principle 2 may also have been empowered to analyze and better understand personal and cultural perspectives on disability and their implications (Kennedy & Menten, 2010). This understanding can begin with recognizing disability as another form of diversity in the classroom and actually including students with disabilities in conversations about diversity without shying away from individual differences (Olkin, 2002). Positive behaviors are supported and encouraged at the levels of the district, the school, the classroom, and the individual students so that behavioral challenges are clearly understood and managed among diverse population of students (Sailor et al., 2006).

ELIMINATING DEFICIT THINKING

Teachers in classrooms where Principle 2 has been effectively implemented also know their multifaceted students and can use this knowledge to help students do their best to learn. Educators in effective classrooms choose to eliminate deficit thinking and its vocabulary from their interactions with students and with colleagues.

For example, when describing a student who has either newly arrived to the United States or has a growing command of English, their teacher would not describe them as the student who "speaks *no* English" but rather as a student who speaks a certain home language, is an emergent bilingual, or who is learning English in addition to his or her home language. Additionally, it is as important for educators to acknowledge the language(s) the student is most likely orally proficient in and may also be literate in. It is important to stress ELs' strengths and acknowledge that even though they may be learning English, they already speak another language and bring a rich culture to their classrooms. They are not a tabula rasa.

Students with disabilities in these classrooms have had patterns of strengths and weaknesses analyzed and documented (Schultz, Simpson, & Lynch, 2012) and understand their own strengths and preferences (Weishaar, 2010). In addition, the delivery of instruction under Principle 2 focuses on engagement, representation, and expression that guide student meaning making through their individual strengths and preferences. Individual disabilities are seen in the context of the successes and contributions these individuals can make, and again, judgments are based on the individual student rather than on any broad descriptive category (Armstrong, 2012).

Student collaborations and cooperative learning opportunities are carefully designed and closely monitored under Principle 2 to maximize the positive effects of peer-mediated learning. Educators in these classrooms recognize the benefits of frequently using cooperative learning strategies to developing healthy peer relationships among students with and without disabilities (Putnam, Markovchick, Johnson, & Johnson, 1996; Taylor, Peterson, McMurray-Schwartz, & Guillou, 2002). During preconferences, the design of those groups and their effects can be described and discussed (Carter, Cushing, Clark, & Kennedy, 2005; Hendrickson, Shokoohi-Yekta, Hamre-Nietupski, & Gable, 1996). During observations, the ways in which student cooperative groups function and are assessed can be determined as can their effect on establishing a climate of diversity. Group learning can serve as an important peer-mediated learning strategy in inclusive classrooms (Keel, Dangel, & Owens, 1999; Maheady, Harper, & Mallette, 2001; Malmgren, 1998). The general tone and tenor of the school can be reflected in classroom activities such as cooperative learning as well, so discovering and engaging in issues critical to equitable access such as instructional leadership, the uses of assessment, and levels of adult collaboration in the school overall are important topics in the process of evaluation (Voltz & Collins, 2010). Relationships between adults on teaching teams as they reflect diverse viewpoints can be explored while troubleshooting difficulties and facilitating improved communication as part of the evaluation process (Rice, Drame, & Owens, 2007). Administrators should be willing and eager to learn from these conversations as well.

Classrooms where diversity is employed to enhance learning consistently emphasize student choice. For students with disabilities, because of fear of choice, poor personal awareness, or a lack of knowledge of strengths and weaknesses, this may require teaching making choices (Cote Sparks & Cote, 2012; Shevin & Klein, 2004). Accommodations, modifications, and curricular adaptations can also be implemented through the IEP and taught as elements of making choices, particularly when using technology (Marino, 2009; Smith, Dittmer, & Skinner, 2002). Research has also highlighted the need to provide students, including those with severe intellectual disabilities, options to respond to reading comprehension tasks (Hudson, Browder, & Wakeman, 2013). Students who are consistently provided choices may interact with their colleagues and their teacher more frequently and respectfully.

WHAT PRINCIPLE 2 MEANS FOR ELs

Preparing to meet the needs of ELs first involves recognizing the strengths they bring to the classroom, be they resiliency or linguistic, cultural, and/or experiential strengths. To prepare to instruct ELs, all teachers will need to know their students' backgrounds, including language(s) spoken in the home, English language proficiency, culture, previous education experiences, and life experiences. As teachers get ready to implement instruction for ELs, they will also need to consider students' identities as language learners and be aware of how comfortable their students feel taking risks with the language. For example, teachers will need to know whether their ELs like speaking in English in whole-class discussions or whether they prefer to work in pairs or small groups.

In addition to focusing on ELs' backgrounds that will affect how they are instructed, teachers of ELs will also need to consider the strategies they will use to teach ELs. Since all teachers of ELs are also language teachers, they will need to teach ELs academic language as well as content to foster ELs' success in both areas, providing temporary scaffolding techniques to support ELs in the classroom. Staehr Fenner (2014, p. 150) outlines the following considerations in designing effective instruction for ELs:

- Be cognizant of their cultures and background experiences, and build on these factors during instruction.
- Create content and academic language objectives based on content standards as well as English language development standards. [Content and language objectives do not need to be separate and may be integrated.]
- To guide instruction, analyze the academic language demands of any text given to students.
- Plan for how they will be instructed before, during, and after reading complex text.
- Design appropriate assessments, so they can demonstrate what they know and can do in the English language and with the content.

The College- and Career-Ready Standards (CCRS) Lesson Evaluation Rubric in Table 5.1 is a tool that can help teachers and evaluators determine how much consideration has been given on preparing to teach ELs (Staehr Fenner & Snyder, 2014). It can also be used to evaluate how suitable a teacher's own CCRS-aligned lesson is for ELs during the lesson planning phase and to gauge the usefulness for ELs of a content lesson the teacher has developed or lessons that have been developed by another teacher or a curriculum writer.

WHAT PRINCIPLE 2 MEANS
FOR STUDENTS WITH DISABILITIES

Principle 2 is based on teachers' appreciation and knowledge of student diversity and the creative use of that diversity for the benefit of all learners in the classroom. Teachers' outlooks and attitudes regarding diversity

Table 5.1 College- and Career-Ready Standards Lesson Evaluation Rubric: Meeting the Needs of English Learners

Lesson Criteria	Lesson Does Not Meet the Needs of ELs	Lesson Partially Meets the Needs of ELs	Lesson Meets the Needs of ELs
Alignment between lessons, tasks, CCRS,[a] and ELD standards	The lesson plan does not contain ELD[b] standards or the tasks in the lesson do not align with the CCRS and ELD standards described.	The lesson contains both CCRS and ELD standards. However, the lesson tasks are not fully aligned with the standards. The lesson may or may not contain student-friendly objectives, or student-friendly objectives are not well developed.	The lesson documents clear alignment between the lessons, tasks, CCRS, and ELD standards. The CCRS and ELD standards and objectives are integrated into instruction. The lesson includes student-friendly objectives.
Regular practice with complex text and its academic language	There is limited opportunity for students to learn and practice academic language. There are few strategies to support EL engagement and participation.	The lesson contains some opportunities for ELs to practice academic language. There are some strategies to support EL participation and engagement. However, not all activities contain such strategies, or the strategies do not appropriately account for ELs of varying proficiency levels.	Academic language instruction is woven throughout the lessons. Each lesson activity provides scaffolding for ELs of varying proficiency levels. Lesson includes strategies to support EL engagement and participation (e.g., providing/accessing background knowledge, flexible grouping, sentence stems or sentence frames, visuals).

(Continued)

Table 5.1 (Continued)

Lesson Criteria	Lesson Does Not Meet the Needs of ELs	Lesson Partially Meets the Needs of ELs	Lesson Meets the Needs of ELs
Reading, writing, and speaking grounded in evidence from text, both literary and informational	The lesson does not contain questions that require close reading and analysis of the text for a response, or the questions are not appropriately scaffolded for ELs. The lesson does not offer opportunities for students to practice the four language domains (speaking, listening, reading, and writing).	The lesson contains questions that require close reading and analysis of the text, but the questions are not appropriately scaffolded for all levels of ELs. The lesson offers opportunities for students to practice some of the language domains.	The lesson contains text-dependent questions scaffolded for ELs (e.g., use of sentence stems and/or sentence frames, unfamiliar vocabulary defined within the question). Students have opportunities to practice all four language domains throughout the course of the lesson.
Building knowledge through content-rich nonfiction	Background knowledge is not provided for ELs. The lesson does not include a variety of strategies to support the development of ELs' content knowledge such as modified texts or home language support.	Background knowledge is provided for ELs, but it may be too much, too little, or not concisely taught. The lesson includes some vocabulary instruction. Some modified texts or home language support may be provided. Strategies are not differentiated by proficiency level.	An appropriate amount of background knowledge is concisely taught to ELs. The lesson includes an appropriate amount of targeted vocabulary instruction. Modified texts and home language support are provided as needed. These strategies meet the needs of students at varied proficiency levels.
Assessment	The lesson does not include formative or summative assessments of both content and language development.	The lesson includes formative and/or summative assessments to assess students' academic language and content development. However, these assessments do not take into account students' varying proficiency levels.	The lesson includes formative and/or summative assessments to effectively assess ELs at different proficiency levels' academic language and content development. Performance-based rubric(s) are provided.

a. College- and Career-Ready Standards

b. English language development

must be based on the same commitment to equal access that is the hall-mark of Principle 1. Added to that principle is the active support and integration of student diversity into lesson design, development, and implementation.

For students with disabilities, this means a classroom that is student centered. Students with disabilities are seated among their peers, scattered throughout the classroom, and an observer is unable to tell who among the class has a disability and who does not. The environment in the classroom is welcoming. Students are happy. They enjoy being with this teacher and with one another. They are eager to engage with the skills and content of the classroom. They are confident citizens who are well respected by the adults in the room and by their colleagues in the learning process.

The general education teacher and the special education teacher together, if the classroom is cotaught, have equal command of content and a clear and complimentary understanding about their students and the range of strengths and talents with whom they work. These teach-ers can employ multiple means of coteaching from "one teach, one assist" through "parallel teaching" and "station teaching" to "team teaching" with equally positive results. Their delivery of instruction is seamless, with each teacher confident, as a result of the coplanning process, in the exper-tise of his or her colleague and the direction of the lesson. Expectations have been clearly delineated, and there is never a threat of one or the other teacher capitulating or deviating from the agreed to social, emotional, and academic outcomes. The focus of the lesson is directly and unrelentingly on skills and content, and the teachers manage a full range of strategies, including flexible grouping on a regular basis, to engage and support learner growth.

In classrooms where the general education teacher works singly, it is clear that he or she has become educated in the understanding and use of the opportunities provided when working with diverse populations of students. Through the use of high expectations for all students, well rein-forced and practical routines, predictable and consistent consequences, and immediate and targeted feedback, the teacher manages the classroom structure so that students feel safe and respected. The teacher has put in place protocols whereby students are accountable to one another for the comportment and conduct of the lessons. Each student has a firm grasp of the lesson objectives and the goals and outcomes for the unit and the year. Students with disabilities regularly review their annual goals and benchmarks and can, sometimes with assistance, articulate their pro-gress toward those goals. As in other classrooms, simple and clear rules of responsible conduct prominently posted, evidence of student work, and student progress both individually and collectively documented and displayed are hallmarks of classrooms where diverse student needs are met. In addition, students are aware through visual displays and from classroom conversations that may be the topic of evaluators' pre-observation meetings, that personal success can be modeled and measured by numerous examples of achievement by persons with disabilities.

The strengths of each student find emphasis in the manner that the lesson is delivered, and their understanding is expressed. It is evident that various forms of student style preferences and multiple intelligences have been thoroughly designed and integrated into the fabric of the lesson. Assessment strategies reflect the range of styles and preferences in the classroom, and students are comfortable with the choices provided as well as with the levels of challenge being offered. Preferences and intelligences are mixed and matched, access to individual help and support is ensured, and students feel empowered to ask questions and ask for help. Assistive and regular classroom technologies are in full and frequent use, and both general education and special education teachers have been educated in their use and in troubleshooting the machinery.

Adequate and appropriate considerations have been given to the categories of disability in the classroom through careful planning and creative implementation. Students with issues of mobility have clear access throughout the classroom to peers and resources in the same way that their nondisabled colleagues have. Students with behavioral issues have specifically designed supports and well-documented plans to help accommodate and mitigate issues as they arise, and adult interventions are available for them as well that have been developed and orchestrated in advance. Students with disabilities in reading and mathematics have several options provided for engagement, representation, and expression, and they are confident in their ability to contribute to class discussions and to small-group interactions. Resources for students with blindness or visual impairments are available electronically, aurally, or by Braille. Students with autism have been provided visual aids and organizers, while students with attention disorder have adequate accommodations for movement and engagement. Students with intellectual disabilities also have adult support if necessary and through pace and repetition, they are provided opportunities to connect with skills and content and to practice skills through different content circumstances. Students with disabilities are given equivalent choices to the ones provided for their nondisabled peers and they are engaged in group and classwide decision making and classroom governance. Students with disabilities are provided identical opportunities to exercise responsibility as are their nondisabled peers. In short, students with disabilities are shown the same dignity and respect as shown to nondisabled students and are encouraged and supported to learn in ways that are fair and that indicate high expectations.

PROCESS OF INTEGRATING PRINCIPLE 2 IN TEACHING

The groundwork for realizing Principle 2 in teaching begins on the first day of school and is emphasized every day thereafter. This process occurs through the careful building of community in the classroom, through the conscious effort of acknowledging and building on student strengths and preferences, through the careful grouping of learners, and through the integration of student choice. Schoolwide and administrative supports help the implementation of Principle 2 through engendering positive behavioral supports and creating a community of safety, health, and respect. Adults (parents included) with diverse strengths, needs, and cultures are also acknowledged and woven into the fabric of life at the school. Seeking to understand (Covey, 2007) is the first priority for relationships among all the members of the community. For example, school publications, including codes of conduct and regular newsletters, are provided to families in their language of preference, and website information is accessible through different languages and to individuals with disabilities. Principle 2 applies to the pre-observation conference and to the observation itself, but there may be some indicators that educators can discuss in the post-observation meeting that evaluators can be made aware of.

PROCESS OF INTEGRATING
PRINCIPLE 2 FOR ENGLISH LEARNERS

Knowledge of students presents itself with a number of opportunities for both evaluator and teachers. For educators of ELs, Principle 2 requires both macro- and microlevel knowledge of linguistically diverse populations and their strengths as well as needs within school communities. To successfully implement and uphold Principle 2, educators must deepen and widen their sense of responsibility for ELs including providing cultural, linguistic, and social support.

For educators of English learners, it is important to realize that English learners are not a monolithic group. English learners differ in a number of ways but what does unify them is that they speak home languages other than English. For evaluators, knowledge of the EL population across all grade levels, including the number of monitored students (those who have reached proficiency within the past two years), home languages spoken by

ELs, whether they are long-term ELs, and the number of students dually identified as an EL with a learning disability is essential. For the teacher, knowledge of the same data is needed but at the classroom level. The data may continuously change as students move in or out of communities; it is important for educators to regularly ask for and be notified of changes. Most likely, the ESOL teacher is aware of the data that are required to inform Principle 2.

Being aware of and being able to articulate an understanding of one's EL population is undoubtedly part of preconference conversations. Also part of those conversations is the need to be able to describe and clarify the model (e.g., coteaching, dual language, leveled ESOL courses) of language support implemented at the school. Clarifying the model of language support will assist teachers and evaluators in understanding their role in a student's academic experience. In-depth knowledge of the language model will include the process by which ELs are identified, required assessments, and parent notification. The ESOL teacher is a go-to resource for collecting and updating EL information.

From a curricular standpoint, it is essential that both the evaluator and teacher be well versed in both content and language standards, curriculum, curriculum maps, curriculum guides, assessments (including any performance-based rubrics), and grading practices for ELs at all their grade levels. Having knowledge of what is expected to be taught and assessed by teachers of ELs and mastered by students is an essential part of the evaluation process. Administrators have the opportunity to support all teachers and personnel who work closely with linguistically diverse learners by creating a school community where language, culture, and differentiated instruction are valued and supported. The teacher can demonstrate his or her understanding of differentiating for ELs based partly on the student's English language proficiency level. Other factors, such as a student's learning style, developing all domains of language (speaking, listening, reading, and writing), classroom configurations and the content being taught should be considered as part of pre-observation conversations as well. For teachers to know not only how to differentiate due to an EL's language proficiency level but also why that specific type of differentiation will provide students access to content concepts is key for successful school communities that serve ELs. That depth of knowledge by both evaluators and teachers takes a high level of investment so that there is a thoughtful knowledge base that supports differentiated instruction and not a random use of teaching strategies. Principle 2 presents opportunities to improve not only teacher practice and student outcomes but school communities that serve diverse learners as well.

PROCESS OF INTEGRATING
PRINCIPLE 2 FOR STUDENTS WITH DISABILITIES

Potentially, from preconference discussions and from the evaluators' knowledge of the character of the student body, the population of students in the classroom has been established as reflecting the natural proportion of students with disabilities to students without disabilities. The evaluator has been advised and educated and, consequently, understands not only the range of disabilities but the types of student responses and behaviors that can occur in this particular classroom mix.

Teacher thinking is critical to understand for Principle 2 to be fully evident. Focusing on the needs of groups of students with disabilities (classifications of disability) within the classroom may be a starting point to describing and discussing the approaches to learning that the teacher envisions. Centering the pre-observation conversation on specific students in the classroom may help determine the nature and extent of the differentiation involved in the instruction as well as how well the teacher understands the student's strengths and the barriers to student learning. Also important to the process is capturing the methods by which individual student outcomes can be measured and articulated as well as focusing on whole-group outcomes. Conversations can use the framework provided by UDL—engagement, representation, and expression (Rose & Meyer, 2002)—to center on the nature of differentiation in the classroom. As teachers describe the lesson that evaluators will witness, evaluators can gauge the degree to which student engagement, multiple means of representation of skills and content through scaffolds and supports, and varied assessment strategies are present within the lesson.

As has been seen, administrative support for students with disabilities is crucial for the achievement of these populations. It goes without saying that the teaching necessary to ensure their success does not take place in a vacuum. Rather, as leaders and as evaluators, administrators, and persons responsible for the supervision of personnel in schools must create an environment where good teaching can thrive. Building trust is an important first step (Tschannen-Moran, 2009). Beyond that, the same attitudes, beliefs, and strategies that build community and develop academic success in classrooms are similar to the ones that help create a sense of belonging, emotional safety, and professional engagement for teachers, support personnel, and related service providers. Administrators should be open to creating supports for students with disabilities through the redeployment of available paraprofessional personnel. The responsibility for the successful advancement and graduation of all learners falls to the principal.

Necessary allocation of time, especially for coplanning, and reasonable distribution and access to materials and resources in the service of all learners are important prerequisites to ensuring that all students, particularly those in these vulnerable populations, succeed. Without these essential components being in place, conversations between evaluators and teachers may focus less on valuing diversity and on building community and more on acrimonious debates about how all students can be best educated. Open and honest conversations during team and faculty meetings and during professional development opportunities throughout the school year can focus on the beliefs and attitudes as well as the methods that lead to a greater sense of community in classrooms. Valuing diversity as strength in the community can be explored.

PRINCIPLE 2 QUESTIONS FOR DIALOGUE

Questions to consider during these opportunities for dialogue between teachers and evaluators may include the following:

- Does our school utilize strategies that help *all students* develop ongoing, natural friendships and supportive relationships with other students and teachers? How do the adults in our school model and support respectful friendships and relationships with all community members?
- Do *all students* in our schools have opportunities to engage in co-curricular and extracurricular programs? If not, how can we redesign our co-curricular and extracurricular offerings to ensure that every student has access to them?
- Does our school provide a variety of individualized, coordinated services designed to address the unique strengths and challenges of *all students*, such as pre-referral services, English for Speakers of Other Languages (ESOL) and/or dual language programs and services, response-to-intervention systems), schoolwide positive behavioral supports and anti-bullying programs? How can we improve these systems of support for *all students*?
- Does our school help *all students* make successful transitions (e.g., between classes, from elementary to middle school, from school to work/postsecondary education) and develop self-determination?
- Does our district achieve and sustain a 100% graduation rate with *all students* advancing to fruitful and self-fulfilling postsecondary opportunities? If not, what steps can we take to help students make successful transitions and develop self-determination, and how can

we reduce the rate at which students leave school before achieving a high school credential?

- Are our school's services, policies and practices diversified? Do they take into account the cultural, linguistic and experiential backgrounds of all students and their families? Who is represented in our community, and how can we provide them a voice regarding our school's services, policies and practices? (August, Salend, Staehr Fenner, & Kozik, 2012, pp. 2–4)

LOOK-FORS FOR PREPARING TO SUPPORT DIVERSE LEARNERS

Look-fors for Principle 2 should be evident in both the pre-observation meeting and during the observation itself. They may also be evident in the post-observation. The pre-observation conversation can focus on the community of the classroom and the environment that the teacher has created for his or her learners. Using community-building practices with strong evidence bases such as responsive classroom will certainly indicate a conscious effort on the part of the teacher to engender a sense of social engagement, emotional safety, and belonging for students. Tables in this section can help educators document their general understanding of concepts embodied by Principle 2 and how they can prepare to support ELs and students with disabilities. Each table provides a space for evaluators to indicate whether evidence has been found for each of the look-fors as well as a place for comments related to the look-for. Some of the look-fors pertain more to pre- or post-observation conversations, and others lend themselves more to observation of classroom instruction. The sample look-fors provided are meant as a starting point for educators' conversations about teacher evaluation that is inclusive of ELs and are by no means an exhaustive list. Educators are encouraged to adapt these look-fors so that they reflect educators' unique contexts.

Look-Fors for Teachers of English Learners

First and foremost, teachers of ELs should be able to articulate high expectations for their diverse learners that demonstrate an understanding of what ELs can do with language at their English language proficiency level. To formulate these expectations, teachers of ELs must know the home language and proficiency level of their students as well as any background factors that may affect their performance in the classroom. The higher the level of literacy an EL possesses in the home language, the more quickly that EL should acquire literacy in English, as skills developed in one language tend to transfer to an additional language.

For example, consider the situation of Ms. Bethea, a third-grade teacher. Ms. Bethea teaches Adira, an EL at the intermediate level who is literate in Arabic, as well as a student named Masira, an Arabic speaking EL also at the intermediate level but who has not developed literacy skills in Arabic. Ms. Bethea may set different expectations for the type of writing both students will produce in English and should develop different types of supports for each student's writing. While the teacher must recognize that Adira and Masira will develop English proficiency at different rates, she must still give both students access to challenging content in English but with appropriate, differentiated scaffolds and supports that may be unique for each student.

As part of Principle 2, all teachers of English learners should be able to articulate how ELs' culture and previous educational experiences can affect how they interact with students and teachers. They need to be aware of the many different types of ELs in their classrooms and how they must adapt their instruction to meet their ELs' needs. For example, ELs who have not been previously schooled in the United States may have a tendency toward rote learning instead of student-centered learning. Level of English proficiency notwithstanding, those students may feel more comfortable copying information from a whiteboard than working in small groups. As a result, teachers of these students will need to provide them extra support to transition them into group work. Students with interrupted formal education (SIFE) or students who have experienced gaps in their education for reasons such as poverty or war may not be used to school routines that non-SIFE students adhere to (DeCapua & Marshall, 2011). For example, SIFE students may not understand classroom expectations for taking turns or procedures for dismissal. ELs who have not been schooled in the United States may not be familiar with concepts such as a school yearbook, pep rallies, or attendance policies that teachers may take for granted. Long-term ELs who may have been born in the United States but who have not reached proficiency in English after several years of instruction may require extra support of their literacy skills in order to make progress in English.

Teachers of ELs should be able to articulate an understanding of how ELs' cultures may influence their behavior and conduct. They should be able to cite examples of how ELs' cultures are included in classroom instruction and which types of adjustments they make to their classroom environment to accommodate ELs' cultures. Along those same lines, teachers of ELs should be able to articulate and also model expectations of classroom routines for ELs who are not familiar with cultural expectations that play out in the classroom. Even if ELs have been schooled solely in the United States, they might not be familiar with the expectations at the classroom level. Therefore, teachers should model expectations for routines such as the collection of homework, expectations for when students can leave their seats, procedures for seeking permission to visit the restroom, and expectations for standing in line. Even if they were born and schooled in the United States, ELs' home cultures may influence how they participate in classrooms on a day-to-day basis. For example, in some cultures, standing in line is much less organized than in the United States, and people tolerate closer distances (i.e., the concept of personal space is not the same). By consequence, ELs may not adhere to the teacher's expectations of maintaining space between students and keeping hands to oneself while standing in line.

Beyond the impact of culture on students' behavior, culture may also influence how students work together. Teachers of ELs should be aware of the potential influence of culture on aspects of student engagement such as body language. For example, ELs might show respect for the teacher by not making direct eye contact. In addition, a student's culture may also influence the way in which he or she organizes oral discourse and structures writing. These student outcomes may fall outside teachers' expectations for students, and all educators of ELs should be familiar with the potential impact of culture on ELs' work products.

In addition to being aware of the influence of culture on ELs' behavior and work, all teachers of ELs must demonstrate awareness that appropriate scaffolding needs to be provided in instruction so that ELs can interact with challenging content. To demonstrate this awareness, teachers of ELs need to be familiar with different types of scaffolds that are appropriate for ELs at different levels of proficiency.[3] By default, they also need to know the proficiency levels of their ELs and also know which types of scaffolds their ELs tend to respond best to. For example, teachers of ELs may find that sentence frames tend to work better for their ELs at beginning and intermediate levels of proficiency, while word banks and glossaries are effective for a wider range of their ELs. All teachers of ELs should collaborate with ESOL teacher(s) to determine which types of scaffolds will be most effective for their students.

Finally, teachers of ELs should be able to explain how their classroom's physical space affects ELs' opportunities to participate in the classroom and supports their acquisition of English. For example, teachers should be able to talk about and demonstrate how classrooms are configured so as to promote ELs' interactions with other students and with the teacher. Classrooms should be set up in a way that promotes partner and small-group interaction with ELs and other students so that ELs can practice and apply language structures they are learning throughout their school day.

Table 5.2 highlights key components of sample Principle 2 look-fors that are specific to all teachers of ELs.

Look-Fors for Teachers of Students With Disabilities

In terms of what to look for during the process of teacher evaluation for educators of students with disabilities, much depends on the kinds of disabilities present in the classroom and their relative intensities. Teachers should exhibit a clear basic understanding of the social and academic barriers that may be present among the 13 categories of disability determined

Table 5.2   Principle 2 Look-Fors for All Teachers of ELs

Principle 2 Look-For	Evidence Found: Yes or No	Comments
Articulates high expectations for ELs, including a nuanced understanding of expectations for what ELs can do with language at their English language proficiency level and the supports necessary for each level		
Describes the role of home language literacy skills and the strategies used to support English acquisition		
Articulates how ELs' culture and previous educational experiences affect how they interact with students and teachers		
Articulates how ELs' culture may influence their behavior and work produced		
Describes a variety of strategies to effectively scaffold material for students of varying proficiency levels		
Describes configuration of classroom space so as to support EL's opportunities to participate in classroom activities and their acquisition of English		
Describes plans for lowering students' affective filter and encouraging risk taking in English		

by federal regulations and among the students in the classroom with any of these disabilities or with co-occurring disabilities. Teachers should be able to describe the adaptations, modifications if necessary, and accommodations that help govern the delivery of instruction to these students. At the same time, educators being evaluated should be able to express the methods by which student strengths and challenges have been determined, how these strengths and challenges will be incorporated into the lesson being observed, and how these strengths and weaknesses affect teacher decision making in the classroom (Schultz et al., 2012). Also, teachers should be able to articulate their high expectations for students with disabilities and have access to grade-level appropriate materials, skills, and content.

In addition, all teachers should be able to describe the social and emotional connections that these students enjoy in the classroom and what means are being implemented to make sure of these connections, such as morning meetings, peer-mediated learning, and heterogeneous grouping. Teachers should be able to articulate how their efforts at encouraging community are connected to the goals, objectives, and accommodations for students with disabilities in their classrooms. Also, all teachers should be able to describe the adaptations for these students that will result in greater engagement and connection to the classroom community. Through the planning process, all teachers should be able to express an understanding of each student's strengths and weaknesses, learning preferences, and the effects that a disability may have on the student's classroom performance. Teachers should be invited to describe the behaviors of students with more profound disabilities and their efforts to work with the students in the class in developing an atmosphere that is safe, friendly, respectful, and conducive to learning.

During the observation, an evaluator should be attuned to the emotional tenor of the classroom, focusing on the comfort level of students and watching the lesson from the point of view of the student. The observer can be aware of signs of disengagement and resistance on the part of students. Likewise, watching for how peers interact with one another and what supports are in place for constructive responses to various behaviors can help measure levels of community in the classroom. How well teachers keep students on task, how they handle disruptions to the flow of teaching, and the respect and positive regard they provide students can also be among the look-fors that observers can hope to see. Specifically, during the instruction of classrooms inclusive of various disabilities, the look-fors shown in Table 5.3 can help the process of observation. Table 5.3 provides key components of sample Principle 2 look-fors that are specific to all teachers of students with disabilities.

Table 5.3	Principle 2 Look-Fors for All Teachers of Students With Disabilities

Principle 2 Look-For	Evidence Found: Yes or No	Comments
Articulates a clear, basic understanding of the social and academic barriers that may be present among the 13 categories of disabilities in general		
Articulates a clear, basic understanding of the social and academic barriers that may be present among the students in the classroom with disabilities or with co-occurring disabilities		
Describes the adaptations, modifications, and accommodations being used with students and how they support students' learning		
Articulates high expectations for students with disabilities		
Describes access to grade-level appropriate materials, skills, and content		
Describes the social and emotional connections that these students enjoy in the classroom and what means are being implemented to make sure of these connections		
Describes adaptations for students that will result in greater engagement and connection to the classroom community		
Describes implementation of classroom practices that show respect for students, help students stay engaged and on-task and, minimize classroom disruptions		
Keeps students on task, adeptly handles disruptions to the flow of teaching, demonstrates respect and positive regard for students		

Look-fors for All Teachers of ELs and Students With Disabilities

Table 5.4 outlines sample look-fors for teachers of ELs as well as students with disabilities. The look-fors provided in this table are applicable

Table 5.4	Principle 2 Look-Fors for All Teachers of ELs and Students With Disabilities

Principle 2 Look-For	Evidence Found: Yes or No	Comments
Describes a classroom that has a high degree of structure in which students' roles and responsibilities are clear		
Articulates the multiple ways that diverse learners will be engaged in the lesson, how the information provided during the lesson will be represented, and how students will express the learning that they have achieved		
Describes how diverse students interact and work cooperatively with others		
Articulates high expectations for all students		
Recognizes the role students' culture and prior educational background play in their classroom behavior and learning preferences		
Describes the strategies used to determine students' strengths and challenges and how this knowledge of strategies results in effective classroom instruction		
Describes the strategies for supporting students' social and emotional connections and community building in the classroom		
Describes significant variation in the pace and duration of lessons and activities based on students' backgrounds and needs		
Describes how students help one another with skills and content		
Describes how a safe environment is established with encouragement for positive behavior while ignoring minor inappropriate behavior		

for teachers of both groups of students. Although ELs and students with disabilities leverage many unique characteristics that are not common across both groups of students, there are look-fors that apply to all teachers of ELs as well as students with disabilities.

SAMPLE FROM RHODE ISLAND
STATE TEACHER EVALUATION RUBRIC

Pages 137–138 show an example of how Rhode Island educators have designed their teacher evaluation rubrics that serve as examples of Principle 2 (Rhode Island Federation of Teachers and Health Professionals, 2012). For this rubric's component, Designing Coherent Instruction, the rubric first outlines four levels of performance applicable to teachers of all students. It then highlights considerations specific to all educators of English learners and also considerations specific to all educators of students with disabilities that detail how these diverse populations of students must be included teacher evaluation. These extra considerations describe how ELs and students with disabilities' outcomes may differ from non-ELs and students without special needs. The rubric includes considerations for both populations of students in the two additional rows of the rubric that reference the elements found in Principle 2, such as front-loading information for ELs and UDL for students with disabilities. These additional considerations for ELs and students with disabilities, coupled with the rating of "highly effective," provide one state's expectations for educators in meeting Principle 2: preparing to support all learners.

PRINCIPLE 2 SCENARIOS

Following are scenarios that provide examples of pre- and post-observation conversations between educators and their evaluators regarding Principle 2. Note how these teachers clearly articulate how they designed and executed the lesson observed in order to support the needs of all learners in their classes.

Middle School EL Scenario

Mr. Holborn, an eighth-grade mathematics teacher, has been teaching for over 10 years. He is actively involved in his school community and serves on the board of the local teachers union. Mr. Holborn mentors preservice teachers and is assigned as the chair of the mathematics department this year. He teaches five 90-minute blocks of mathematics class per day in an urban school. Approximately 80% of the student population at the school receives free and reduced lunch. The class observed has 24 students, 11 males and 13 females. Half of the students in Mr. Holborn's class are identified as English learners

RHODE ISLAND RUBRIC SAMPLE

Standard 1: Planning and Preparation

Component 1.3: Designing Coherent Instruction

A teacher translates instructional outcomes into learning experiences for students through the design of instruction. Even in classrooms where students assume considerable responsibility for their learning, teachers must design instruction that is coherent and balanced between careful planning and flexibility in execution. Teachers design instruction that reflects the needs of 21st-century learners and include opportunities to solve problems, collaborate, innovate, and create using high-level cognitive processes and communication tools and media (Danielson's FfT, 2007).

Elements / Performance Indicators	Ineffective	Developing	Effective	Highly Effective
1.3.a Learning Activities, Lesson Structure, & Content –Related Pedagogy R1PTS 1,2,3,4,5	Learning activities are not suitable to students or to instructional purposes, do not reflect instructional purposes, do not reflect the range of pedagogical approaches suitable to student learning of the content, and are not designed to engage students in active intellectual activity. The lesson has no clearly defined structure, and/or time allocations are unrealistic.	Only some of the learning activities are suitable to students or to the instructional outcomes and reflect a limited range of pedagogical approaches or some approaches that are not suitable to the discipline. Some represent a moderate cognitive challenge, but with no differentiation for different students. The lesson has a recognizable structure, although the structure is not uniformly maintained throughout.	Learning activities are suitable to students or to the instructional outcomes and reflect teacher's familiarity with a range of effective pedagogical approaches in the discipline. Most represent significant cognitive challenge, and with some differentiation for different groups of students, help students to construct content knowledge and build 21st-century skills.	All learning activities are highly suitable to diverse learners, support the instructional outcomes, and reflect a wide range of effective pedagogical approaches in the discipline. They represent significant cognitive challenge, and with differentiation for individual students help students to construct content knowledge and build 21st-century skills. The lesson structure is clear and allows for different pathways according to diverse student needs, anticipating student misconceptions and the needs of 21st-century learners.

(Continued)

(Continued)

RHODE ISLAND RUBRIC SAMPLE

Elements / Performance Indicators	Ineffective	Developing	Effective	Highly Effective
		Progression of activities is uneven, with unreasonable time allocations.	The lesson has a clearly defined structure on which activities are organized. Progression of activities is even, with reasonable time allocations.	The progression of activities is highly coherent with appropriate time allocations.
Considerations for ELLs:	<td colspan="4">• Learning activities and lessons should incorporate academic language. • Progress and progression of activities may take longer, and more front-loading of information may need to happen to make sure that ELLs understand. • Teachers will need to have access to specialists or support personnel knowledgeable about ESL.</td>
Considerations for SWDs:	<td colspan="4">• Learning activities and lessons should incorporate Universal Design for Learning (UDL) • Learning activities and lessons need to be tailored to students' instructional and developmental levels. • Teachers will need to have access to specialists or support personnel knowledgeable about disabilities.</td>

a. ELLs = English language learners

b. SWDs = students with disabilities

c. UDL = universal design for learning

who are Spanish speakers from Central America. A fourth of the students speak Spanish. He also has three Vietnamese students who are newly arrived to the United States. The majority of the students are at intermediate to advanced levels of English language proficiency and some are long-term ELs..

Mr. Holborn completed the state's approved endorsement for teaching English learners recently and was instrumental in arranging to have the endorsement courses taught to educators at his school. Even as an experienced teacher, he acknowledged the linguistic diversity of his school community and wanted to be more prepared to meet the needs of those students. Although evidence for Principle 2 can usually be found during the pre-observation, this post-observation conversation between Mr. Holborn and his principal Ms. Ray reflects the teacher's commitment to supporting the needs of all learners.

Post-Observation Conference Conversation

Ms. Ray: *Tell me more about the lesson that I observed. I noticed that you were introducing some new concepts.*

Mr. Holborn: *Yes, we are in the middle of our unit on consumer math. The students tend to enjoy this unit because I used examples of things they are interested in buying and already have at home.*

Ms. Ray: *I noticed that. You had the students in groups with varying tasks. Tell me about those groups.*

Mr. Holborn: *The groups have been working together since the beginning of this unit. I tried to balance the groups out by language level. Since I have mostly intermediate English learners, I have them assigned to multilevel language and math ability groups. I really want them to have a variety of models from their peers. Sometimes they listen to each other more than me. (Mr. Holborn chuckles)*

Ms. Ray: *I understand; their peers are very important to them. Here are some of my notes. You had four different groups; one group was comparing cell phone service plans, a second group was using iPads to research and calculate tip percentages, a third group was using calculators to calculate compound interest word problems, and you were with the fourth group working on math concepts around the city. Is that accurate?*

Mr. Holborn: *Yes, that's right. I had just reviewed the directions for each group. I have the directions in writing for each group to refer to as well. It can take a couple of class periods for each group to rotate through each assignment. The students use a group checklist to help them stay on task. They also know they'll have to complete a short written summary for me at the end of class, something like an exit ticket.*

Ms. Ray: *How have you integrated your students' background knowledge into instruction?*

Mr. Holborn: *For example, I learned that most of my students take public transportation to school. The group I mostly worked with was using maps of the city transit system to figure out the most economical way to get from one part of the city to another. We have been following the urban planning committee's plan to add an additional bus line for commuters.*

Ms. Ray: *How have your students responded to the use of exit tickets?*

Mr. Holborn: *So far so good. It's helped me address their concerns for future classes, too. I have even adjusted the group tasks based on the feedback they've given me.*

Ms. Ray: *That's great, I'm glad the students have taken an interest in consumer math.*

Mr. Holborn: *I am, too. I know that the students are working on persuasive essays in English language arts class. They are working on different arguments for and against the proposed bus line. What they are learning in math is helping them in English language arts class too.*

Mr. Holborn's cross-curricular approach to teaching consumer mathematics helps his students to make connections not only to other content areas but to real-world experiences as well. By applying critical thinking skills learned in mathematics, they will have more of a sense of responsibility as learners and consumers. Mr. Holborn was able to articulate his grouping strategies and how he supports the groups to work independently and cooperatively. The evaluator captured active student engagement and identified that part of the lesson for Mr. Holborn to explain his planning and assessment of the tasks as part of the post-observation conversation.

Elementary School Students With Disabilities Scenario

Ms. Haight has been teaching students with disabilities as part of a coteaching team in an inclusive kindergarten classroom for 5 years. The school where she works is in a rural part of the state with a free and reduced lunch rate of 47%. This year the class of 22 students in which Ms. Haight works has welcomed six students with disabilities, four with speech and language impairments and two boys, Zach and Ollie, who are students with autism. Mr. Ludezma, the Director of Special Education, will be observing Ms. Haight teaching in the classroom that includes two assistants for each of the children with autism and a speech therapist who pushes in three times a week for literacy instruction. The decision had been made during a daily co-planning session that included Ms. Haight and the general education teacher, Ms. Carmichael, that Ms. Carmichael would take the role for this lesson on initial letter sounds in words of working with the majority of the class. Ms. Haight would parallel teach the lesson with the two students with autism and three other students who could benefit from close monitoring and more individualized attention in a responsiveness to intervention model. The speech therapist, Ms. Jacks, will circulate the class, helping students with their letter sounds while focusing on the three students with speech and language impairments. While the class takes attendance, the lunch count, and practices the calendar and the weather for today, Ms. Haight and Mr. Ludezma talk during the pre-observation conference about the lesson he will be observing later this morning.

Pre-Observation Conference Conversation

Mr. Ludezma: *I see you're going to be identifying initial letter sounds in class today. Talk a little bit about the teaching you will be doing.*

Ms. Haight: *As you know, I coteach the class with Ms. Carmichael, and usually when we meet and co-plan we talk about the roles we will take in the class. Today, I will be parallel teaching with Zach and Ollie and three other children who are finding some challenges in their letter identification and initial sounds. Ms. Carmichael will lead the class in a song: "At the Teddy Bear Picnic," and the class will be asked to hold up the picture card that Ms. Carmichael describes like "Can you find the bear with the red apple?" or "Can you find the bear with the pink towel?" Then she'll ask, "What is the first letter in the word apple? And*

"What sound does the letter a *make in the word* apple*?"
We've got about 10 cards that show teddy bears holding
things or doing things. Meanwhile, I'll be working with
the small group of five on the same skill, only I'll be providing some additional prompts and cues by pointing to
the pictures or lining them up so that the correct one is
closest to me and giving Zach and Ollie and the others
more time to think through the sounds. Then on the car-
pet, Ms. Carmichael will read "Crazy Town Upside Down.
"While she does that, I'll read the book with my five children. It's a good book to read for them because it lets you
trace the letters with your finger, so I asked that we use it.*

Mr. Ludezma: *How will you know if the lesson has been successful?*

Ms. Haight: *All three of us, Ms. Carmichael, Ms. Jacks, and I, will be
keeping a running record of how well students can identify
the initial sounds in the words we ask them about.*

Mr. Ludezma: *Is there anything you'd like me to look for during the
lesson?*

Ms. Haight: *Yes. Depending on the day, Zach and Ollie can be engaged
with the learning at very different levels. Zach can be
pretty verbal, although he tends to disengage from what's
going on pretty easily. Ollie never speaks, although his
engagement can be high. His attention can wander, but
he'll come back to focus quickly if I address him. He loves
animals, though, so his focus should be pretty keen. I've
only begun working with the other three in this group, so
I want to have their full attention and learn more about
how they learn. Could you pay attention to how each child
is engaged in the lesson and suggest some ways that I
might not be using to keep them all focused?*

Mr. Ludezma: *I'll do my best. I look forward to the lesson.*

Importantly in the scenario, Ms. Haight has acknowledged a number
of different ways in which the diversity of the learners in this kindergarten
class can be addressed. First, she and the general education kindergarten
teacher have developed a plan for the lesson that includes a clear understanding of their coteaching roles and responsibilities. In addition, they
have solicited the speech therapist in not only monitoring youngsters in
her own group but in helping monitor other members of the class. Their

coordinated effort will allow them to represent and assess the learning from multiple perspectives. Second, although Ms. Haight has just begun working with three additional students in a response to intervention second-tier small group, the teachers in this scenario have a clear understanding of the various strengths, intelligences, interests, and barriers that characterize their students' learning, and they may be able to capitalize on this knowledge in different ways. Ms. Haight's suggestion of the book indicates her and Ms. Carmichael's understanding that tactile modalities can be important and can help with student engagement. Finally, even within the small group with whom she'll be working, Ms. Haight acknowledges the differences within the disability spectrum— the fact that no two individuals with disabilities are alike.

QUESTIONS FOR COLLABORATIVE CONVERSATIONS

To begin a discussion about the extent to which Principle 2 is embodied in educators' current teacher evaluation systems, educators can consider the following questions as part of self-reflection or discuss them in pairs or groups:

- How would you summarize the essence of Principle 2: preparing to support all learners?
- Which elements of Principle 2: preparing to support all learners resonated the most with you?
- Which look-fors of Principle 2 are you ready to integrate into your teacher evaluation system to provide equal access to ELs and students with disabilities?
- How will you integrate these look-fors into your teacher evaluation system?

CHAPTER SUMMARY

This chapter focused on the second principle, preparing to support all learners. The need for Principle 2, which builds from concepts in Principle 1, was explored by focusing on the diversity that ELs and students with disabilities bring as well as the effects of teaching framed in diversity. Look-fors, a sample teacher evaluation rubric, and scenarios for ELs and students with disabilities highlighted ways in which the elements of Principle 2 can be manifested in pre-observation conversations, including ways in which the classroom environment can affect the instruction of these students. In addition, sample teacher evaluation rubrics were shared that provide examples of the various elements contained in Principle 2.

NOTES

1. See Chapter 3 for more information on UDL.

2. Some ELs are also dually identified as needing special education services.

3. See Chapter 2 for more information on scaffolding instruction for ELs.

Principle 3: Reflective Teaching Using Evidence-Based Strategies

6

Many feel evaluations often focus on easy-to-observe practices such as classroom management and whether students are on task rather than looking for substantial evidence to address that all students can master the actual learning goals and objectives.

Ms. C. Hentz, Academic Data Coach

INTRODUCTION

This chapter focuses on Principle 3: reflective teaching using evidence-based strategies. Principles 1 and 2 outline the types of knowledge and dispositions teachers must have to help English learners (ELs) and students with disabilities succeed; they also describe what a well-organized and welcoming environment looks like, a place where different learners with varied strengths and backgrounds can work together. In addition to these areas of teaching ELs and students with disabilities, educators must focus on teachers' skill levels, using effective strategies to reach and teach all learners. Therefore, Principle 3 aims to highlight a teacher's ability to design, develop, implement, and assess effective instruction for all learners. This chapter explores the need for Principle 3 by reviewing the types of classroom strategies that result in effective classroom teaching in the service of all learners. The principle is then investigated for the benefits it provides ELs and students with disabilities as a result of reflective teaching using evidence-based strategies.

As is true for Principles 1 and 2, discussion of Principle 3, reflective teaching using evidence-based strategies, includes consideration of the processes involved for being aware of Principle 3 and identifying effective teaching practices firmly in the repertoire of professional staff. This chapter continues with a series of identifiable look-fors that evaluators can witness in effective classrooms where the teaching strategies are designed and implemented so that ELs and students with disabilities have opportunities for success. A sample teacher evaluation rubric from New York State as well as scenarios at the end of the chapter are designed to provide a firmer foundation for both teachers and evaluators in how explicit evidence for Principle 3 is manifested in the evaluation process and where, during observations, adherence to this principle can be made clear.

FOCUS OF PRINCIPLE 3: REFLECTIVE TEACHING USING EVIDENCE-BASED STRATEGIES

Principle 3 definition: Educators' classroom instruction embodies the tenets of universal design for learning (UDL). Instruction is individualized, student centered, varied, appropriately challenging, standards based, and grounded in evidence-based practice. Educators build instruction with their diverse students' unique strengths, challenges, backgrounds, experiences, and needs in mind.

Evidence for Principle 3 is what typically comes to mind when one thinks of classroom observations that are a part of teacher evaluation systems. Through scheduled observations and unscheduled walk-throughs, teacher performance in classrooms is documented and evaluated. Principle 3 highlights the use of techniques and strategies that engage, enhance, and ensure diverse student learning on classrooms. As such, the principle depends on the implementation of the principles of UDL (Rose & Meyer, 2002) as a means to include and differentiate instruction for all students, particularly ELs and students with disabilities. As an evaluator, using a UDL framework for evaluation of diverse learners means paying close attention to how the principles of UDL are manifest in lesson design and implementation.

Simply put, UDL focuses on the why (engagement), the what (representation), and the how (expression) of learning in classrooms. Fundamentally, UDL relies on the use of flexible materials and media that provide students options for learning and that respond to the particular strengths, needs, and preferences that different learners display. The principles of UDL can apply to teaching all learners, as various strategies, technologies, and media can enhance experiences for everyone in the classroom (Edyburn, 2010).

Observations focused on the UDL framework will uncover a seamless design in the delivery of content and skills to diverse students. UDL requires that teachers think through lessons carefully and deliberately and make whatever formats students use easily available, with the skills to use these formats taught as well. With UDL, the purpose behind the lesson is clear, and elements of novelty and relevance are apparent. All students use the options available to them to participate in the lesson as appropriate, including the use of screen technologies and manipulatives, while accommodations and modifications are also employed to assist with all students' access to the curriculum. Several means to gauge students' level of understanding of the lesson are used in different modalities (e.g., visual, auditory, kinesthetic) and through various intelligences (Gardner, 1983). Appropriate classroom accommodations that support ELs as well as students with disabilities are encouraged in the process. Figure 6.1 provides a visual representation of the three different elements of UDL.

EVIDENCE OF ENGAGEMENT IN UDL CLASSROOMS

Engagement for all learners is firmly established as part of lesson planning and in providing instructional delivery. The relationships between the teacher and his or her students as a result are warm and respectful. The teacher is clear as to the direction of the lesson, the essential question(s) of the unit, and the objectives for the unit, all of which have been made clear, visually or otherwise, to the students in the classroom. For ELs in particular, the teacher communicates the content as well as the academic language objectives of the lesson to students in a form they will understand. In a dual-language classroom setting, the objectives may be for home language or partner language development and may be presented in the home language.

When working in a UDL framework, the teacher also understands the larger context and relevance of the lesson for all learners and is able to communicate the application of the skills and content students are learning. The application and content is taught explicitly—that is, clearly and systematically (Seo, Brownell, Bishop, & Dingle, 2008). As new content is provided, academic vocabulary, academic language, concepts inherent in the material, definitions, problems and their solutions, and strategies for learning are taught, reviewed, periodically summarized, and practiced by

Figure 6.1   UDL Learner Differences

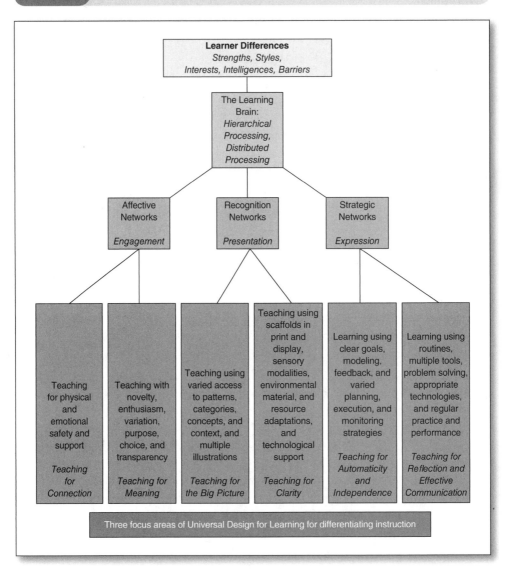

students. Beyond explicit teaching, learners are coached, and their progress is continually monitored and assessed.

EVIDENCE OF REPRESENTATION IN UDL CLASSROOMS

Representation in the UDL framework highlights the multiple ways in which information can be provided and various skills practiced. Although not wholly dependent on technology, Principle 3 also pinpoints the use of structure and routine in classrooms. This structure includes focusing the teacher on articulating both careful unit and lesson design and on expressing intended and actual student outcomes that may become topics of a post-observation conference. Students should appear well versed in the routines of the classroom and should follow these routines with minimal to no interventions from the teacher. In the case of ELs who are new to the U.S. education system, teachers will take the time to ensure students are able to follow clear classroom routines. By the same token, lessons should be designed and implemented so that students can regularly attempt understanding and application of skills and content through guided and independent practice and receive feedback about the relative success of their attempts.

In terms of representation, there can also be regular adjustments and adaptations in place for learners as the teacher becomes aware of how diverse students are engaging with the lesson. These adjustments and adaptations can take the form of scaffolds. To provide effective scaffolds for diverse learners, teachers need to exercise elements of Principle 2 since scaffolds should be tailored to students' backgrounds, including their disabilities and linguistic, cultural, and socioemotional strengths as well as areas of need. Because no two diverse learners are exactly the same, the types and amounts of scaffolding used for one (e.g., visuals, home language support) might vary from the types and amounts of scaffolding used for another student (e.g., adaptive technology, graphic organizers) with a different background.

For example, even with a strategy such as inquiry-based instruction for science, which has been shown to yield positive results for student achievement in the discipline (Scruggs & Mastropieri, 2007), students with disabilities may need additional scaffolds for learning in the form of direct guidance (Palincsar, Magnusson, Cutter, & Vincent, 2002). ELs at lower levels of English proficiency may benefit from the scaffolds of directions and written materials presented in their home language if they are literate in that language. Detailing scaffolds to learning should be evident in teacher thinking and in the implementation of the observed lesson. These can include visual and graphic representations of content, cues and prompts, flexible grouping of students, varied questioning techniques, and reviewing and summarizing lesson information.

EVIDENCE OF EXPRESSION IN UDL CLASSROOMS

Expression in the UDL framework aims to develop multiple means of assessing student understanding of what is taught. In the case of ELs, teachers and schools are accountable for these students' achievement in content and also their growth in English language proficiency. For students with disabilities, a critical emphasis in evaluating and documenting their instruction is on determining not just what the instruction may look like in the classroom but also what the outcomes are like for the students being taught (Heward, 2003). Therefore, some system for developing both groups' long-range goals as well as for monitoring student progress toward those goals should be in place for the evaluator to see (Stecker, Fuchs, & Fuchs, 2005; Wiggins & McTighe, 2005c).

The systematic monitoring of progress toward long-term goals for students with disabilities and all diverse learners should be technically adequate—that is, carried through with fidelity and with equivalent forms of measurement. The monitoring of all students should lead to education decisions about individual student learning as well as program impact through diagnostic thinking (Capizzi & Fuchs, 2005). Wiggins and McTighe (2005c) contend that learning goals depend on essential questions developed through "big-picture" thinking by teachers about the skills and content they need to provide their students to ensure success. Consequently, to be certain that Principle 3 is in play for teachers during the design, implementation, and assessment of lessons, pre- and post-conferences can elicit teacher thinking and reflection on observed lessons in an effort to understand the strategies used in the context of larger concepts and outcomes for diverse learners.

WHY PRINCIPLE 3 IS NEEDED FOR TEACHERS OF ENGLISH LEARNERS

Principle 3 is crucial to ensure that all teachers who work with ELs employ UDL-aligned strategies so that ELs at varying levels of English language proficiency receive the kind of support they need to be successful in acquiring academic language simultaneously with challenging content. While College- and Career-Ready Standards (including the Common Core State Standards) hold promise for setting high expectations for ELs, teachers will need guidance and support in bringing those standards to life for ELs during instruction so that ELs can be positioned for success. All teachers of ELs will need to include ELs' culture in instruction, teach academic language, and appropriately scaffold instruction for ELs at different levels of English language proficiency. For teachers to be recognized for their efforts in adjusting their instruction for ELs, it is essential to base teacher evaluation in regard to look-fors that highlight specific strategies teachers should be using for ELs in inclusive classrooms.

One area in which teachers of ELs must be skilled is in knowing about their ELs' cultures and including their ELs' culture in instruction when possible. There has not yet been a direct relationship proven through empirical research in terms of student outcomes and including culture in instruction (August & Shanahan, 2006). However, literature reviews related to effective programs for ELs have repeatedly found that such programs exemplify a strong and intentional community of respect and acceptance, both within and beyond the school (Ochoa & Cadiero-Kaplan 2004; Williams, Hakuta, & Haertel, 2007). Thomas and Collier's (1997) classic findings also suggest that a cultural atmosphere that demonstrates acceptance of ELs can make a difference in EL student outcomes. Schools and districts that view ELs' culture as a valuable asset rather than a problematic deficit tend to create positive environments that are more conducive to ELs' success.

In addition to including their ELs' culture in instruction, teachers also need to analyze the academic language found in the materials they use during instruction and explicitly teach the linguistic structures ELs need to fully participate in lessons. For example, prior to basing a lesson on the use of a particular text, teachers of ELs need to analyze the academic language found in that text, anticipate language that might be particularly challenging to ELs, and explicitly teach ELs examples of academic language. Teachers will need to be on the lookout for potentially problematic language for ELs at three levels: the lexical/vocabulary level, the grammar/syntax level, and the discourse/organization level. Once they have identified especially challenging words, phrases, complex sentence structures, discourse, and organization in the texts[1] they are using, teachers need to weave in instruction on these features of academic language so that ELs can acquire academic language in tandem with content.

A final area in which Principle 3 calls on all teachers to be teachers of language is through necessitating the use of appropriate scaffolds during instruction. Scaffolding techniques supported by recent research include (1) teaching a set of academic vocabulary intensively across several days using a variety of techniques, (2) integrating oral and written English language instruction into content area teaching, (3) providing regular structured opportunities to develop written language skills, (4) providing small-group instructional intervention to students struggling in literacy and English language proficiency (Baker et al., 2014), and (5) drawing from students' home language skills and knowledge during instruction (Francis, Rivera, Lesaux, Kieffer, & Rivera, 2006).

While many scaffolds[2] are also beneficial for all students (e.g., graphic organizers, having students summarize and paraphrase), home language scaffolds are of unique benefit to ELs. Multiple research studies indicate that ELs draw from conceptual knowledge and skills acquired in their home language and apply that knowledge and those skills to learning an additional language (Dressler & Kamil, 2006). In addition, instructional methods that help ELs use their home language knowledge and skills promote literacy development in an additional language (August, Branum-Martin, Cardenas-Hagan, & Francis, 2009; Carlo et al., 2004; Liang, Peterson, & Graves, 2005; Restrepo et al., 2010).

Some ways to include home language support for ELs include having glossaries that feature home language translations, providing supplemental reading or video clips in students' home language, assigning bilingual homework activities, and pairing ELs who are at beginning levels of language proficiency with bilingual partners so that they can discuss the academic topic in a student's home language and/or in English. In addition, teachers can instruct students on how to use home language cognate knowledge to unlock the meanings of unknown words in English when their language shares cognates with English

WHY PRINCIPLE 3 IS NEEDED FOR
TEACHERS OF STUDENTS WITH DISABILITIES

Although full inclusion of students with disabilities has been a goal for a number of years (Will, 1986), research on successful strategies for engaging these students, representing skills and content, and assessing learning for this population has been sporadic. The advent of the Common Core State Standards would seem to herald enhanced possibilities for achievement for students with disabilities (Parrish & Stodden, 2009). Like annual goals, these standards represent specific targets for learners, thus making the acquisition of these standards possible. Proven instructional strategies as well as a focus on professional collaboration[3] can benefit students with disabilities in their meeting these instructional standards (Bulgren, Sampson Graner, & Deshler, 2013).

The development of responsiveness to intervention (Fuchs, 2003; Fuchs, Mock, Morgan, & Young, 2003) suggested another potential direction for the identification and management of learning disabilities, representing by far the greatest number of children needing special education, predicated on notions of validity and fidelity rather than on previously held notions of discrepancy and deficit. This new direction also laid bare the effects of poor teaching as leading to the increased struggles of children and young people in reading and in mathematics (Hollenbeck, 2007). Teacher thinking in terms of fully understanding student needs as well as strategies to address these needs should be part of the conversations in the evaluation process, and the manifestation of this thinking should be evident in classroom observations. Hence, the potential for teaching well so that all students advance in the curriculum has become a rallying cry for educators and policymakers interested in equity and a globally proficient workforce.

Although slow to develop, the research base for successfully teaching students with disabilities has been growing, and various strategies have been researched, analyzed, and developed in addition to those characterized by responsiveness to intervention. Expectations should be clearly high for students with disabilities, and positioning them as having and developing expertise along with their nondisabled peers can have significant impact on their learning (Tobin, 2007). Learning must be well organized; routines and procedures should be in place and followed (Tobin, 2007). Preteaching strategies, particularly in content area classes, can also be focuses of preconference conversations (Berg & Wehby, 2013). Beyond attitudes and the relationships that teachers seek with students, based on the research evidence, peer-mediated learning in various forms seems to be one of the keys to helping students with disabilities succeed academically that evaluators can expect to see in classrooms (Mastropieri et al., 2006). So, for example, collaborative strategies such as Numbered Heads Together when used regularly can increase academic performance and help develop on-task behaviors (Haydon, Maheady, & Hunter, 2010). Other strategies may include collaborative learning strategies for reading and for vocabulary acquisition (O'Brien, 2007; Shook, Hazelkorn, & Lozano, 2011).

For students with disabilities and for all learners, direct explicit instruction and strategy instruction remain as having significant impact on the development of skills and understanding within the K–12 curriculum (Flores & Kaylor, 2007). Explicit instruction focuses on critical content and skills that are sequenced logically as well as analyzed, taught, and synthesized. In addition, the lesson is well organized; goals and objectives are clear and explicit; examples and nonexamples are provided; learners are supported by guided and independent practice; and there is frequent teacher-student and student-student interaction. Finally, student progress is monitored closely; feedback is immediate, affirming, and corrective; the pace is brisk; the knowledge imparted is organized; and ample time is allotted for distributed and cumulative practice (Archer & Hughes, 2011).

The emphasis on feedback throughout the learning process is important, too, because regular well-conceived assessments and the data they provide are the cornerstone of good teaching. Thus, conversations about assessment should be a priority for evaluators as well as observed evidence of the use of active and continual methods of determining and documenting student understanding (Wiggins & McTighe, 2005c). In addition, teacher attitudes and philosophies about grading practices for students with disabilities and about the application of appropriate accommodations and modifications should also be described and discussed (Kurth, Gross, Lovinger, & Catalano, 2012).

WHAT PRINCIPLE 3 MEANS FOR ELs

While many strategies that benefit ELs also have the added benefit of supporting non-ELs (e.g., explicitly teaching academic language, using graphic organizers), effective teaching of ELs often goes beyond what can be defined as "just good teaching." Authors de Jong and Harper (2008) refer to the phenomenon of providing ELs the type of specialized support they need that takes their unique cultural and linguistic variables into consideration as "good teaching *plus*." Principle 3 helps define a sample of research-based, observable teacher behaviors for all teachers who work with ELs that exemplify "good teaching plus" for ELs. Included in these behaviors are strategies for scaffolding instruction for ELs at different levels of English language proficiency who bring a wide range of backgrounds to the classroom.

Figure 6.2, EL Lesson Implementation Checklist, outlines several elements of effective lesson implementation for all teachers of ELs that can

Figure 6.2 EL Lesson Implementation Checklist

Checklist for Effective EL Instruction	Yes	No	Comments
Have I created content and language objective(s) for the lesson—either separate or integrated?			
Did I share the lesson objectives in student-friendly language with my ELs?			
Did I analyze the academic language demands of the text(s) used in the lesson[4] prior to teaching the lesson?			
Did I teach salient academic language found in the text(s) to ELs during the lesson?			
Did I determine ELs' level of background knowledge of the topic?			
Did I provide ELs with the right amount of concise background knowledge they needed to access the content of the lesson without giving the content away?			

Checklist for Effective EL Instruction	Yes	No	Comments
Have I provided effective scaffolds (e.g., home language support, graphic organizers, sentence frames and/or stems) for ELs at different levels of English language proficiency so they can access the content of the lesson?			
Have I incorporated instruction of each language domain (speaking, listening, reading, and writing) in the lesson?			
Have I provided frequent opportunities and support for ELs to interact with each other and with me about the challenging content?			
Have I provided support (e.g., modeling, sentence frames, and/or sentence stems) for ELs to use academic language when they interact with each other and with me?			
Have I provided support to ELs in guessing unknown words and phrases (e.g., using cognates, using prefixes and suffixes)?			
Do the questions I used during instruction offer ELs opportunities to cite textual evidence and use higher-order thinking skills? Are these questions scaffolded for ELs at different levels of proficiency?			
Have I provided extra support through the use of materials in the students' home languages for ELs at lower levels of proficiency (e.g., video clips, texts in the home language for students literate in the home language, website URLs?)			
Have I designed and implemented at least one formative assessment to assess ELs' acquisition academic language and content in the lesson?			
Did I determine the language domain(s) and the purpose for the assessment(s) used?			
Was my assessment aligned to content and language objectives?			
Did I share a student-friendly version of the assessment rubric or scoring guide with students so they would be aware of my assessment expectations?			

Source: Adapted from Staehr Fenner (2014).

be used as part of Principle 3 and can be integrated into pre- and post-observation conversations. This checklist can be used as a catalyst for the pre- and post-observation discussion with an evaluator. It can also be used in conjunction with the look-fors checklist found at the end of the chapter to provide examples of scaffolds needed for the instruction of ELs during instruction.

WHAT PRINCIPLE 3 MEANS FOR STUDENTS WITH DISABILITIES

Once teachers have fully understood the law and equal access, developed attitudes that all children can succeed, and focused on the diversity in their classrooms as a strength and necessary for learning, designing and implementing strategies in relentless pursuit of optimal learning is the logical next step. With truly inclusive classrooms flourishing, students with disabilities can expect to be exposed to differentiated teaching methods that apply the UDL framework regularly and successfully.

Students with disabilities are part of a classroom environment where routines and procedures ensure safety and regularity and the fullest use of the time available. They participate in flexible groups, are regularly called on to contribute to class discussions and activities, engage in the class fully comfortable and with a sense of belonging, and are challenged with high expectations of what they can accomplish. They, along with their nondisabled peers, are provided options for how they engage and interact with content and materials and choices for how they are evaluated as to the success of their understanding. Multimedia resources are readily available and used; textbooks, for example, are provided in digital formats so that students with disabilities, when appropriate, can read what they choose, write at least once a day, and discuss what they are reading and writing with their peers (Allington & Gabriel, 2012). In addition, they listen to a fluent adult read text, and their own fluency and comprehension is frequently checked and assisted (Allington & Gabriel, 2012). This focus on literacy, adjusted to various academic content areas, should be the approach throughout the PreK–12 curriculum because it combines the principles of direct instruction with sound practice, such as student choice and collaborative learning (Marzano, 2002).

The supports provided by well-designed scaffolds in the form of prompts and cues, graphic and visual representations, summarizing and taking notes, setting objectives, and continual feedback among others can provide students with disabilities with secure means of access to the general education curriculum. There is evidence of progress monitoring in the classroom as well as evidence that student achievement data is shared regularly with students (and with parents and other teachers), provided in a graphic format for ease of understanding so that students are invited to monitor and adjust their own progress.

Finally, classroom management for students with disabilities may appear different for different students, depending on the disability and the plan for managing behavior in the individual classroom. So evaluators need to be versed in methods of redirecting student behavior, signal interference, proximity interference, and planned ignoring among others in an effort to understand how students with various disabilities are provided behavioral supports (Brownell, Smith, Crockett, & Griffin, 2012). Self-modeling, a successful intervention that videotapes disruptive behaviors for students with intellectual disabilities in inclusive classrooms, can also be described and discussed (Bilias-Lolis, Chafouleas, Kehle, & Bray, 2012). Pre-observation conversations about what evaluators can expect to see coming into inclusive classrooms can help the process of understanding how different management techniques can be applied. Also, in postconference meetings, discussing how successfully and how consistently these management techniques were applied can help teachers hone their approach and keep them accountable to their own thinking and planning. In short, as with all the principles elaborated in this book, evaluator knowledge of the range of potential strategies and interventions for students with disabilities as well as their openness to learning from their teachers will contribute to the overall success of students with disabilities in inclusive classrooms.

PROCESS OF IMPLEMENTING PRINCIPLE 3

Understanding the design and implementation of evidence-based teaching can be addressed throughout the evaluation process. It can begin with the pre-observation conference, with a focus on the conception of the lesson to be observed and the assessments the teacher intends to use to gauge the lesson's success. The understanding can continue through the observation, with the evaluator particular attentive to the agreed-upon strategies as well as the flow of the lesson and the success of the lesson from the perspective of the students participating. The understanding can extend to the post-observation conference when a review of the lesson as well as the outcomes and assessment practices employed by the teacher can be the focus of much of the reflection and conversation.

It is important during the preconference for the evaluator to establish with the teacher what he or she might expect to see in this population of students, given the range of disabilities that may be present in the classroom. Therefore, it may be valuable to review the portions of the teacher evaluation rubric that require specifically that students initiate learning activities—for example, by expressing their own questions, offering their own graphic organizers, or generally enriching the comprehension and learning in the class. For some students with low-incidence disabilities, these behaviors may still be developing and yet to be realized. The pre-observation conference can focus in part on the challenges in documenting these particular behaviors and in how the challenge of students' engaging in these behaviors is being met.

Conversations that teachers have with one another about students and about student work can provide topics of conversations with evaluators. Time as well as a structure should be provided for these teacher-to-teacher conversations to happen on a regular basis. For example, it may be appropriate for a teacher being evaluated to share assessment data and student work with an evaluator, perhaps during a post-observation meeting, in the same way that he or she is used to describing and discussing student artifacts in meetings with colleagues. This conversation can be particularly beneficial in determining the achievement levels of ELs and students with disabilities when the artifacts are compared with annual goals, objectives, and learning benchmarks.

PRINCIPLE 3 QUESTIONS FOR DIALOGUE

The importance of the process of providing teachers professional development on critical learning for developing Principle 3 cannot be overlooked. In fact, a continual focus on exemplary evidence-based instruction throughout the school and district is vital to achieving and maintaining success for ELs, students with disabilities, and all learners.

- Does our school provide *all students* with access to a challenging, high-quality, and developmentally appropriate curriculum aligned to the state's standards[5] within and across content areas? If so, how can we improve this access? If not, how can we improve the quality of the curriculum and redesign curriculum delivery to make sure it is fair and provides equal access for *all students*?
- Does our school give *all students* access to effective and varied instructional practices and an appropriate amount of instructional time? If so, how can we ensure continual improvement of these practices and instructional time allocations? If not, in what ways do we need to change our instructional practices and time

allocations so that *all students'* strengths, challenges, diversities, backgrounds, language needs, styles, abilities, and preferences are addressed?

- Does our school provide *all students and teachers* access to current and innovative instructional and assistive technologies? If not, how can we find and utilize our available resources so that all students and teachers have access to these technologies?

- Does our school support classroom instruction that is characterized by differentiation, flexible groupings, student- and group-directed learning, high-quality language development, cultural sensitivity and responsiveness, and authentic and relevant learning experiences? If so, how can we continually improve these practices? If not, in what ways can we provide the necessary professional development and support to change our classroom instruction to encourage and sustain these practices?

- Does our school utilize a variety of valid and reliable measures to assess student learning progress and inform instruction? Does our school offer students the appropriate assessment accommodations and alternatives they need to demonstrate their learning? What additional measures, assessment accommodations, and alternatives can we use to evaluate student learning and inform instruction?

- Does our school implement a comprehensive and multifaceted evaluation of all aspects of its programs and make improvements based on the data collected? How do we use data to enhance our educational programs so they benefit *all students*? What additional data can we use?

- Does our school use a variety of strategies and supports to help *all students* develop academic, social, and civic-engagement skills? How can we make sure that meaningful engagement is encouraged, modeled, and celebrated at the school, in the classroom, and with individual students? (August, Salend, Staehr Fenner, & Kozik, 2012, pp. 2–4)

LOOK–FORS FOR REFLECTIVE TEACHING USING EVIDENCE-BASED STRATEGIES

Tables in this section can help educators document their general understanding of concepts embodied by Principle 3, including the use of evidenced-based strategies in the instructions of ELs and students with disabilities. Each table provides a space for evaluators to indicate whether evidence has been found for each of the look-fors as well as a place for comments related to the look-for. Some of the look-fors pertain more to pre- or post-observation conversations, and others lend themselves more to observation of classroom instruction. The sample look-fors provided are meant as a starting point for educators' conversations about teacher evaluation that is inclusive of ELs and are by no means an exhaustive list. Educators are encouraged to adapt these look-fors so that they reflect educators' unique contexts.

Look-Fors for Teachers of English Learners

In terms of look-fors that evaluators could use when determining the degree to which Principle 3 is enacted in all teachers' instruction, of ELs several areas should be evident during classroom observations as well as in conversations between teachers and evaluators. All teachers of ELs should structure their instruction by framing instruction with instructional objectives in mind that define the academic language ELs must use to access content. Such objectives can take the form of separate objectives for content and academic language or integrated content and academic language objectives that outline the academic language ELs will learn to support their learning of content. Another look-for that can be found as part of the start of the lesson is in the way teachers provide directions to ELs. All teachers of ELs should use directions presented in clear language both orally and in writing to the degree possible. Teachers should check for ELs' understanding of directions by having ELs rephrase directions in their own words, translate directions into their home language, and/or monitor ELs' response to directions to be sure these students have understood their task(s).

During instruction, the presence of several types of look-fors can indicate effective teaching of ELs. Teachers can use scaffolding techniques such as home language support, visuals, and graphic organizers[6] to support ELs at different levels of English language proficiency so that they can engage with challenging content. Evaluators should be able to note differences in the amount and type of scaffolding provided to ELs. ELs at higher levels of English proficiency should be provided fewer scaffolds, while ELs at lower levels of proficiency should be given more robust scaffolding during the instruction of content and language. For example, an EL at a beginner level of proficiency who is literate in her home language could be given a home language translation of a text that is also provided in English, a visual of the text, sentence frames to support her answers to questions in English, and a word bank. On the other hand, an EL at the advanced level of proficiency taking part in the same lesson could just be provided a word bank as a support for reading the same text in English.

Another look-for for all teachers of ELs is the use and type of the teacher's questions, including higher-order and text-dependent questions, that are scaffolded for ELs at different levels of English language proficiency. Such scaffolding could consist of providing additional supplementary questions that lead ELs to a deeper understanding of a text or other topic they are discussing in class, providing synonyms for especially challenging vocabulary found in questions, and sentence frames or stems to support ELs' answers to questions and to explain their thinking.

Teachers of ELs can also provide supports so that ELs can participate in discussions in pairs, small groups, and/or with the entire class. Such supports might consist of modeling classroom discussions, sentence frames/stems, and word banks to support their interactions in class and explain their thinking. Another type of support to ELs that can be evident is voicing the strategy behind the ways in which ELs are placed in pairs or small groups so that they are best positioned to interact with others and put the academic language they are learning into practice. Some look-fors in terms of grouping are placing ELs with more proficient peers, grouping ELs in like language groups so that they can discuss the topic in their home language, and being able to articulate the reason behind a particular grouping strategy.

A different type of look-for for teachers of ELs is the use of supplementary and/or adapted materials to support ELs at different levels of English language proficiency. While the Common Core State Standards call for the use of texts at grade level, ELs—by the very nature of second language acquisition—often read below grade level in English. Teachers of ELs must therefore be able to support ELs with additional materials on similar topics as those being discussed in class in order to support their reading of grade-level text. Such supplementary materials could include texts in students' home languages (if the students are literate in their home languages) and readings at a lower grade level in English on the same topic being discussed. In addition, video clips could be provided in the home language and/or English to build background knowledge on topics that non-ELs may already possess. While ELs should not be denied access to work with grade-level texts in English, they must be provided support through adapted materials as they gain proficiency in English.

A final set of look-fors for teachers of ELs involves the unique nature of creating performance-based assessments that allow ELs to demonstrate their acquisition of academic English and content. Some look-fors include the use of performance-based rubrics and/or checklists that are aligned to the lesson's content and academic language objectives, the inclusion of a rubric shared with students that is written in "student-friendly" language at a level of language that ELs understand, and the sharing of models of expectations for student work. For example, if the lesson culminates in the students writing a paragraph, ELs should be able to see the rubric that will be used to evaluate the paragraph as well as look at a model paragraph that exemplifies high-quality work.

Tables 6.1 shows key components of Principle 3 look-fors as they relate to all teachers of ELs. This robust table will help educators develop a general understanding of concepts embodied by Principle 3 and how educators can teach ELs using evidence-based strategies.

Look-Fors for Teachers of Students With Disabilities

Evaluators of classrooms of teachers of students with disabilities will need to use both pre- and post-observation conversations and the

Table 6.1 Principle 3 Look-Fors for All Teachers of ELs

Principle 3 Look-For	Evidence: Found Yes or No	Comments
Provides clear instructional content and language objectives for each lesson		
Encourages use of home language where appropriate		
Includes ELs' culture in instruction ELs' culture is included in instruction		
Provides directions in . . . in student-friendly language and/or students rephrase directions in their home language or English		
Uses analysis of the academic language in the materials used during instruction to explicitly teach linguistic structures ELs will need to fully participate in the lesson		
Uses performance-based rubrics and/or checklists (written in "student-friendly" language) aligned to the lesson's content and academic language objectives and shares the rubric with students		
Uses a variety of scaffolding techniques (e.g. sentence stems, word banks, glossaries, home language material) to support students of varying proficiency levels		
Provides adapted and supplementary material (e.g., home language text, readings at lower lexile level, videos) as needed to support student access to the content		
Students practice using language in small groups and pair work with support and scaffolding from the teacher		
Includes all four domains of language (speaking, listening, reading, writing) in instruction		

observation itself to determine how Principle 3 is being enacted in the teachers' instruction in the form of various look-fors. First of all, high expectations need to be clearly evident in the instruction of students with disabilities. These can be understood in pre- or post-observation conferences by focusing conversations with teachers on the goals of the lesson for all students and for students with disabilities and the means by which the success of the lesson will be established for these students. Listening for clearly framed goals and objectives that focus on measurable and observable outcomes can help determine whether and how a teacher's expectations are being woven into the fabric of the lesson. Also, questions about the appropriate thinking skills that students with disabilities will likely display and the scaffolds necessary to ensure their success at these skills can help create a broad understanding of teacher expectations during the lesson. Questions about the data available to the teacher and about the nature of the teacher's decisions regarding his or her expectations using that data will help frame an understanding of the teacher's expectations as well. Likewise, discussions about student strengths, styles, interests, and intelligences as well as the barriers to learning that students face and the ways in which these barriers are consciously being addressed can inform expectations. Finally, high expectations will be evident in the classroom as students with disabilities follow routines appropriately, are given responsibility for their learning, participate in classroom activities, interact with classroom peers and the teacher, and are given choices along with other students for the representation and expression of their learning.

In determining look-fors, observations can focus, among other indicators, on the levels of engagement for students with disabilities. Look-fors in effective classrooms include use of student experience, tapping background knowledge, and connecting student understanding to prior knowledge from the unit or units taught. Making the process of tapping previous knowledge clear, teachers can provide videos, include students in conversations about experiences, or have students represent their connection to the lesson through bell ringers and the recognition and development of already acquired patterns and content. Students with disabilities and all students should be regularly provided choices as to how they participate in the lesson. For example, evaluators can expect to witness teachers asking students how they want to read text, by way of paper, by way of a computerized e-reader, or by way of the text displayed on the SMART Board, screen, or some other medium. Depending on the disability, another look-for can be the use of leveled texts that reduce the complexity of the reading load while maintaining the curricular content. Approaches to text should be varied, so that students are not always given the choice of leveled texts nor are they always used as part of the lesson plan. Finally, having had open discussions about difference and disability with their students, teachers can heterogeneously group students in various configurations where nondisabled students and students with disabilities are given opportunities to problem solve together, review and practice work, and teach one another. Desks can be arranged for ease of access and stimulation and clutter can be kept to a minimum.

Varied types of representations are also important look-fors for students with disabilities. Word walls, vocabulary on index cards or associated with electronic or published icons, graphic representations in the form of diagrams or color-coded paper, or bookmarked documents for easy access depending on the content can also keep students with disabilities engaged in the flow of the lesson and contribute to the learning in the classroom. The observed lesson should be provided using multiple modalities. Attention can be paid to (1) students' visual acumen, through adaptations such as preferred seating and enlarged text; (2) aural receptivity, through amplified sound and closed captioning of videos, films, and PowerPoint presentations and podcasts; and (3) kinesthetic preferences, through manipulatives, stress reducers, medicine balls, and ample opportunity for movement. Providing directions simply and clearly can be the mark of a highly effective teacher. Therefore, during observations, directions should be read by students using the necessary assistive technologies and read out loud by the teacher. Academic vocabulary and challenging concepts should be anticipated in the lesson, taught as part of the regular lesson routine through multiple means, and provided in several examples through guided practice. With pretaught lessons, students with low-incidence disabilities can participate in answering higher-order questions and participating actively in classroom discussions. Summaries and taking notes can be emphasized using tape or computerized recording, speech-to-text recognition software, or peer-initiated strategies. Groups should be heterogeneously designed, with students completing work in pairs and triads and in small groups of no more than five individuals. Movement into groups should be anticipated and should be completed with ease and minimal disruption. Groups should be assembled with peer support and active teaching for students with disabilities as well as for all members of the class. All students should be responsible for their learning, for designing curricular goals and objectives, and for monitoring their progress.

Student action and expression as a means of assessing progress should also be evident in look-fors to the evaluator during the observation. The classroom should have a regular routine applied to the lessons, ample space and time for modeling as well as for guided and independent practice and daily evaluation. Regular, planned formative assessments can be discussed and described in either pre- or postconferences. Importantly, however, systematic monitoring of the progress through the lesson of students with disabilities and of all students should be emphasized as part of the evaluation protocol. Thumbs up/thumbs down, using three-colored discs, the use of whiteboards or electronic media such as clickers to check for understanding, or other strategies for formative assessment should be regularly applied with students with disabilities participating using preferred means of self-expression. Tickets out the door, regular journal entries to reflect on the learning taking place, and individual and group summaries can also provide teachers with formative data. In the same vein, summative assessments, ideally, should be performance based, calling on students to collect and connect the skills and knowledge learned from the unit in a coherent, relevant, and meaningful activity. If pencil-and-paper summative assessments are used, they should provide clear, concise directions, ample white space, reading loads ahead of thinking loads, and opportunities for feedback that will advance student learning. Table 6.2 outlines sample look-fors that are applicable to all teachers of

Table 6.2 Principle 3 Look-Fors for All Teachers of Students With Disabilities

Principle 3 Look-For	Evidence Found: Yes or No	Comments
Homework assignments are listed with approximate times for the completion of each assignment		
Presents content material in a variety of ways to support student learning (e.g., word walls, on index cards, graphic representations, on color-coded paper)		
Gives students choice choice in terms of how they learn and practice and are assessed on content		
Monitors student progress closely; feedback is immediate, affirming, and corrective		
Multimedia resources are readily available and used; textbooks are provided in digital formats		
Redirects student behavior, signal interference, proximity interference, and planned ignoring (among other strategies)		
Students are given choices for the representation and expression of their learning		
Emphasizes summaries and taking notes using tape or computerized recording, speech-to-text software, or peer-initiated strategies		

students with disabilities. These look-fors are intended to serve as a catalyst for educators' conversations about the inclusion of elements related to Principle 3 in teacher evaluation systems.

Look-fors for All Teachers of ELs and Students With Disabilities

Table 6.3 provides sample look-fors that are applicable to teachers of the combined group of ELs and students with disabilities. While the look-fors in Tables 6.1 and 6.2 are applicable to only ELs and students with disabilities respectively, Table 6.3 presents look-fors that share commonalities across both groups of students.

Table 6.3 Principle 3 Look-Fors for All Teachers of ELs and Students With Disabilities

Principle 3 Look-For	Evidence Found: Yes or No	Comments
Content is "chunked" into manageable, understandable parts that students can access easily		
Uses student experiences and his or her own experiences to relate to content and skills in the curriculum being taught		
Directions in the classroom are simple and clear and provided orally and in writing		
Uses strategies that guide students' learning and thinking (e.g., guided reading strategies, read- and think-alouds, review of skills and processes)		
Routines and procedures in the classroom are well established and have been modeled and practiced. The implementation of these routines is effortless and seamless		
Students regularly work in pairs and in groups for the purposes of practice, group work, projects, problem solving, and to assist one another in the learning in the classroom		
Uses different means to access texts that are read for class (e.g., e-readers, audio recordings, graphic novels, storyboards, graphics of narrative plot or subject exposition, home language where appropriate)		
Students are encouraged to think aloud to problem solve.		
All students are provided options for how information and materials are presented to them and used to be most accessible for them		

Principle 3 Look-For	Evidence Found: Yes or No	Comments
Students are provided preferential seating if necessary		
Instructional changes are made as a result of assessment data collected on students (including English language proficiency assessment data for ELs)		
Uses varied forms of assessment, including pencil-paper tests, performance assessments, and daily quizzes and assessment strategies for monitoring and measuring student progress		
Students are given ample time on tasks		
Students read and reread passages of text to one another and ask one another questions about what has been read with and without the teacher listening in		
New academic language is anticipated, pretaught, and taught directly, in context, and through several different examples when encountered during reading		
There is a word wall present in the classroom (when possible) or an academic language list accessible that teachers and students can contribute to on a regular basis		
Models text comprehension skills such as predicting and summarizing		
Some questions are provided to students ahead of the lesson		
Questions are scaffolded so that ELs and students with disabilities can answer them		
Students engage in frequent and active responses to activities and questions, individually and in groups		
Asks a variety of question types including higher-order questions and provides appropriate scaffolding as needed		
Clearly articulates the goals of each lesson along with observable outcomes that will demonstrate that students have met the lesson goals		

SAMPLE FROM NEW YORK STATE TEACHER EVALUATION RUBRIC

Following is an example of how New York State educators have designed their teacher evaluation rubric that serves as an example of Principle 3 (New York State United Teachers, 2013). The sample rubric from

New York State first delineates four levels of performance in the area of establishing instructional groups. It also clearly defines three considerations each for teachers of ELs and teachers of students with disabilities. In the case of teachers of ELs, specific guidelines are given for grouping ELs so that the students can practice the linguistic constructs they are learning in class with peers. For teachers of students with disabilities, the observation considerations indicate that student engagement may "look different" for these students, making educators aware that a successful teacher evaluation rating is indeed possible even when teaching students with disabilities. Considerations for teachers of both populations of students support collaboration with ESOL and special education specialists or support personnel to support classroom instruction.

New York State Rubric Sample

Indicators	Ineffective	Developing	Effective	Highly Effective
A. Establishes instructional groups	Teacher's grouping results in students who are not working with the teacher, are not productively engaged in learning, and/or exhibit disrespect to the teacher and/or other students.	Teacher's grouping results in students in only some groups being productively engaged in learning while unsupervised by the teacher. Student interactions are generally appropriate but occasionally may reflect disrespect for one another.	Teacher's grouping results in small-group work being well organized, and most students are productively engaged in learning while unsupervised by the teacher. Student interactions are generally polite and respectful.	Teacher's grouping results in small-group work being well organized, and students are productively engaged at all times, with students assuming responsibility for productivity. Students work independently and collaboratively to accomplish goals. Student interactions are consistently polite and respectful.
Considerations for ELs	• ELs benefit from interacting with English-proficient peers, and when appropriate, ELs should be paired with English-proficient peers. • When grouping ELs for content instruction, they should be grouped according to their content knowledge level and not solely their levels of English language proficiency. • Teachers will need to have access to specialists or support personnel knowledgeable about English for speakers of other languages (ESOL).			
Considerations for students with disabilities	• Learning goals are appropriate for each student. • Student engagement at "at all times" and assuming responsibilities for productivity may look different for students with disabilities. • Teachers need to have access to specialists or support personnel knowledgeable about disabilities.			

PRINCIPLE 3 SCENARIOS

Following are scenarios that provide examples of pre- and post-observation conversations between educators and their evaluators regarding Principle 3.

Secondary EL Scenario

A tenth-grade math class has two students identified as ELs. One student is a native Urdu speaker. Mandarin is the other student's home language. Both students have advanced levels of English across all domains except writing. Their teacher Ms. Artez is concerned about the allowable accommodations for ESOL students during end-of-year content assessments, especially since the district has recently adopted writing across the curriculum as its focus initiative. As part of student assessments in mathematics, students must respond to open-ended questions related to how they solved equations and which formulas they used (if applicable). This conversation between Ms. Artez and her assistant principal, Dr. Corbin, highlights Ms. Artez's need for more information about what is allowable for ELs and how best to implement those accommodations into classroom instruction.

Preconference Conversation

Dr. Corbin: *Can you tell me about how the formative assessments are going in your class? I understand you have incorporated more writing in your math class this year.*

Ms. Artez: *Yes, I have. I was surprised at how my students responded to the idea of discussing and writing in math class. It has really created more dialogues, and it's interesting to hear about their processes for solving equations.*

Dr. Corbin: *Wonderful to hear. I'd like for you to share that with your team at the next professional learning meeting. I know it might be more challenging to get students used to this way of synthesizing their thoughts in writing.*

Ms. Artez: *I do have a question about grading and assessing their written responses. I have two English learners who appear to need additional time with the written portion of their assignments and assessments. I am wondering if there are any accommodations for them that I am not aware of.*

Dr. Corbin: *Good question. We are scheduled to have the ESOL instructional coach meet with us next week. I'll be sure to reach out to him before then regarding your concerns. I wonder if these students are struggling to demonstrate their understanding in other classes as well or just in your class.*

Ms. Artez: *Since both students are able to communicate well orally in English, my concern is their ability to construct their thoughts in writing. Although they can carry on a conversation with their peers and explain their thinking, writing those thoughts appears to be a challenge. The students are familiar with the rubric, but I think they struggle with being able to earn a high rating because they are taking longer to complete the essays. I'd like to show the EL instructional coach the writing rubric the math team is using this year to assess their written responses. Maybe he can help us with implementing accommodations and help us think about the best way to grade their work.*

Dr. Corbin: *I'll pay close attention to how you're supporting your ELs' written work during your classroom observation as well.*

This scenario demonstrates Ms. Artez's proactive approach to advocating for her EL students. Since a new writing-across-the-curriculum initiative has been implemented, she has noticed her students struggling with their written responses. By bringing her concern to her administrator's attention, together they are planning to address her concerns with the team. By discussing concerns as part of the preconference conversation, both the teacher and evaluator have a better understanding of what the teacher's needs are and how the evaluator can aid in addressing those needs not only for one teacher but for several teachers who work with those students.

Elementary Students With Disabilities Scenario

During this post-observation conference, Mr. Kliewer, a ten-year veteran, reviews the lesson he has taught on *Tuck Everlasting* to his fifth-grade students with Ms. Lodell, the assistant principal. The class of 26 students in an urban school district with an 88% free and reduced lunch rate includes three students with learning disabilities in reading and one student, Patrick, with attention deficit disorder. A special education teacher, Ms. Graham, coteaches the class, and she and Mr. Kliewer coplan during lunch and after school. During the conversation, Mr. Kliewer points to several adaptations that he and Ms. Graham have developed for the lesson, for which the objectives and an agenda were included on the board, using the focus areas described through universal design for learning.

Post-Observation Conference Conversation

Ms. Lodell: *Tell me about the lesson I observed today.*

Mr. Kliewer: *We've been reading* Tuck Everlasting *for about three weeks in and out of class. Children seem to like the book because the characters are interesting and it makes some good points about living well and about being who you are. We start off our lessons the same way each time with my going over the homework. I had them create a Venn diagram comparing and contrasting the Tucks' way of life with the Forsters'. Patrick knew to collect the homework at the start of ELA and drop it off for me at my desk. I checked the homework over while the students completed a "Do Now" in their journals describing their personalities in three sentences. Patrick passed out the worksheets, and Ms. Graham introduced the lesson with a worksheet at the SMART Board with a list of the characters we'd be working with and discussing today while the children followed along at their desks. I modeled how I might look for evidence in the text about the "Man in the Yellow Suit" and how I could use the evidence I found to describe his character in the story. We broke the class up into heterogeneous groups based on five of the characters on the list after asking who wanted to focus on which character. Each student had to contribute to the group with a piece of evidence from the text about their character and then read it out loud and tell what it said about them. A reporter for each group described the results and the evidence the group found to the whole class, and Ms. Graham led a "thumbs up/ thumbs down" for each description when it was done. For homework, I had them draw a picture of what it would be like for them to live forever and how they would like that. We'll present our pictures to the class tomorrow as we start to wrap up reading the book.*

Ms. Lodell: *You've provided me with a good summary of the lesson, including how you handled the Venn diagram for homework, what the focus of the lesson was, and how the basic structure and routine of the class engaged the children for the topic you were presenting. I also like how you and Ms. Graham worked together to introduce the lesson and how you assessed student understanding after each group had spoken. Talk to me about how you differentiated your instruction for all the levels of students in the class.*

Mr. Kliewer: *Well, as I mentioned, Tuck Everlasting is a great read for students at this level. The vocabulary in the book is very rich and can be challenging. So as we've introduced and read each chapter, we had the students look through the text for words they didn't understand and we defined them, then put them on the word wall to be able to remind students what they meant. We try as often as possible to give students choices like that. These were words that they selected, and we let students decide for themselves which characters they wanted to work on in their groups. Ms. Graham pretaught the lesson during resource room and reminded Patrick and the other students with disabilities about the vocabulary and how to find evidence in the text. Ms. Graham and I decided that along with thumbs up/thumbs down, we'd ask one student after each group was done to summarize what he or she heard about the character. That way, students got to hear and think about the character's personalities more than once and from several different points of view. Andrea, one of our students who has a reading disability, has been using a leveled reader for Tuck, so she brought that with her to her group and used it to participate. Kwany, another student whose scores have been lower, although she's not in the special education program, uses both the leveled reader and the regular text. You saw how Patrick helped out as the collector and distributor, and instead of a simple thumbs-up/thumbs down, Patrick uses those laminated colored discs—green, yellow, and red—that you saw him holding up to let us know he understands. He plays with the discs to keep busy sometimes while we're in whole-class discussions. I like to give "visuals" or "musicals" for homework; like a week ago I had students create a rap, for our new vocabulary words, using ideas from the book. Patrick loved that!*

Ms. Lodell: *I noticed another student using those discs as well. It sounds as if you and Ms. Graham working together have come up with some good ways to differentiate instruction using*

UDL such as presenting vocabulary with a word wall and engaging Patrick in the routine of the classroom to keep him focused. I noticed Patrick giggling and flapping one of the pages in front of a student's face before handing her the paper. Talk a little bit about that behavior.

Mr. Kliewer: *I know Ms. Graham spoke to Patrick about his behavior when everyone was lining up for lunch and told him that he wouldn't have the privilege of helping us in the class if he kept that up. You have to pick and choose your battles with Patrick. He was so engaged in the lesson during the "thumbs up/thumbs down-summarize" assessment activity that he was practically jumping out of his skin, wiggling and bouncing, to raise his green disc high in the air. As long as he doesn't annoy other students and distract from their learning, he needs to get his "jumpies" out sometimes.*

Principle 3, with its focus on evidence-based practice and responsive, meaningful teaching and learning for all students, is clearly modeled in the description of the lesson and in Mr. Kliewer's thinking. First, the content is viewed from several different modalities, styles, and intelligences, such as visual, aural, and kinesthetic and interpersonal, verbal, and musical with much of the delivery of instruction tailored to student choices. Second, direct instruction seems to be a regular hallmark of Mr. Kliewer's approach, and Ms. Graham's preteaching the lesson contributes to greater participation among the children with disabilities. Mr. Kliewer's modeling is followed briskly by opportunities for group interaction and peer teaching. Third, from leveled readers to colored discs to special jobs for students who find paying attention difficult, Mr. Kliewer and Ms. Graham have harnessed the power of universal design not only by engaging, representing, and assessing using multiple means but also by extending adaptations made for students with disabilities to other members of the class. Finally, with Mr. Kliewer and Ms. Graham supporting each other, Mr. Kliewer is able to undertake helping Patrick manage his behaviors in ways that keep Patrick connected to the learning while mindful of his effect on other students.

QUESTIONS

To begin a discussion about the extent to which Principle 3 is present in educators' current teacher evaluation systems and to create a plan for implementing Principle 3, educators can consider the following questions as part of self-reflection or discuss them in pairs or groups:

- How would you summarize the essence of Principle 3: reflective teaching using evidence-based strategies?
- Which elements of Principle 3, reflective teaching using evidence-based strategies, resonated the most with you?
- Which look-fors of Principle 3 are you ready to integrate into your teacher evaluation system to provide equal access to ELs and students with disabilities?
- How will you integrate these look-fors into your teacher evaluation system?

CHAPTER SUMMARY

This chapter examined Principle 3, reflective teaching using evidence-based strategies, and how it can frame classroom observation as part of the teacher evaluation process. The chapter first outlined relevant elements of the UDL framework that provide the underpinnings for Principle 3. The chapter provided details on different strategies to use during the instruction and classroom-based assessment of ELs and students with disabilities and provides evaluators with information about specific look-fors that reflect teachers' inclusiveness of these diverse learners during instruction. The chapter also included sample conversations between teachers and evaluators that highlight different nuances of Principle 3.

NOTES

1. Texts can be written, visual, and/or oral.

2. Please see more examples of scaffolding for ELs in Chapter 2.

3. More information on professional collaboration can be found in Chapter 7.

4. Texts can include written texts as well as forms of discourse such as speeches, audio clips, and videos.

5. In the case of ELs, content standards and English language development standards would need to be considered.

6. While these are a few examples of scaffolds for ELs, this is by no means an exhaustive list.

Principle 4: Building a Culture of Collaboration and Community

7

I bring what I know to the table. My experience as a speech patholo-gist has certainly helped me when considering if an English Learner could have a learning disability. Sometimes, I have been the one who initially asks, "Do we need to look further?" I shed light on the dilemma of "Can a student be in both programs?" As we build the capacity of teachers to work with our English learners, so must we build teachers' capacity to consider our students for all of the pro-grams that might help them.

Ms. B. Colonna, ESL Instructional
Program Specialist/Department Chair

CONTENT OF THE CHAPTER

Chapter 7 focuses on the implementation of collaboration among professionals and the creation of a community where English learners (ELs), students with disabilities, and all students can thrive and be success-ful. The development of collaboration and community requires the com-mitment and the effort of everyone who touches the lives of students in schools. Teaching ELs and students with disabilities successfully requires a high degree of collaborative expertise, and it requires an openness to the families and cultures of these students along with keen communication skills and a willingness to be flexible and occasionally make mistakes. As

Ms. Colonna noted above, educators oftentimes have to serve multiple roles as advocates for students. Principles 1 through 3 of equal access, valuing diversity, and using reflection and evidence-based strategies form the foundation for the trust necessary to fully realize the collaboration and community necessary in Principle 4.

This chapter describes Principle 4 and the need for developing the means to cultivate close connections among all the individuals who know and serve diverse students. Then the chapter describes the advantages adherence to Principle 4 can provide ELs and students with disabilities. The chapter also focuses on the process by which Principle 4 can be ensured, and it ends with a set of look-fors that teachers and evaluators can use as evidence when creating strong collaboration and a sense of community in schools. It ends with a sample teacher evaluation rubric from New York State and sample scenarios of Principle 4 in action.

FOCUS OF PRINCIPLE 4: BUILDING A CULTURE OF COLLABORATION AND COMMUNITY

Principle 4 definition: Educators focus on professional relationships and connections to culture and community in the service of all students. They work toward establishing a community that is based on collaboration among educators, students, caregivers, families, neighbors, and other relevant groups. They work cooperatively, communicate regularly, and share resources, responsibilities, skills, decisions, and advocacy.

As College- and Career-Ready Standards (including the Common Core State Standards) are implemented across the country and new protocols for teacher evaluation are put into effect, there is a need for closer collaboration and creating more responsive communities in schools that can bring evidence-based practices to the classroom (Graham & Harris, 2013; Haager & Vaughn, 2013). Professional support for reaching the standards in the form of grade-level and cross-disciplinary teams, learning communities, and the development of professional development plans and mentoring opportunities means that teachers, their colleagues, and evaluators can cultivate methods of connecting with one another and sharing expertise (Shady, Luther, & Richman, 2013). Clearly, when collaboration is established, responsibility for diverse student achievement, accountability to systemic evaluation, and helping all students succeed take on a new and richer meaning.

The education of ELs and students with disabilities by its very nature requires collaboration on many levels within schools. As we have seen, issues of equal access, through the development and implementation of educational plans for ELs and individualized education plans (IEPs) for students with disabilities, already require close coordination among professionals and the establishment of fruitful working connections with the homes and families of these students. Also, the nature of inclusive classrooms demands coordination among various educational professionals, paraprofessionals, and related service providers. Cotaught classrooms naturally tend to foster high degrees of collaboration, and if the coteaching teams are particularly successful, this cooperation can provide outstanding seamless delivery of instruction for ELs and students with disabilities.

COTEACHING AND COLLABORATION

Coteaching relationships are one way to provide important evidence of professional collaboration and the ongoing development of community within the school. At the teacher evaluation preconference, teachers can make evaluators aware of the likely team configurations in which they will be involved during the course of the lesson. During an observed lesson, evaluators can be mindful of the roles each member of the coteaching team has decided to undertake. Coteaching arrangements encompass several different variations, always planned and orchestrated beforehand by the teachers involved. Variations can include arrangements where one person teaches the lesson and the other assists, circulating among the students in the classroom and providing regular check-ins with students to assist and enhance the work.

Variations in coteaching can also include the following:

- One teach, one assist where either the general educator or the ESOL or special education specialist teaches the lesson while the other teacher circulates the classroom providing support
- Parallel teaching in which two teachers teach the same content to the class divided roughly in half at the same time
- Station- or center-based teaching where students and/or teachers circulate to work with different groups of roughly the same proportionate size
- Alternate teaching where a larger group of students receives instruction while a smaller group receives more intensive instruction simultaneously

- Team-teaching where both teachers work together with the whole class, sharing complete responsibility for the delivery of the skills and content in the lesson (Bauwens & Hourcade, 1997; Honigsfeld & Dove, 2010; Wilson & Blednick, 2012)

In each of these arrangements, ELs and students with disabilities are heterogeneously grouped among their peers. The high quality of the coteaching relationship can be evident during the observation itself in the seamless quality of the teaching. The collaboration necessary for successful coteaching can also be an important strand in the discussions between teachers and evaluators, often during the post-observation conference.

Successful coteaching requires that fundamental attitudes or dispositions be present as well as skill sets that may exist in addition to those displayed in relationships with students while teaching. Coteachers need to share a vision for the education of ELs and students with disabilities, delineating clear and high expectations for all learners. For ELs, teachers must believe that students can acquire language and content simultaneously and be included in classrooms that contain non-ELs. For students with disabilities, teachers must believe together that inclusion can succeed as a means to educating students with disabilities. Planning time needs to be available for coteachers, and the planning they do together needs to be undertaken so that they are equal partners in the process. Roles and responsibilities are decided on and clarified. Coteachers are advocates for their professional development needs, enhancing their relationship as well as their teaching methods. The classroom procedures established by the coteachers are mutually agreed to. Coteachers are also involved in continual reflection, problem solving, and professional improvement (see Maryland State Department of Education, n.d.). Probing the professional relationship that coteachers have with one another and the extent to which these variables are addressed in ongoing discussions can be an important topic to discuss during post-observation conferences.

Depending on the demographics of the districts that teachers of ELs find themselves in, coteaching between a content teacher and a teacher of English for speakers of other languages (ESOL) or bilingual teacher may not always be possible. For example, in districts with smaller numbers of ELs, it may not be feasible to have an ESOL teacher in every school. In cases where ESOL teachers are itinerant, serving multiple schools, coteaching will be nearly impossible with each content teacher that serves an EL. In such cases, collaboration between ESOL and content teachers becomes more challenging but even more crucial. Some ways that ESOL and content teachers can collaborate when they do not have the luxury of coteaching or common planning time include sharing information and planning electronically or by phone. In instances where there are only a few ELs in a school, it might be helpful to group them with one or two grade-level or content teachers who are open to teaching ELs (and non-ELs together in the same classroom) using research-based strategies and to provide those teachers with the professional development to incorporate EL strategies effectively. Grouping ELs with fewer content teachers will also make it easier to foster collaboration between ESOL and content teachers. Evidence of such collaboration in settings in which coteaching is not possible can be collected during pre- and post-observation conferences.

PARAPROFESSIONALS IN SPECIAL EDUCATION

Paraprofessionals[1] are also important members of the collaborative team providing instruction for students with disabilities. To begin, the type and amount of instruction that paraprofessionals provide might require clarification, including understanding the caseloads of special educators and their resulting efficacy (Suter & Giangreco, 2009). Making sure that the highest-quality instruction is being provided to student with disabilities is paramount (Carter, O'Rourke, Sisco, & Pelsue, 2009). Clearly describing and developing responsibilities and intended tasks for paraprofessionals as well as education in supervision and delegation for teachers of students with disabilities is also necessary (French, 2001, 2002). Evaluators should be cautious to make sure that teachers remain responsible for planning and implementing instruction for students, conducting assessments, assigning grades, signing formal documents, attending meetings, and remaining the primary communicator to student families (Carnahan, Williamson, Clarke, & Sorensen, 2009; Causton-Theoharis, 2009; Etscheidt, 2005; Giangreco, Doyle, & Suter, 2012; Liston, Nevin, & Malian, 2009). It may be important to discover during pre- or post-observation conversations what arrangements have been made for the supervision of the paraprofessionals in the classroom by the general and special education teachers of record. In addition, how well the paraprofessionals on the team provide support as evident during the observed lesson can also be an important topic of conversation.

COLLABORATION WITH CAREGIVERS OF ELs

In the same way, parents, caregivers[2], and families of ELs and students with disabilities should be included as part of the decision-making team and as part of the ongoing conversation that involves the fullest education of their children. Elevating caregivers' role means acknowledging the important position caregivers hold in the process of educating children and understanding the culture and dynamic of the home, the expectations and aspirations of the student's family for the future, and the resources available for supporting the educational enterprise.

Under Title I and Title III requirements, caregivers of ELs must be notified at the following times (Forte & Faulkner-Bond, 2010):

1. When the student has been recommended for language-support services

2. When the student has taken annual statewide content assessments

3. When the language instructional program in the student's district did not meet Title III accountability targets

4. When the student's district did not make annual yearly progress (AYP) for the limited English proficient subgroup

Beyond these required points of contact, both Title I and Title III require that caregivers of ELs be involved in the students' education and that communication be provided "to the extent practicable, in a language such parents understand." Principle 4 undergirds the need to reach out in often creative ways so that caregivers of ELs will feel welcome in the school and engaged with their child's education.

COLLABORATION WITH CAREGIVERS OF STUDENTS WITH DISABILITIES

Although caregivers of students with disabilities are required by law to be part of the team that develops the IEP (Heyward, 2009), sometimes they are absent from the process, and this absence can be construed as their lack of involvement in their child's education. Before making assumptions, educators should initiate the means to connect with caregivers, offering them choices for participating in school activities and setting up regular communication channels, including daily logs (Staples & Diliberto, 2010). Probing these kinds of caregivers outreach and methods of involvement can be part of the conversations that teachers and evaluators have with one another during post-observation conferences.

Relationships between teacher and families of students with disabilities begin with IEP meetings that function harmoniously and offer support for all participants (Lytle & Bordin, 2001), including related service providers (Diliberto & Brewer, 2012). These meetings focus first on student strengths (Kozik, 2012; Lytle & Bordin, 2001) and require careful preparation to ensure collegiality, accuracy, and transparency (Weishaar, 2010). IEPs also need to be written constructively to maximize each student's potential, integrate skills through goals that apply in multiple real-life settings (Diliberto & Brewer, 2012), and use goals that reflect high expectations and the best thinking of the entire IEP team (Capizzi, 2008). The document should accurately reflect the student at the heart of the IEP discussion and include elements of long-term planning (Meaden, Sheldon, Appel, & DeGrazia, 2010) with input on the student's future and the family's aspirations. Examples of IEPs can be provided as part of the meetings carried out for teacher evaluations.

Beyond the development of the IEP, teachers should also be able to provide evidence of frequent communication with parents and students and the treatment of both parents and students as partners in the educational process. General educators working with students with disabilities in inclusive settings, as well as their special education counterparts, acknowledge the importance of close home-school communications (Berry, 2011). Strategies such as daily notebooks (Hall, Wolfe, & Bollig, 2003), flexibility in scheduling conferences, and remote access to homework assignments (Epstein, Munk, Bursuck, Polloway, & Jayanthi, 1999) can be indicators of educator flexibility and the careful development of family involvement. It can be made clear through post-observation conferences that teachers of students with disabilities have considered the supports that families have learned to use at home and applied these when appropriate (Edwards & Da Fonte, 2012).

In addition, connection with students' families can help educators understand student feelings about school as well as some of the ways to motivate students (Brownell, Smith, Crocket, & Griffin, 2012). How teachers help families manage different kinds of transition and plan for changes in the student's life can also be important to the post-observation conference (Fenlon, 2011; Heatherington et al., 2010; Martinez, Conroy, & Cerreto, 2012). Finally, strong and fruitful relationships with students are necessary for academic success, and they begin with welcoming environments where diversity is valued as described in Chapter 5. Analyzing and understanding the community of the classroom and the involvement of students may extend to discussing student choice making (Cote Sparks & Cote, 2011).

ROLE OF DIVERSE STUDENTS IN COLLABORATION PROCESS

In addition to including their families, diverse students themselves need to be part of the collaboration process as well. English learners should be aware of how they are acquiring language and the rate at which they are progressing; they should also know about their educational options. Students with disabilities should be involved in collaboration not only through the development of their IEPs (Martin et al., 2006); rather, both groups of students should actively reflect and participate in the process of their education. Some teacher evaluation rubrics often underscore the need to have student voices as part of the process of engagement and learning in classrooms, and student responsibility for their learning in the process is emphasized (Danielson, 2007; New York State United Teachers, 2012). For ELs and students with disabilities, unique considerations about the role of students themselves in their education must be a part of teacher evaluation.

Educators should be aware of the stages of second language acquisition for ELs, and teachers should be able to include ELs in their own meta-awareness of the strategies they use to acquire language. Evaluators should be aware of the components to self-determination for students with disabilities: choice making, decision making, problem solving, goal setting and attainment, self-advocacy and leadership, self-management and self-regulation, and self-awareness and self-knowledge (Lane, Carter, & Sisco, 2012). They should be able to document these components within observations and throughout the pre- and post-observation conference process. Understandings about involving students in these components and discussing the barriers to the development of self-determination in ELs and students with disabilities can be discussed as well (Cho, Wehmeyer, & Kingston, 2011).

WHY PRINCIPLE 4 IS NEEDED

TESOL International Association (2010) outlines five domains and 11 professional teaching standards that define how the teaching of ELs differs from teaching non-ELs. Table 7.1 indicates the areas in which effective teachers of ELs must have expertise.

TESOL (2010) conceptualizes the domain of professionalism as the driver of all other aspects of teachers' interactions with ELs. It is especially crucial for all teachers of ELs to be adept at the domain of professionalism that is required to support ELs, including drawing from an understanding of ESOL research and history of the field of ESOL. In addition, all teachers of ELs must focus on developing professionally to build professional relationships with colleagues, caregivers of ELs, communities, and advocate for ELs.

Similarly, the Council for Exceptional Children ("Council for Exceptional Children's Position," 2013) acknowledges the complexity of

Table 7.1 TESOL Domains and Standards

TESOL Domain	TESOL Standard(s)
Language	• Language as a system • Language acquisition and development
Culture	• Culture as it affects student learning
Instruction	• Planning for standards-based ESL and content instruction • Implementing and managing standards-based ESL and content instruction • Using resources and technology effectively in ESL and content instruction
Assessment	• Issues of assessment for English language learners • Language proficiency assessment • Classroom-based assessment for ESL
Professionalism	• ESL research and history • Professional development, partnerships, and advocacy

educating students with disabilities. The complexity not only has to do with understanding 13 categories of disability and working with students who represent significant variations within those categories. The complexity also extends to the range of relationships required for teachers of students with disabilities to cultivate as defined in professional tasks such as coteaching, consultation, case management, and home-school relationships. This range of relationships points to the need to provide ample support for all teachers of ELs and of students with disabilities, with the means built into teacher schedules so that the complexity of these tasks can be undertaken successfully. Systemic supports for teachers in inclusive classroom settings need to be in place for ELs and students with disabilities to be successful (De Bortoli, Foreman, Arthur-Kelly, Balandin, & Mathisen, 2012).

Evidence for Principle 4 will likely become clear during a pre- or post-observation conversation and may also be evident during the observation itself. The focus of evaluating teacher performance for collaboration and community is on the initiation and cultivation of professional connections with colleagues, paraprofessionals, related service providers, and the families of ELs and students with disabilities. The quality of these connections extends the conversation to the methods and strategies teachers employ to make sure that all students are supported by mutually respectful and culturally responsive connections that reflect high expectations for academic achievement.

In addition, working relationships between coteachers and collaborators can be examined through the teacher evaluation process. Although the effects of coteaching on student achievement remains an area of study (Magiera & Zigmond, 2005), well-designed and expertly executed coteaching partnerships can enhance student learning and academic success (Honigsfeld & Dove, 2010; Kozik, Osroff, Lee, & Marr, 2010). Discussions can focus on the philosophies for educating students with disabilities held by coteaching partners if these relationships, under the scrutiny of observation, prove to be problematic (Carter, Prater, Jackson, & Marchant, 2009). Conversations between evaluators and teachers can focus on the availability and use of coplanning time. Issues such as setting agendas, deciding on roles and responsibilities, developing professional rapport, addressing student concerns, and regularly assessing the quality of the team's efforts can be highlighted and addressed in these discussions (Murawski, 2012). Team configurations can be described, and evidence of these working relationships can be observed (Bauwens & Hourcade, 1997; Murawski & Spencer, 2011; Wilson, 2012).

WHAT THE PRINCIPLE MEANS FOR ELs

Principle 4 sets high expectations for the level of collaboration that is crucial for all educators of English learners to share the responsibility for students' academic achievement as well as for their personal growth. In comparison to students with disabilities, there is no federal legislation requiring any one document such as the IEP to guide the way in which ELs are educated. Instead, policies for ELs' education vary by school, district, and state. In the absence of a binding document such as an IEP, it often falls upon educators within schools to build and sustain professional relationships to create an inclusive environment for ELs as well as their families or caregivers. Some districts have implemented a document similar to the IEP to drive the collaboration process for ELs. Manassas City Public Schools in Virginia, for example, has implemented an ESOL Instructional Plan that brings each EL's teachers together quarterly to discuss each student's progress and determine classroom supports.

One way Principle 4 is manifested is through providing some guidelines for establishing a community necessary for ELs' success that is supportive of ELs through collaboration among stakeholders, including educators, students, caregivers, families, neighbors, and other relevant groups. In particular, Principle 4 seeks to help teachers articulate the ways in which they serve as a catalyst of collaboration with the goal of holistically supporting ELs. Collaboration begins at the classroom level, with content and ESOL or bilingual teachers engaging in discussions about how to best draw from each EL's cultural and linguistic strengths as well as meet each student's unique academic needs. Collaboration then extends beyond the classroom to the content or grade level, to guidance counselors as well as all teachers who interact with each EL. In addition, collaboration must also occur at the schoolwide level so that all educators share in the education of each EL in the building. Beyond the school level, collaboration must also take place with ELs' families or caregivers as well as with the EL's community.

As part of Principle 4, educators engage in regular communication as well as share effective resources for supporting ELs' achievement. Since research on effective instructional strategies for ELs continues to grow (Baker et al., 2014; Goldenberg, 2008), it is of utmost importance for educators to foster an open environment in which sharing of resources for ELs is expected. By creating open lines of communication with EL families and caregivers as well as developing stronger ties with all who work with ELs at the school and community level, educators expand their advocacy efforts on behalf of those ELs who are still developing their own voice in their education.

WHAT PRINCIPLE 4 MEANS
FOR STUDENTS WITH DISABILITIES

For students with disabilities, Principle 4 means a well-functioning IEP with all the education professionals, related service providers, and special education and school administrators knowledgeable and working to remain in support of one another and on the same page. If Principle 4 is fully realized, a student with disabilities can expect instruction and related services to be provided in classrooms that are inclusive and where disability is seen as part of diversity rather than an isolating phenomenon that requires segregation from other similar age peers. At least two fully certified educators are in charge of the learning taking place for all the students in the classroom. All students in the class have the advantage of at least two good adult minds to help explain content and to develop skills in ways that can appeal to a broader swath of the classroom population and to the students with disabilities. Concepts are explained and modeled several different ways; practice becomes truly guided with careful oversight of regular representation and expression, and the likelihood of the immediate feedback necessary for the strongest learning to occur is increased with cotaught models. Most of all, individual preferences and ways of learning are spoken to so that the complex differentiation and the resources necessary for universal for learning (UDL) to become fully realized in the classroom have been understood and methods have been designed to fully incorporate learner strengths. As colleagues, coteaching partners manage behaviors in the classroom equitably and with one another's full and planned-for support. The student with disabilities feels valued as a contributing member of the classroom community.

If a paraprofessional is required as part of the IEP, that person is confident with and capable of the roles and responsibilities of the position. So the paraprofessional speaks to the student and to others in the class in age- and gender-appropriate language and fosters a sense of belonging inside the classroom. Interactions with other students are encouraged and allowed to develop in that the paraprofessional does not hover and interrupt the natural flow of friendships being formed and work being completed in the classroom. Also, the paraprofessional and the other educators responsible for the student's education regularly provide choices and focus on ensuring active decision making as well as regular reflection. Students with disabilities experience learning as appropriate to their needs in much the same way that nondisabled students work in the classroom.

With Principle 4's emphasis on collaboration and community in place, home and school work in close coordination with one another. Students with disabilities are likely to be asked by their families about their progress at school; regular notes from teachers and assignments are reviewed, discussed, and returned for which the students are given responsibility. Life at home and life at school coexist seamlessly with the same kinds of procedures for discipline and high expectations in place at both locations. Importantly, parents and caregivers of students with disabilities hold the school and its educators in high regard. They have become fully engaged in the system so that their feelings and ideas regarding the education of their children matter. They are routinely listened to and, consequently, routinely listen to the professionals in charge of their children's education. They are aware of their responsibilities with regard to their children, especially when it comes to communicating with the school and connecting with their students in ways that are consistent and fruitful for their growth. Like the students' educators, parents and caregivers vested under Principle 4 are able to articulate the progress students are making as well as the barriers that may exist and ways of overcoming them.

Under Principle 4, IEP meetings are conversations among equals with all the various points of view being represented on the final document. The pros and cons of various teaching methods and adaptations are discussed and enough time is provided, through professional arrangements such as miniconferences, that all the participants feel comfortable with the outcomes. Students with disabilities are fully a part of their IEP meetings and have been since their arrival in the school system. These meetings provide opportunities for students to reflect on their growth and their progress, to more fully understand areas of need and concern, to request adjustments to their plans and programs, and to witness the care and consideration that those planning for their education enjoin on their behalf. It is clear to them that their opinions, preferences, and aspirations for themselves matter in the process of becoming educated.

PROCESS FOR INTEGRATING PRINCIPLE 4

Although it is crucial for teachers of ELs and students with disabilities to collaborate, traditionally, teachers do not always collaborate regularly with one another. Their focus might be more on the classroom and their work within it; hence, much of their professional lives can be spent in isolation from one another. By the same token, traditional professional development days can be spent in frustration with little or no personal application of the skills and content being presented. Professional development does not necessarily mean a dependence on outside sources to educate teachers in new ways of attending to student learning. Professional development also means the work that teachers do with one another in collaborative relationships. Embedded professional growth and development can take the form of professional learning communities, book circles, reading groups, team meetings, and regular conversations among teachers about student work as well as planning for units and lessons. School systems may consider rewarding teachers with contact hours for these kinds of activities.

Developing Principle 4 for school personnel can require a greater commitment of time as well as a greater sensitivity to the needs of educators working with ELs and students with disabilities on the part of administrators and those responsible for the professional development of teachers. This principle focuses the evaluation process fundamentally on personal connections and requires subtle considerations on the part of evaluators because these relationships can be hard to orchestrate and maintain. So, for example, questions about monitoring the performance of paraprofessionals in classrooms may compromise the comfort of teachers being evaluated and also may require soul-searching on the part of the evaluators themselves. Like students, teachers cannot be expected to be proficient at responsibilities for which they have had no education or training. Not all teacher preparation programs focus prospective candidates well enough on issues of collaboration with other adults and initiating full partnerships with caregivers and with families. Like the other principles, however, Principle 4 is tailored to involve the school community through the proactive development of the evaluation process and to ensure that the system is accountable for providing the means for individual professional growth of its members. Therefore, the conversations in regard to Principle 4 are critical because the evaluator must also assume the role of a person available to problem solve with the observed teacher and to ensure that the resources are available for teachers to fully carry through on the roles and responsibilities this principle encourages.

As has been true for the other three principles, the success of Principle 4 rests on a school environment that is abundant with continual discussion and dialogue about teaching and learning as they relate to ELs and students with disabilities. Faculty meetings, opportunities for evaluation by school administrators, and classroom visits by peers as well as impromptu conversations can focus with laser-like sharpness on necessary attitudes, values, and strategies for encouraging student success.

PRINCIPLE 4 QUESTIONS FOR DIALOGUE

In the school, ELs and students with disabilities are everybody's students and therefore everyone's responsibility. As such, discussions at faculty meetings and at post-observation conferences can include the following questions to spur further reflection and exchanges of ideas:

- Do our educators, students, families, caregivers, and community members collaborate to communicate, share resources and expertise, make decisions, and solve problems related to the education of ELs and students with disabilities?
- Does our school provide educators with adequate time and structures to collaborate with each other and to communicate with diverse students' families, caregivers, and community members?
- What can we do to improve our system of collaboration and professional development to ensure better sharing of resources, decision making, and problem solving for diverse students?
- Does our school provide the resources, adult supports, time, scheduling arrangements, and high-quality professional development to educate *all students* in inclusive classrooms? What can we do to encourage focused and fruitful collaboration and high-quality professional development?
- Does our school communicate a sense of community where individual differences are valued? How can we create an even stronger sense of community? (August, Salend, Staehr Fenner, & Kozik, 2012, pp. 2–4)

LOOK-FORS FOR BUILDING
A CULTURE OF COLLABORATION AND COMMUNITY

During pre-observation conferences in which lessons are discussed and during observations, evaluators can expect to hear and see evidence of inclusive attitudes toward ELs and students with disabilities and knowledge and accountability to the law by teachers. Post-observation conferences afford evaluators another opportunity to follow up with teachers regarding the ways in which teachers focus on professional relationships and connect with students' cultures and the community. Tables in this section can help educators document their general understanding of concepts embodied by Principle 4. Each table provides a space for evaluators to indicate whether evidence has been found for each of the look-fors as well as a place for comments related to the look-for. The sample look-fors provided are meant as a starting point for educators' conversations about how well they are building a culture of collaboration and community that benefits their ELs. Educators are encouraged to adapt these look-fors so that they reflect their unique contexts.

Look-Fors for Teachers of English Learners

In terms of teachers of English learners, Principle 4 look-fors may include oral or written evidence of planning conversations between content and ESOL or bilingual teachers, collaboration between content and ESOL or bilingual teachers about strategies to use to support the instruction of ELs, or the sharing of professional development opportunities related to ELs. These look-fors are not necessarily observable during one conversation or setting but can be demonstrated and documented on an ongoing basis. The post-observation conference can also focus on how teachers make decisions regarding the kind of coteaching or collaboration strategies exhibited during the lesson that was observed and evidence of collaboration.

Another area of look-fors for teachers of ELs is in actively supporting and promoting EL caregivers' and families' involvement in their children's education. Even though it may be challenging for families of ELs to come to the school building, teachers should be able to document regular contact with ELs' families. Teachers of ELs will undoubtedly need to approach EL family involvement differently than with non-EL families. For example, when contacting families, teachers should use the language and form of communication that is most comfortable for the family. In many cases, translated documents will need to be used for families who read their home language. In addition, many EL families may prefer to communicate by phone or in person instead of in writing. In cases where there is a parent liaison available at the school, teachers should be able to discuss how they are collaborating with that liaison to more effectively engage with EL families. Where there is no parent liaison (or a parent liaison who does not speak the languages the families represent), teachers will need to use interpreters to communicate with EL families by phone or in person.

When it comes to connecting with EL families, teachers may have to use some creative measures. As evidence for Principle 4, in cases where teachers have not experienced success in EL parents coming to the school, they may be able to cite going to families' places of work or meet with them at a time that is convenient close to their place of residence. Some teachers of ELs may describe home visits with EL families in order to foster a deeper connection with families of ELs and build more solid relationships (Staehr Fenner, 2014). Teachers should describe attempts to address factors that may impede EL families' coming to school for meetings and events such as lack of child care, lack of transportation, or language barriers. In such cases, teachers could describe their efforts to provide child care, ride sharing, or vouchers for public transportation, and interpreters to decrease potential barriers to EL families' involvement in school-based activities.

Evidence for Principle 4 found in discussions between teachers and evaluators can also include the regularity and quality of teacher interactions with the larger community in which ELs live. Such discussions can be about the awareness of community resources that could be of assistance to EL families, such as multicultural counseling centers, opportunities for ESOL classes for families, and pathways to general equivalency diplomas for those families who would qualify. While teachers of ELs might not be involved directly in providing such community resources to EL families, they should be aware of the types of resources that exist so they can assist in connecting EL families with appropriate supports as necessary.

Finally, all teachers' advocacy for ELs plays a prominent role in their own professional responsibility (Staehr Fenner, 2014). Teachers must develop their advocacy skills for ELs and their families in order to share the responsibility and also the joy of teaching ELs. As part of Principle 4, teachers should be able to describe ways in which they advocate for ELs who are in the process of developing their own advocacy skills. Some ways in which teachers could advocate for ELs include ensuring that ELs are considered when school and district policies are created, speaking out on ELs' behalf when curricular decisions are made, and doing their part to make sure EL families feel welcome in the school. To become more effective advocates for their students, teachers may consider joining a local and/or national EL teachers' organization, attending professional conferences, and reading materials that highlight strategies for effectively teaching ELs. Table 7.2 shows sample look-fors that are specific to for all teachers of ELs.

Table 7.2 Principle 3 Look-Fors for All Teachers of ELs

Principle 4 Look-For	Evidence Found: Yes or No	Comments
Communicates with families of ELs in a language and form they understand		
Supports EL family engagement and involvement		
Is creative in involving EL families—for example, making home visits and/or visiting the workplaces of students' families		
Articulates awareness of community resources that are of benefit to ELs		
Involves ELs in actively reflecting on and participating in the process of their education		
ELs are aware of how they are acquiring language, the rate at which they are progressing, and should know about their educational options		
Helps ELs recognize the strategies students use to acquire language		
Explains and documents how he or she collaborates with students, caregivers, families, and the community to support ELs' personal growth		
Collaborates with others (e.g., ESOL or bilingual teachers) in lesson planning and implementation to support ELs' academic growth		
Shares professional development opportunities related to ELs		

Look-Fors for Teachers of Students With Disabilities

Evidence for Principle 4 comes largely out of conversations with teachers and can be based on the evidence that teachers provide. Open discussion about assumptions and stereotypes regarding family structures, working caregivers, and the availability of time to help with homework and attend meetings can be explored. For students with disabilities, evaluators may also want to probe whether or not an attitude of "ableism," the belief that able-bodied people are superior to people with disabilities, exists in the teacher they are evaluating, in the special education program, and at the school where they work. Exploring these attitudes is critical, not only to the full inclusion of students with disabilities but also for the fruitful and meaningful connections that should be the hallmark of personal and professional collaboration under Principle 4. Parents of children with intellectual disabilities tell of being isolated after the birth of their son or daughter, with medical providers growing reserved and even unwelcoming when the soft signs of Down syndrome might be apparent in a newborn (Esposito, 2004). Shame can be a dominant emotion in families, driven as it is by cultural beliefs about deficiency and the prevalence of a deficiency model throughout the American educational system. Therefore, evaluators need, first and foremost, to be dedicated to ensuring that all children and their families develop to their fullest and greatest potential.

Look-fors for Principle 4 can be witnessed most often either during the post-observation conference or during the observation itself—the former in cases of collaboration with families and the community, the latter as indicative of professional collaboration in the classroom. Levels of contact with families, daily, weekly, and quarterly logs, regular progress reports, school-to-home notebooks, and documented telephone conversations with caregivers are artifacts for which the evaluator can look and on which the evaluation conversation can focus. Teachers should be prepared to provide these pieces of evidence as positive indications of their working to afford the student with disabilities the best possible access and education. Descriptions of IEP meetings as well as uniquely and individually constructed IEPs are also look-fors that can be shared. Finally, to further validate the evaluation process for teachers of students with disabilities, having an evaluator sit in on a parent-teacher conference to document the results as part of the evaluation portfolio can determine additional rich look-fors to assess a teacher's relationship to caregivers and to the community. Witnessing caregiver-teacher conversations that are positive, where the parent is encouraged to speak first and often and where student artifacts are provided as data for teacher decision making, can be rich in look-fors to evaluate teachers under Principle 4. Teachers can also provide documented evidence of these conversations during post-observation conferences.

Observations within inclusive classrooms can extend to look-fors involving the implementation of coteaching and the support of service providers and paraprofessionals in the classroom. Teachers can choose to alert evaluators of varying professional arrangements in pre-observation conferences, or questions about these look-fors can extend into post-observation conversations. Look-fors regarding professional collaboration can be focused on well-defined roles within the classroom so that each professional is implementing instruction with maximum efficiency and efficacy. Evaluators can be on the look-out for coteaching relationships in which the special educator functions as a teaching assistant rather than as a certified teacher. Although the one-teach/one-assist model may be adapted to the lesson plans that day and observed, it is worth confronting any underuse of personnel. Hence, questions about the professional contributions of both teachers and how they can be enhanced might extend to becoming look-fors during the post-observation conference. Coteaching in whatever form it takes should be seamless and satisfying for the professionals involved. The best coteaching, calling on the five models available for teachers to consider (Bauwens & Hourcade, 1997; Honigsfeld & Dove, 2010; Wilson & Blednick, 2012), occurs when the observer, witnessing relationships much like the meld of students in an inclusive classroom, cannot tell the general educator from the special educator. Look-fors in these cases include both teachers providing equal, accurate, and targeted content and skill instruction and support. Additional look-fors, offered at post-observation conferences, can also be evidence of successful coplanning, student artifacts of both general education and special education students, and assessments shared for all students in the observed classroom.

Finally, teachers of students with disabilities are responsible for collaboration with service providers and for the supervision of paraprofessionals. Look-fors may include ample space within the classroom for service providers to work with students with disabilities, the seamless integration of these services into the lesson, and the application of provider expertise to the classroom. So, for example, an occupational therapist may not only provide instruction and practice for a person with cerebral palsy in adjusting a pincer grip on an object but may also provide support and instruction to other students and to the whole class in some of the best ways to hold and control a pencil. Finally, paraprofessionals should be supervised in the performance of their tasks. Look-fors may include the fading of support for select students with disabilities as well as healthy social interactions that students with disabilities enjoy without the paraprofessional intervening. Likewise, the comfort of the paraprofessional in assisting the student; in assisting with the planning, development, and implementation of center-based activities; or in assisting other students in ways that prove fruitful can also be look-fors in effective inclusive classrooms and part of the observation and post-observation conference. Table 7.3

Table 7.3	Principle 4 Look-Fors for All Teachers of Students With Disabilities

Principle 4 Look-For	Evidence Found: Yes or No	Comments
Provides space for service providers and paraprofessionals to work with students in the classroom		
Service providers and paraprofessionals are effectively integrated into the classroom routine		
Initiates the means to connect with parents or caregivers, offering them choices for participating in school activities and setting up regular communication channels, including daily logs		
Establishes and maintains relationships with families of students with disabilities during IEP meetings		
Provides evidence of frequent communication with parents and students and the treatment of both parents and students as partners in the educational process		
Documents components to self-determination for students of disabilities		

provides sample look-fors that educators can use to determine how well they are integrating Principle 4 into their support of students with disabilities in classrooms and schools.

Look-fors for All Teachers of ELs and Students With Disabilities

Table 7.4 shows key components of Principle 4 look-fors as they relate to both groups of diverse learners. These components are applicable to both groups of students due to their similarities.[3] This table will help educators document a general understanding of concepts embodied by Principle 4 and how educators can build a culture of collaboration and community to support both groups of students.

Table 7.4	Principle 4 Look-Fors for All Teachers of ELs and Students With Disabilities

Principle 4 Look-For	Evidence Found: Yes or No	Comments
Uses different modes to communicate with families of ELs according to the family's background and preferences (e.g., notes, e-mails, phone calls, home visits)		
Attempts to address factors that may impair families' participation in school events (e.g., child care, work schedules, language barriers)		
Effectively participates in a planning meeting that includes coteachers, service providers, and/or paraprofessionals		
Effectively and respectfully communicates with caregivers during an IEP meeting, English language service planning meeting, and/or conferences		
Communicates with families to share information about classroom or home-based behavior management strategies, grading policies, teacher philosophy, and teacher expectations		
Selects conference times based on the needs of caregivers and sends notes or e-mails or makes phone calls to thank caregivers for attending in order to foster caregiver attendance at conferences		
Advocates for ELs and students with disabilities in the classroom context and beyond the classroom level		
Shares resources to support ELs and students with disabilities		

SAMPLE FROM NEW YORK
STATE TEACHER EVALUATION RUBRICS

Following is an example of how New York State educators have designed one of their teacher evaluation rubrics that serves as example of some elements of Principle 4.

New York State Rubric Sample

This rubric highlights New York's Element VII.1: Teachers reflect on their practice to improve instructional effectiveness and guide professional growth. The rubric displays how teachers plan their own professional growth with the unique foci of serving ELs and students with disabilities in mind. The rubric also highlights the need for collaboration with specialists or support personnel who are trained in working with English learners and/or students with disabilities.

Teachers set informed goals and strive for continuous professional growth.

In a world of rapidly expanding access to information, opportunity, and technology, educators have a responsibility to continually prepare themselves to align instruction with transforming student needs. Continued professional growth and development is essential to creating dynamic learning environments. Teachers use information from a variety of sources to inform their professional development and practice.

Element VII.1: Teachers reflect on their practice to improve instructional effectiveness and guide professional growth.

NYSED Indicators: *Examine and analyze formal and informal evidence of student learning. Recognize the effect of their prior experience and possible biases on practice. Use acquired information to identify strengths and weaknesses and to plan professional growth. New York State United Teachers (2013)*

Indicators	Ineffective	Developing	Effective	Highly Effective
B. Plans professional growth	Teacher rarely uses reflection or other information to identify strengths and weaknesses or bias to plan professional growth.	Teacher occasionally uses reflection and other information to identify strengths and weaknesses or bias to plan professional growth. Teacher may need guidance selecting appropriate professional opportunities.	Teacher uses reflection and other information to identify strengths and weaknesses and bias to plan professional growth.	Teacher regularly uses reflection and other information to identify strengths and weaknesses and bias to plan professional growth. Teacher seeks out professional growth opportunities to address areas of weakness.
Considerations for ELLs:	• Areas of weakness generally include lack of knowledge and skills in helping ELLs access grade-level content and develop second language proficiency (academic language necessary to master content standards in a second language). • Teachers will need to have access to specialists or support personnel knowledgeable about ESL.			
Considerations for SWDs:	• Areas of weakness generally include lack of knowledge and skills in helping students with disabilities access grade-level content. • Teachers will need to have access to specialists or support personnel knowledgeable about disabilities.			

PRINCIPLE 4 SCENARIOS

Following are scenarios that provide examples of pre- and post-observation conversations between educators and their evaluators regarding Principle 4.

Elementary EL Scenario

This scenario describes one teacher's approach to collaborating with his colleagues and describing that process to his administrator, Ms. Ali. This conversation is part of his post-observation meeting. Mr. Ahmad, first-grade teacher, works with a paraprofessional, Ms. Issa, and two other first-grade teachers, Ms. Katz and Ms. Doleman. Together, the teachers planned and facilitated a parent meeting to explain the annual language assessments administered in first grade. This meeting was part of a larger schoolwide meeting focused on explaining the English language assessment to parents and caregivers. There are 67 first-grade students enrolled at this school. Over 70% of the first-grade students are identified as English learners. The primary languages spoken by the ELs are Arabic, Amharic, Tagalog, and Spanish.

Post-Conference Conversation

Ms. Ali: *Congratulations on hosting a successful parent meeting. Tell me about the parent surveys.*

Mr. Ahmad: *Thank you. Yes, we did have a great turnout. We were so glad to have so many families attend. The team planned for months for this meeting. We wanted to provide an opportunity for the families to meet us as a team and for us to explain the English language assessment to them. The language assessment the first graders take is very different from the kindergarten version. The parent surveys we collected were very helpful. The surveys were translated into different languages.*

Ms. Ali: *So overall you found the meeting successful? Would you change anything about the meeting if you were able to?*

Mr. Ahmad: *The parents wanted more information about how the English language assessment would be used and administered in first grade. Ms. Issa, two other interpreters, and I were able to talk with family members who were just learning English. They found that most beneficial. What the team and I would do differently would be to have condensed the handouts. Some parents also asked about information on the school's website. They asked if information was available in their language online. Maybe in the future we could post some of this information online in various languages for them to view at home.*

Ms. Ali: *That is a great idea. We'll have to research online vendors that offer website translations.*

Mr. Ahmad: *The parents definitely thought the information presented was helpful. We don't want to overwhelm them. If we could streamline the process of how the information is presented—that would be an improvement.*

Ms. Ali: *I agree. I appreciate your taking the lead on this. I believe parent meetings about English language assessments are really needed across the district. I'm glad we are able to inform parents about these important aspects of their children's education. I have one last question for you. Was there anything in particular that your team highlighted for parents?*

Mr. Ahmad: *Yes, in fact there was. Families often ask us what they can do to help their children learn English. We tell them to maintain their home language. If they have books at home to read to them and if they can continue having conversations with them in their home language, students will learn English with a better foundation of their home language. We also assured them that this was not a pass/fail assessment but rather an assessment that monitors students' progress in English.*

Ms. Ali: *Right, that assessment is not like typical assessments. Those were good points to highlight. Thank you for sharing that advice. We all need to be reminded of the importance of maintaining one's home language and focusing on and celebrating progress.*

This postconference conversation highlighted key components of Principle 4—collaboration and advocacy. Mr. Ahmad and his team provided an opportunity for ELs and their families to learn more about the English language assessment administered in first grade. The teacher also reinforced that it is crucial for EL families to speak their home language with their children to provide them a solid foundation in language and literacy that will transfer to English. Since this meeting was part of another schoolwide meeting, they were able to maximize attendance.

Secondary Students With Disabilities Scenario

Mr. Karpinski, the high school principal, and Ms. Sackett, a fifth-year biology teacher, have been discussing a lesson Mr. Karpinski observed earlier in the day. They work in a rural junior/senior high school with a 53% free and reduced lunch rate. The ninth-grade biology lesson, taught with a class of 20 students, focused on concepts in genetics—specifically, using Punnett squares to determine heterozygote and homozygote expressions of dominant and recessive genes through genotype and phenotype. Four students with disabilities are included in the class—two with learning disabilities in reading, one with a learning disability in mathematics, and one, Alana, with an emotional disability. Alana is accompanied throughout the day by a teaching assistant, Ms. Ford. Ms. Hargreaves, the special educator, comes into the class to coteach on Days 1, 3, and 5. She consults with Ms. Sackett for classes like this one on Days 2, 4, and 6. Their coplanning takes place over lunch once a week with the ninth-grade team and by e-mail. The post-observation conversation has been a review of the lesson, begun with homework of facial characteristics and hair color cut out from magazines and identified as phenotypes with corresponding genotypes diagrammed. After pairs of students completed a word web of the vocabulary for the unit as a further review, Ms. Sackett walked them through a series of guided notes based on a PowerPoint presentation focused on creating Punnett squares to represent genotype. The conversation shifts to an incident in the classroom.

Post-Observation Conference Conversation

Mr. Karpinski: *Ms. Sackett, tell me about what happened with Alana in the back of the room halfway through the guided note-taking activity!*

Ms. Sackett: *As I understood what happened, Alana couldn't help herself but react by throwing her pencil, knocking over her chair, and stomping out of the room. She means well. Sometimes, Ms. Ford can hover a little too much and, for ninth graders, that can feel pretty upsetting. It actually started with her bending over Cody's paper and pointing to something he needed to write and Cody's blurting out an invective at Ms. Ford to leave him alone. That triggered Alana because she doesn't do well when people are angry around her, so she reacted and left the room. You saw I caught Ms. Ford as she went out the door after her because Alana's IEP specifies she can leave for time-out whenever she needs to, so I figured she'd head down to the guidance office since she knows her own IEP and its accommodations. I suggested Ms. Ford stay with us in the classroom at that point, although the outburst had rattled her, too. I tried to get back to teaching as quickly as possible, but taking five minutes to debrief the incident with the class seemed appropriate.*

Mr. Karpinski: *So you saw that what happened wasn't Alana's fault and you responded, first, by making sure she could get to a safe place and then to work with your students on what had happened. I noticed that you began that conversation by noting that everyone is different and everyone's level of tolerance for different behaviors is different.*

Ms. Sackett: *It seemed like the right thing to say at the time, although, when I asked the students about what they thought, Cody's response in calling Ms. Ford "a witch" was inappropriate.*

Mr. Karpinski: *Cody and I had a talk after you sent him to my office and I finished the observation, and I tried to reinforce his need to behave respectfully and gave him a week of after-school detentions and called his parents. I'll make sure he follows up with an apology to Ms. Ford with my being present.*

Ms. Sackett: *That would be great. I'll check in with Ms. Hargreaves and Ms. Ford when she comes off the bus tomorrow to debrief the event and to help her process what happened. In the meantime, Ms. Hargreaves and I called Alana's mom at lunchtime to let her know what happened. Whenever the students we share are involved, we call the parents on the speaker phone together to make sure that we touch base, describe the incident, and discuss the results.*

Mr. Karpinski: *How did Alana's mom react?*

Ms. Sackett: *She was fine with what happened and how it was handled. Ms. Hargreaves and I have spoken to her several times during the year so far, first as individuals to introduce ourselves so that she knew Alana was in the biology class and that she could call either of us with any concerns she had; then together on a speaker phone to report to her a couple of times that Alana had been exercising some great self-control and that she was carrying about a B average in biology.*

Mr. Karpinski:	*So Alana's mom knows you from the positive messages you've been able to deliver.*
Ms. Sackett:	*Yes, and she knows we're working in Alana's best interest. She's a bright girl.*
Mr. Karpinski:	*Well, it seems as though the incident has worked out, although I'm concerned about Ms. Ford's hovering behaviors.*
Ms. Sackett:	*So am I. I know that Ms. Hargreaves is helping supervise Ms. Ford in the delivery of her services, but sometimes I don't know what to do because Ms. Ford doesn't quite know how to give students the space they need. Maybe if we could talk together with her, with your help at drafting an agenda for the conversation, and give her some research on fading support for students and modeling the behaviors, we could make her relationships with students more fruitful and less obtrusive.*
Mr. Karpinski:	*I'd be happy to help.*

This post-observation conference illustrates some of the ways in which Principle 4 can emerge through observations and in post-observation conferences. Note that Mr. Karpinski invites Ms. Sackett to tell the story of the incident rather than rushing to any kind of judgment or deciding too quickly who is at fault. First, although Ms. Hargreaves was not present for the class, she and Ms. Sackett clearly have a close collaborative relationship with one another that extends to talking with parents together. The conversation with Alana's mother began with their contacting her separately and delivering the same message so that Alana's mother did not feel overwhelmed and understood that the content in the class, biology, and Alana's special education services were academically equally important. Second, Ms. Sackett makes the decision to help Ms. Ford manage the situation, both after Cody's outburst and through targeted professional development regarding her work with Alana, thereby making sure to explain how Ms. Ford can perform her responsibilities more successfully. Also, as a general education teacher, Ms. Sackett has read and understands Alana's IEP, and she takes full responsibility for dealing with Alana's behavior as would the special educator according to that document. In addition, she supports Ms. Ford and the class by dismissing Cody from the room immediately, and Mr. Karpinski supports the process with reasonable and restorative consequences. Finally, Ms. Sackett takes the time to collaborate with her students in attempting to talk through and learn from the incident because emotions at the point can be running high and engagement is paramount to learning.

QUESTIONS

To begin a discussion about the extent to which Principle 4 is present in educators' current teacher evaluation systems and to create a plan for implementing Principle 4, educators can consider the following questions as part of self-reflection or discuss them in pairs or groups:

- How would you summarize the essence of Principle 4: building a culture of collaboration and community?
- Which elements of Principle 4, building a culture of collaboration and community, resonated the most with you?
- Which look-fors of Principle 4 are you ready to integrate into your teacher evaluation system to provide equal access to ELs and students with disabilities?
- How will you integrate these look-fors into your teacher evaluation system?

CHAPTER SUMMARY

This chapter focused on Principle 4: building a culture of collaboration and community. The chapter began with considerations for teacher evaluation systems that are inclusive of ELs and students with disabilities as espoused by Principle 4. Such considerations included coteaching and collaboration, paraprofessionals in special education, and collaboration with caregivers of ELs as well as students with disabilities. The role of diverse students in the collaboration process was also highlighted. Next, the chapter examined why Principle 4 is needed and looked at examples of what Principle 4 means for ELs and students with disabilities. The chapter was rounded out with the process for integrating Principle 4, look-fors, a sample rubric, and scenarios for both groups of students.

NOTES

1. Paraprofessionals may also be referred to as instructional assistants.

2. The term *caregiver* encompasses parents, families, and any adult responsible for the direct care, protection, and supervision of the student.

3. For dually identified students (i.e., ELs who also have a documented disability), look-fors would apply to both groups of students.

Empowering Educators Through Coaching

8

How will this tool be used? Constructively (to promote teacher development) or destructively (to "get a teacher out")?

Dr. M. Williams, EL Coordinator

Chapter 8 sets the four principles examined in this book in the practical context of implementing teacher evaluation protocols that are inclusive of all learners. The focus of this chapter is on coaching, in part because coaching best approximates the process by which teacher evaluation protocols can realize their most potent effects and in part because the evaluation process, like much coaching, takes place in one-to-one settings (teacher to evaluator). As Dr. Williams states above, educators need to know how to use teacher evaluation to improve teachers' performance, especially when it comes to working with English learners (ELs) and students with disabilities.

The chapter first defines coaching as well as the circumstances under which coaching through teacher evaluation protocols can most likely succeed. The chapter goes on to discuss why coaching is needed as a construct within schools and how evaluators can successfully help to create higher-performing teachers of diverse learners and more effective classrooms. Next, the chapter describes components of coaching, such as how to get started, types of questions to ask, and strategies. The implications of well-designed and thoughtfully developed coaching attitudes, constructs, and strategies for improved student outcomes for ELs and students with disabilities are then discussed, followed by a series of considerations for evaluators and teachers as part of establishing coaching relationships.

DEFINING AND UNPACKING COACHING OF DIVERSE LEARNERS

Unpacking the definition and the purpose of coaching can be helpful to teachers and evaluators alike. Definitions of coaching in organizations such as businesses and not-for-profits abound (Joo, 2005). Descriptions range from emphases on "systematic feedback" to "one-on-one interventions" (Joo, 2005, p. 467). Purposes for coaching extend from "equipping people with tools, knowledge, and opportunities" to improving "personal satisfaction" and "organizational performance" to "enhancing interpersonal awareness" (Joo, 2005, p. 467). Coaching, in general, can be defined as *the facilitated learning of professional people to maximize their personal and professional mastery to realize the desired community outcomes. The goal of coaching is to constructively engage a person's expert performance in continual repeated applications in his or her chosen enterprise.* Here, the enterprise being referred to by the definition is teaching, and the purpose is to continually improve the education of ELs and students with disabilities.

Coaching educators of diverse learners can require additional knowledge, sensitivity, application, and understanding. Because ELs and students with disabilities have gained access to the educational system through legal precedent and government mandate, knowing the ways in which their education is determined by regulation is critical. Because ELs and students with disabilities represent a unique and varied population of people with individual strengths and specific challenges, an awareness of the differences and opportunities their educational profiles provide can enhance a teacher's expertise. A teacher's performance can find greater definition and control by having been coached into developing evidence-based practices and greater reflection. Finally, encouraging dialogue about the many ways in which teachers' students can continue to draw support from families, communities, and the professionals with whom they work can spur even greater performance overall.

Therefore, coaching teachers for working with diverse learners can be defined as *the facilitated learning of professional people to maximize their personal and professional mastery, to realize access to the general education curriculum, to capitalize on the diversity of their communities, to hone and extend their professional practice, and to fully use school and community support in the interests of diverse learners. The goal of coaching is to constructively engage a person's expert performance in continual, repeated, and reflective applications in teaching inclusive classrooms.*

Well-coached teachers in an environment that is not conducive to learning, to collegiality, and to shared responsibility for diverse learners' success may not perform at levels high enough to ensure student success. Therefore, the positive culture, the character of the school and the daily investment of its professional staff in the goal of educating young people well can be a critical factor in maximizing the effects of good coaching.

WHAT COACHING IS AND IS NOT

Coaching conjures many different images in the minds of most people. When people think of coaching, they typically think of an athletic coach, someone who paces the sidelines and animates player performance by yelling instructions and encouragement. Yet it is the more personal relationship that this coach may enjoy with his or her players—working with them individually or in smaller groups to assist them in developing their skills and a mind-set that may lead to the team's winning—that better reflects the kind of coaching most appropriate under teacher evaluation schemes. Coaching cannot be a harangue about a litany of problems seen in a teacher's performance that an evaluator feels qualified and obligated to point out and remedy. Also, coaching teachers throughout the pre- and post-observation process can never appear as a means to a "gotcha," suggesting that the evaluator is somehow biased in favor of creating a negative evaluation of the teacher.

Instead, the primary goal of coaching educators is to help them become better and more reflective practitioners. Helping them to understand more about how they teach and why they teach that way requires that the evaluator and teacher establish and maintain a sound professional relationship. A high level of trust is required from all parties before praise and constructive criticism can take place. Additionally, the professional relationship requires the acknowledgment that both parties— teacher and evaluator—have a responsibility for ensuring the success of the evaluation process as well as a recognition of the ultimate benefits of the process: better student outcomes and personal and professional mastery. The emphasis in the definition of coaching is on "facilitated learning," which means that the person who is the coach and the evaluator operates as a guide for the process of reflection and improvement during pre- and post-conferences.

WHY COACHING IS NEEDED
AS PART OF TEACHER EVALUATION SYSTEMS

Coaching acumen is a critical skill for any professional who can have an effect on the delivery of instruction in the classroom. Teacher evaluation can never be about "catching" professional performance at levels that are less than satisfactory or less than exemplary. Although some researchers argue against the combination of coaching with evaluation (Tschannen-Moran & Tschannen-Moran, 2011), coaching as a function of teacher evaluation can be viewed as a practicable and necessary means to guiding professionals toward the school's goal of teaching all students to the highest degree and to the best results possible. Considering the reality of educational politics in the 21st century, often there is not enough time or personnel to work with staff as both an evaluator and also as an administrator. Most often, they are one in the same.

Given the profound emphasis placed on teacher evaluation throughout the United States, coaching can be seen as taking an important place in the overall leadership and professional development scheme in schools (Simkins, Coldwell, Caillau, Finlayson, & Morgan, 2006). Some would argue that rearrangements of the hierarchy so that power in the school is shared in the manner of distributive or collective leadership engender the most positive outcomes for staff and for students (Leithwood, Harris, & Hopkins, 2008; Leithwood & Mascall, 2008). Obviously, administrators do not have to oversee student achievement alone. A culture of respect and collaboration can extend the coaching conversation to the support available from the entire community of professionals, paraprofessionals, literacy coaches, special education teachers, English for speakers of other languages (ESOL) teachers, counselors and school psychologists, and related service providers included.

Coaching for differentiated instruction for ELs and for students with disabilities can require wider and wider circles of influence among school personnel. Management techniques for students with autism, for example, might be included in the conversation of cafeteria workers, bus drivers, and office support staff. Along the same lines, helping newly arrived ELs acclimate to their schools might require different types of conversations among those same stakeholders. Through using coaching as a tool during evaluation, leaders can design stronger supports for diverse learners.

CONDITIONS FOR OPTIMAL TEACHING

As has been noted in each chapter of this text, developing the conditions for optimal teaching and student success through conversations at faculty meetings and through responsive and well-executed professional development opportunities is a precondition for successful teacher evaluation. Learner-centered professional development is critical (McLeskey, 2011), and a culture of collaboration with teachers and among teachers themselves (Waldron, McLeskey, & Redd, 2011) is a necessary prerequisite. As such, there needs to be an entire culture and climate to support teachers (Correa & Wagner, 2011). Coaching, mentoring, teaming, professional learning communities, book groups, curriculum mapping, and the like—indeed all those activities where teachers and administrators talk with one another dedicated to a single purpose—can enhance classroom performance (McLeskey, 2011).

In these circumstances, coaching protocols can operate closely with teacher evaluation responsibilities; the relationship between the two can be understood, and its benefits can be clear. For any coaching process to work, close collaboration among professionals is essential (Silva & Contreras, 2011). Also, the school principal is often the one on whom most of the coaching responsibilities fall (Nidus & Sadder, 2011), establishing coaching protocols and encouraging regular dialogue with teachers about elements such as student work can encourage better teacher evaluation.

KEY CHARACTERISTICS OF COACHING FOR TEACHERS OF DIVERSE LEARNERS

Several additional considerations must be made when coaching teachers of diverse learners such as ELs and students with disabilities. These characteristics include developing strong relationships with teachers, using an appreciative inquiry or strengths-based approach to the coaching, and teacher-centered coaching. Figure 8.1 below provides a visual representation of the relationships between teachers' and evaluators' practice through coaching to meet the needs of all diverse learners.

Figure 8.1 Evaluators and Teachers Meeting the Needs of All Learners

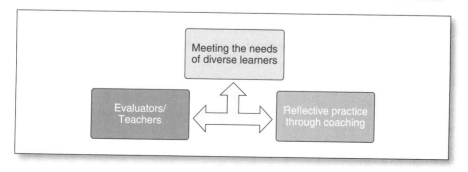

DEVELOPING STRONG RELATIONSHIPS
AND TRUST WITH TEACHERS OF DIVERSE LEARNERS

It is important that an evaluator develop strong professional relationships with teachers of diverse learners and also trust the professionalism of the teacher and work to ensure personal trust over and against considerations of hierarchy or school bureaucracy. If the "community outcome" of continual improvement of *all* student achievement has been made clear by the school's leadership, any teacher's professionalism should be dedicated to that purpose and understood in the evaluator-teacher relationship. The evaluator creates the circumstances, provides the resources, and observes the expected results so that teachers emerge regularly as both enlightened and eager for still more growth. Recognizing teachers as advocates for their students, for themselves, and for their teaching as well as engaging teacher thinking about the design, development, and implementation of units and lessons can help navigate bureaucracy and create trust.

Personal and professional development require trust based on expertise (Cunningham & McNally, 2003) and the ability of the coach to differentiate, through careful listening and empathy, for each member of the professional staff (Zepeda, 2007). Evaluators must continually update knowledge and skill proficiency along with teachers (Brady, 2007). After trust helps secure the relationship and conveys the empathetic response of the coach, the conversation can then turn to the future and the improvement and growth of the person's performance.

USING AN APPRECIATIVE INQUIRY
OR STRENGTHS-BASED APPROACH TO COACHING

Even when faced with a teaching observation that recommends significant changes be made, the premise of teacher evaluation should be on a teacher's recognizing where and how the need for improvement arose in the process of designing, implementing, and evaluating learning. For teachers of diverse learners, this process may take additional time and awareness on both the teacher and evaluator's part to recognize areas of need. The goal of the coaching process for educators of diverse learners is for teachers to become better practitioners. The coaching process is both personal and professional, so it is important to make transparent the deeper motivations for the process—namely, that all students, including diverse learners, will learn to their best potential and the highest expectations of teachers and adults in the community. Reaching and teaching ELs and students with disabilities in inclusive settings requires a steadfast commitment on the part of both the teacher and the evaluator for exploring the range of strategies and supports that could be made available for student learning.

By the same token, "mastery" on the teacher's part is the individual focus of evaluation. The goal of coaching as defined here; that is, to "constructively engage" a teacher through this facilitated relationship toward a *reiterative* "application" of "expert performance," means that the coach must solicit meaning and build on that meaning until teaching mastery exists continually in the person's classroom. Coaching as understanding meaning can often be a positive experience. Coaching, when done thoughtfully, carries with it an "aha" moment at which point the person being coached becomes clear about how his or her performance exhibited expertise or how it *could* exhibit expertise given changes in practice, more time, and continued reflection.

The Role of the Coach

In describing the coach's role and the coaching relationship, Tschannen-Moran and Tschannen-Moran (2010) rely on *appreciative inquiry* to define and enhance the work. Appreciative inquiry is a nonproprietary means of personal and organizational development that is in large part predicated on the notion that in every human situation something works (Hammond, 2001). The kind of coaching described by Tschannen-Moran and Tschannen-Moran (2010) requires an important skill set that school leaders and evaluators must cultivate to be successful, so the circumstances under which the coaching takes place are also critically important.

Thus, as the engagement of expert performance as part of the goal of coaching is examined, it becomes important to recognize that through education and experience, all teachers have particular levels of expertise, depending on the skills and the circumstances being observed. Even in a classroom observation in which the need for significant improvement on the part of the teacher is noted, there are "strengths, vitalities, aspirations, and possibilities" (Tschannen-Moran & Tschannen-Moran, 2010, p. 125) upon which good teaching can build. Given this mindset, evaluators' helping teachers achieve personal and professional mastery through continued and observed "application," through additional chances to reflect, through a supportive culture that relentlessly pursues excellence, and through a collegial and collaborative process, becomes more likely. So, for example, instead of focusing on what did not happen in the lesson, brainstorming evidence-based techniques for a student with emotional and behavioral disabilities and calling forth the expertise of both teacher and evaluator can provide improved results for students from diverse populations.

TEACHER-CENTERED COACHING

The evaluation process should be teacher centered, and the evaluator can keep an eye on trends and patterns in observations and in conversations and use forums such as faculty meetings and professional learning communities to engender professional growth. A coach is in an ideal position to help generalize good thinking about effective practices for diverse learners. The evaluator as coach is also aware of potential connections that exist at the school that may improve practice. Coaches can develop and encourage connections and mentoring relationships among teachers. Through classroom visits, a teacher's strengths can be showcased for other teachers whose practice could benefit through shared resources and experiences.

For the purposes of this book, coaching and, by extension, the entire process of evaluating teachers, must be viewed as an effort that is teacher centered and that

- is collaborative between the evaluator and the teacher,
- is designed to capitalize on strengths and decrease barriers to exemplary performance,
- leads to mastery of the skills of teaching, and
- is dedicated to continually improving student outcomes.

The purpose of coaching is helping teachers make meaning of their performance by examining the process of decision making from thinking through and creating the lesson to execution of the lesson to reflection. In this way, coaching carries with it the principles of constructivism—namely, that teachers build meaning from contextual understanding through an interactive process. The coach can therefore act like a facilitator to help the teacher make this meaning apparent for him or her.

This encouraging meaning making does not mean that the coach cannot offer suggestions that might improve teaching and learning or, in some cases, assist with subpar teaching through remedial plans or close attention to decisions the teacher is making that may not be in the best interest of students or of the goal of improving student outcomes. Often, the evaluator is also the supervisor of personnel at the school and responsible even in part for the hiring and the staffing of teachers, related service providers, and paraprofessionals. In such cases, it may be important for evaluators to delineate for the teacher how and when the conversation is focused on coaching and how and when the conversation is focused on supervision and evaluation during the process of pre- and post-observations. For example, the evaluator can shift seats during the conference, particularly post-observation, from a place across from the teacher to a seat directly next to the teacher. The evaluator can then provide more in-depth remediation. After the shift, the evaluator can return to his or her original seat and can help establish these changes in role in a teacher's mind.[1]

It is important for the evaluator to understand how teachers think about their practice and what steps they go through in making their educational decisions. Coaching models other than the ones alluded to here exist that may serve to help inform drawing forth teacher expertise and its application. Some coaching is primarily solution focused and can make teachers aware of "blind spots" in their performances (Cunningham & McNally, 2003), places they might otherwise have overlooked in the design, implementation, and evaluation of learning for all students. Effective coaching, like effective evaluation, relies on the use of data (Nidus & Sadder, 2011). In the case of coaching, these data are gathered from the observation and from the conversations held pre- and post-observation.

Effective coaching requires a keen sensitivity to a person's tone of voice, to his or her body language, to the nature and quality of the eye contact, as well as to the text of the conversation shared between teacher and evaluator. Different coaching models require attention to these dimensions of personal communication to different degrees. However, practiced coaches will combine keen observation of the teacher in the conversation with continual check-ins about the accuracy of these implications for teaching performance. Effective coaches will risk being wrong with an observation or a stated implication, knowing that continual clarification and feedback will better approximate the path any teacher needs to take toward greater mastery of the art and science of teaching.

REFLECTIVE QUESTIONS TO BEGIN THE COACHING PROCESS

To establish the practice of coaching as part of teacher evaluation, initial questions must be answered by both evaluators and teachers.

1. How much coaching is occurring already?

2. What kind of coaching is happening?

3. Who are the participants?

4. How much coaching includes the strengths and challenges of ELs and students with disabilities?

By asking and answering these questions and collecting evidence and documentation, an evaluator or teacher can prepare to guide conversations so that all principles are addressed thoroughly regardless of the teacher evaluation framework used. These questions are starting points for much broader, transparent conversations.

Much like the look-fors presented in previous chapters, Figure 8.2 provides an example of a self-assessment completed by a teacher named Ms. Kahala that illustrates how teachers of diverse learners can prepare for the coaching processes. By providing a starting point for coaching conversations as well as collecting evidence and documentation of areas checked as "yes" and identifying areas in need of further action or checked, "no," an evaluator and teacher can prepare to guide evaluation conversations. In having a conversation centered on this needs assessment, all four principles for inclusive teacher evaluation can be addressed thoroughly regardless of the teacher evaluation framework being used.

From a coaching perspective, it would be important to acknowledge the areas Ms. Kahala has checked as "yes" prior to discussing the areas checked as "no." This example shows that the teacher has a foundation of awareness and need for further action based on how she answered the questions and comments she provided. In addressing areas of need, it is also important for the coach to ask, "How might I help you here?" This question presents an opportunity to affirm the partnership between evaluator and teacher in order to improve student achievement for all students before the evaluator provides answers or explanations.

WHAT COACHING MEANS
FOR TEACHERS OF DIVERSE LEARNERS

The conversations during the pre-and post-observation conferences are about the decisions the teacher has made during the course of the planning, implementation, and assessment of the lesson. According to Costa and Garmston (2002) and the Cognitive Coaching^{SM} Model, coaching should focus on moving teachers to the greater realization and application of five states of mind: craftsmanship, interdependence, efficacy, consciousness, and flexibility. For teachers of ELs and for students with disabilities, this realization and application of five states of mind could be

Figure 8.2 Ms. Kahala's Needs Assessment

Diverse Learners Needs Assessment Questions	Yes	No	Further Action
Do I know the backgrounds of all of my students, especially those with diverse learning needs?	✓		
Do I have or have access to all of the documents I need that tell me about my students (e.g., IEPs, home language surveys, registration forms, English language proficiency, etc.)?		✓	Not sure I have all info needed; find this info
Have I met and/or been in contact with the families and/or caregivers of my students?	✓		See notes from conference and e-mail log
Have I met with other teachers and/or support personnel who provide services to my students with diverse learning needs?	✓		
Do I plan regularly with other teachers and/or support personnel who provide services to my students with diverse learning needs?		✓	Create schedule to co-plan w/ Mr. Ngu
Am I aware of and do I regularly implement appropriate strategies that allow my diverse students access to the content being taught?		✓	Working on this; need to implement formative assessments; follow up on professional development plan due soon!
Do I regularly use accommodations based on my students' IEPs, ELP levels, and learning needs?	✓		
Do I understand the additional assessments my students take?		✓	Need to get an update from Mr. Ngu
Do I use the data from various assessments to help plan instruction for my diverse students?		✓	Need to get an update

manifested in improved attention to strategies that may help diverse students gain access to understanding and using skills and content.

Likewise, effective coaching can have positive effects for ELs and for students with disabilities by putting teachers in touch with one another and by emphasizing the positive consequences that teaming can have on their students' education. These benefits extend to the need for connection among all the different professionals and teams involved in working with ELs and with students with disabilities and the inclusion of the home and family in decision making. As a result of coaching conversations, ELs and students with disabilities may begin to work within a clearer framework like the principles that undergird Universal Design for Learning (UDL). A coach can solicit a teacher's commitment to carrying through on developing and implementing the principles of UDL for ELs and for students with disabilities. Conceivably, coaching a teacher may also involve increasing awareness of the legal and social justice basis for providing both groups of students with complete and equal access to the general education curriculum. Finally, coaching conversations may create the circumstances for teachers to develop the flexibility necessary to work with diverse populations of students. Thus, questions during coaching opportunities should focus on probing the decisions teachers can make to become more effective. Suggestions from the coach, as well as solicited thinking from the teacher, should focus on establishing these directions and the means to realizing them in practice.

COACHING AND EVALUATION CONSIDERATIONS

Viewing the pre- and post-observation conversations as opportunities to articulate one's craft as a practitioner is an essential part of advocating for oneself. Using that time to ask clarifying questions helps the evaluator to become better prepared for the evaluation. For example, if a component of the teacher evaluation addresses the use of technology, teachers of diverse learners may need to clarify what technology they use and why that technology is the most appropriate for their students. At the same time, an evaluator has to ask probing questions that allow teachers to expand on their initial plans or further explain a lesson observed. A teacher's commitment to a new strategy or course of action that will likely improve outcomes for students can also be a form of risk taking. Evaluations do not necessarily have to capture teachers "sticking to the script" but rather being comfortable enough with their own ability as creative practitioners to try something new or different to address the needs of their diverse students. For teachers and evaluators, the considerations that follow are starting points for both the pre- and post-observation conversation where applicable. Oftentimes, the pre- and post-observation conversations may reveal a need for professional learning about a particular issue and/or student population. Hence, improving outcomes schoolwide may be an approach to supporting all educators of diverse learners.

Further, the evaluator or coach should recognize, enhance, and celebrate the teacher's role as advocate for his or her ELs and students with disabilities. Often, a teacher's advocacy for his or her students can be received as advocacy for his own practice. Conversations around advocacy might focus on the evidence base of the practice as well as the rationale for its implementation in the inclusive classroom. A coach's careful listening to his or her teacher's advocacy efforts for diverse learners means acknowledging the thinking that has gone into the selection and use of the practice. For example, a coach might observe that a child with Down syndrome is being encouraged to read using contextual clues rather than syllabification. The subsequent conversation about the connections between speech impairments and reading can serve to enhance both the teacher and the evaluator's understanding of intellectual disabilities and the development of literacy.

Table 8.1 provides questions and considerations for teacher and evaluators based on the four principles of inclusive teacher evaluation for diverse learners. These questions and considerations for professional learning are not at all exhaustive but rather reflect a sample of questions and considerations and how they relate to each principle. The guiding questions and pre- and post-observation questions are relevant both to the coaching conversation and to sustained professional development through learning communities.

CONCLUSION

Coaching in the broader context of the community can create and enhance support systems for diverse students that can better ensure their achievement. Depending on the coaching model, ELs and students with disabilities can benefit from teachers who are well coached. Teaching populations of ELs and students with disabilities demand flexibility and attention to detail and a level of risk taking that evaluators, through trusted relationships, should elicit in the teachers with whom they work. Clarifying high expectations, enhancing collaboration, implementing UDL, and honing teaching strategies as coaching outcomes can encourage a redoubling of efforts to secure success for these vulnerable populations of learners.

Table 8.1 Inclusive Principles, Guiding Questions, Considerations for Professional Learning Communities, and Conversation Questions

Inclusive Principles	Guiding Questions	Consideration for Professional Learning Communities	Pre- or Post-Observation Conversation Questions
1. Committing to equal access for all learners	• Are teacher evaluations based on the state's teaching standards using relevant indicators in a performance-based evaluation system that is inclusive of ELs and students with disabilities? • Can teachers articulate a vision and a commitment to educating *all* students? • Do classroom personnel have full access to IEPs, 504 plans,[a] and English language proficiency levels and assessment data as appropriate? • What more does the teacher need to improve access for ELs and for students with disabilities to the general education curriculum?	Inclusion of all teachers of ELs and students with disabilities regarding curriculum mapping, formative and summative assessments, teaching strategies, professional learning communities, and other leadership opportunities	• Is a plan articulated that demonstrates a clear vision of access for all students within the classroom?
2. Preparing to support diverse learners	• How are all students nurtured and supported in ongoing and respectful relationships within the classroom, school, and the greater community? • How well are systems of support such as prereferral strategies, response-to-intervention, English for speakers other languages (ESOL) programs and services, first and second language support programs, and/or positive behavioral interventions implemented at the levels of the classroom and school? • How are systems of support in place through classroom and school to make sure that all learners are successful and graduate to meaningful college and/or career opportunities? • How are student strengths and differences acknowledged, celebrated, and built upon?	How are schoolwide communities (e.g., administrative, professional learning, parent/teacher organizations, community-based organizations) inclusive of all learners and their families?	• What has been planned for the lesson and what will be observed during the lesson? • Why have those instructional strategies been chosen? For whom have they been chosen? Why? • How will you know the instructional strategies were effective?

Inclusive Principles	Guiding Questions	Consideration for Professional Learning Communities	Pre- or Post-Observation Conversation Questions
3. Reflective teaching using evidence-based strategies	• How are all students provided effective and varied instructional strategies and appropriate amounts of instructional time so that they can access high-quality, appropriately challenging curriculum and content? • How are language-rich, culturally responsive, flexibly grouped, student-initiated, and authentic and relevant learning experiences manifested in the classroom? • How and when are innovative and assistive technologies used for students who can benefit from them?	How are effective teaching practices communicated and evident throughout all classroom communities for diverse learners?	• Have goals been set for the next observation that are clear and that connect individual practice with an evaluator's perspective on what needs improvement? • Is there a plan to monitor and adjust learning based on improved decision making and more informed practice? • Has the need to gather more data or to work with or understand the available data better been discussed and resolved by the teacher and the evaluator?
4. Building a culture of collaboration and community	• How are problems resolved and decisions made in connection and collaboration with families/caregivers of ELs and students with disabilities and the community? • How are supports, such as scheduling arrangements, parent and professional conferences, and resources for professional development and planning used? • To what degree do educators work cooperatively, communicate regularly, and share resources, responsibilities, skills, decisions, and advocacy for the benefit of *all students?*	How do diverse learners and their advocates address and resolve issues (e.g., administrative, parent/teacher, community based) related to their learning experiences?	• Have you worked with colleagues to have more information about diverse learners and their needs? • Have you talked through a potential solution to a problem, or have you seen a problem from several different points of view? Give an example.

a. Section 504 is an antidiscrimination, civil rights statute that requires the needs of students with disabilities to be met as adequately as the needs of the nondisabled are met. The 504 plans are the documents that outline how the student's needs will be met.

ADDITIONAL DISCUSSION QUESTIONS

Table 8.2 outlines additional discussion questions to use with colleagues in reflecting on and applying themes from this chapter. Each set of questions is grouped by topic.

Table 8.2 Coaching Topic and Discussion Questions

Coaching Topic	Discussion Questions
Urgent need for coaching	Are teachers prepared for and aware of the needs of ELs and students with disabilities who are in inclusive classrooms and learning environments? If not, what professional learning opportunities can be provided to focus on the needs of diverse learners?
Inclusive teacher evaluation frameworks	How can the four principles be incorporated into various frameworks used to evaluate teachers of diverse learners? How will professional learning communities include the needs of diverse learners in order to build teacher capacity to teach all students?
Principle 1	How are diverse learners fully included within the classroom community? How are barriers recognized and addressed so that students are afforded equal access to the content? How are the strengths and abilities of students recognized and capitalized upon?
Principle 2	To what extent are teachers able to articulate the needs of ELs and students with disabilities who are part of classroom communities? To what extent are high expectations communicated and reflected in teaching, learning, and assessment practices?
Principle 3	How will appropriate differentiation be demonstrated? What best practices will be included in the lesson specifics for ELs and students with disabilities? What is the intent behind the use of these practices?
Principle 4	How is the teacher independently engaging in professional development and taking advantage of learning opportunities focused on diverse learners? How are support personnel included in and prepared for planning and instructional delivery for diverse learners?

NOTE

1. For more information, contact thinkingcollaborative.com or Thinking Collaborative Adaptive Schools and Cognitive Coaching P.O. Box 630860, Highlands Ranch, CO 80163.

References

Abedi, J. (2002). Standardized achievement tests and English language learners: Psychometrics issues. *Educational Assessment, 83*(3), 231–257.

Abedi, J. (2006). Psychometric issues in the ELL assessment and special education eligibility. *Teachers College Record, 108*(11), 2282–2303.

Abedi, J., & Dietel, R. (2004, Winter). *Challenges in the No Child Left Behind Act for English Language Learners* (CRESST Policy Brief 7). Retrieved from https://www.cse.ucla.edu/products/policy/cresst_policy7.pdf

Adamson, F., & Darling-Hammond, L. (2012). Funding disparities and the inequitable distribution of teachers: Evaluating sources and solutions. *Education Policy Analysis Archives, 20*(37).

Alford, B. J., & Niño, M. C. (2011). *Leading academic achievement for English language learners: A guide for principals*. Thousand Oaks, CA: Corwin.

Allington, R. L., & Gabriel, R. E. (2012). Every child, every day. *Educational Leadership, 69*(6), 10-15.

Allor, J. H., Mathes, P. G., Jones, F. G., Champlin, T. M., & Cheatham, J. P. (2010). Individualized research-based reading instruction for students with intellectual disabilities: Success stories. *TEACHING Exceptional Children, 42*(3), 6–12.

Alquraini, T., & Gut, D. (2012). Critical components of successful inclusion of students with severe disabilities: Literature review. *International Journal of Special Education, 27*(1), 42–59.

American Institutes of Research. (2012). *Reauthorizing ESEA: Making research relevant: Students with disabilities, a pocket guide.* Retrieved from http://www.air.org/sites/default/files/downloads/report/1278_PG_SpEd_d6_FINAL_508_compliant_0.pdf

American Youth Policy Forum. (2009). *Moving English language learners to college- and career-readiness* (ELL issue brief). Washington, DC: Author.

Americans with Disabilities Act of 1990, 42 U.S.C.A. §12101 *et seq.* (West 1993).

Archer, A., & Hughes, C. (2011). *Explicit instruction: Effective and efficient teaching.* New York, NY: Guilford.

Arias, B., & Morillo-Campbell, M. (2008). *Promoting ELL parental involvement: Challenges in contested times.* Tempe: Arizona State University, Educational Policy Research Unit.

Armstrong, T. (2012). First, discover their strengths. *Educational Leadership, 70*(2), 10–16.

August, A., Branum-Martin, L., Cardenas-Hagan, E., & Francis, D. J. (2009). The impact of an instructional intervention on the science and language learning of middle grade English language learners. *Journal of Research on Educational Effectiveness, 2*(4), 345–376. doi:10.1080/1934574090321 7623

August, D., Estrada, J., & Boyle, A. (2012). *Supporting English language learners: A pocket guide for state and district leaders.* Washington, DC: American Institutes for Research.

August, D., Salend, S., Staehr Fenner, D., & Kozik, P. (2012). *The evaluation of educators in effective schools and classrooms for all learners.* Washington, DC: American Federation of Teachers.

August, D., & Shanahan, T. (Eds.). (2006). *Developing literacy in second-language learners.* Mahwah, NJ: Lawrence Erlbaum.

August, D., Staehr Fenner, D., & Snyder, S. (2014). *Scaffolding instruction for English language learners: A resource guide for English language arts.* Washington, DC: Center for English Language Learners at American Institutes for Research. Retrieved from https://www.engageny.org/resource/scaffolding-instruction-english-language-learners-resource-guides-english-language-arts-and

Bacon, J., & Ferri, B. (2013). The impact of standards based reform: Applying Brantlinger's critique of "hierarchical ideologies." *International Journal of Inclusive Education, 17*(12), 1312–1325.

Bailey, A. L. (2010). Implications for assessment and instruction. In M. Schatz & L. C. Wilkinson (Eds.), *The education of English language learners: Research to practice* (pp. 222–247). New York, NY: Guilford Press.

Bailey, A., Butler, F., & Sato, E. (2007). Standards-to-standards linkage under Title III: Exploring common language demands in ELD and science standards. *Applied Measurement in Education, 20*(1), 53–78.

Bailey, A., Butler, F., Stevens, R., & Lord, C. (2007). Further specifying the language demands of school. In A. Bailey (Ed.), *The language demands of school: Putting academic English to the test* (pp. 103–156). New Haven, CT: Yale University Press.

Baker, S., Lesaux, N., Jayanthi, M., Dimino, J., Proctor, C. P., Morris, J., . . . Newman-Gonchar, R. (2014). *Teaching academic content and literacy to English learners in elementary and middle school* (NCEE 2014-4012). Washington, DC: U.S. Department of Education, National Center for Education Evaluation and Regional Assistance, Institute of Education Sciences. Retrieved from http://ies.ed.gov/ncee/wwc/publications_reviews.aspx

Ballantyne, K. G., Sanderman, A. R., & Levy, J. (2008). *Educating English language learners: Building teacher capacity.* Washington, DC: National Clearinghouse for English Language Acquisition.

Batalova, J., Gelatt, J., & Lowell, B. L. (2006). *Immigrants and labor force trends: The future, past and present.* Washington, DC: Migration Policy Institute. Retrieved from http://www.migrationpolicy.org/ITFIAF/TF17_Lowell.pdf

Bauwens, J., & Hourcade, J. J. (1997). Cooperative teaching: Pictures of possibilities. *Intervention in School and Clinic, 33*(2), 81–85, 89.

Bell, C. A., Gitomer, D. H., McCaffrey, D. F., Hamre, B. K., Pianta, R. C., & Qi, Y. (2012). An argument approach to observation protocol validity. *Educational Assessment, 17*(2-3), 62–87.

Berg, J. L., & Wehby, J. (2013). Preteaching strategies to improve student learning in content area classes. *Intervention in School and Clinic, 49*(1), 14–20.

Berliner, D. (2006). Our impoverished view of educational reform. *Teacher's College Record, 108*, 949–995. Retrieved from http://www.tcrecord.org/content.asp?contentid=12106

Berman, M. S. (2000). Self-concept and academic differences between students with learning disabilities in inclusive and non-inclusive classrooms (Unpublished doctoral dissertation). Temple University, Philadelphia, PA.

Berry, R. A. W. (2011). Voices of experience: General education teachers on teaching students with disabilities. *International Journal of Inclusive Education, 15*(6), 627–648.

Bilias-Lolis, E., Chafouleas, S. M., Kehle, T. J., & Bray, M. A. (2012). Exploring the utility of self-modeling in reducing disruptive classroom behavior in students with intellectual disability. *Psychology in the Schools, 49*(1), 82–92.

Blanton, L. P., Sindelar, P. T., & Correa, V. I. (2006). Models and measures of beginning teacher quality. *Journal of Special Education, 40*(2), 115–117.

Blecker, N. S., & Boakes, N. S. (2010). Creating a learning environment for all children: Are teachers able and willing? *International Journal of Inclusive Education, 14*(5), 435–447. doi:10.1080/13603110802504937

Board of Education of the Hendrick Hudson Central School District v. Rowley, 458 U.S. 176, 200 (1982).

Bon, S. C., & Bigbee, A. (2011). Special education leadership: Integrating professional and personal codes of ethics to serve the best interest of the child. *Journal of School Leadership, 21*(3), 324–359.

Bowman-Perrott, L. J., Herrera, S., & Murry, K. (2010). Reading difficulties and grade retention: What's the connection for English language learners? *Reading & Writing Quarterly, 26*(1), 91–107.

Brady, C. (2007). Coaches' voices bring 6 lessons to light. *Journal of Staff Developments, 28*(1), 46–51.

Breiseth, L. (2011). *A guide for engaging ELL families: Twenty strategies for school leaders.* Washington, DC: Colorín Colorado. Retrieved from http://www.colorincolorado.org/principals/family/

Brock, L. L., Nishida, T. K., Chiong, C., Grimm, K. J., & Rimm-Kaufman, S. E. (2008). Children's perceptions of the classroom environment and social and academic performance: A longitudinal analysis of the contribution of the "responsive classroom." approach. *Journal of School Psychology, 46*(2), 129–149.

Brown, M. R., Higgins, K., Pierce, T., Hong, E., & Thoma, C. (2003). Secondary students' perception of school life with regard to alienation: The effects of disability, gender, and race. *Learning Disability Quarterly, 26*(4), 227–238.

Brownell, M. T., Smith, S. J., Crocket, J. B., & Griffin, C. C. (2012). *Inclusive instruction: Evidence-based practices for teaching students with disabilities.* New York, NY: Guilford.

Bulgren, J. (2002). *The educational context and outcomes for high school students with disabilities: The perception of parents of students with disabilities.* Washington, DC: U.S. Department of Education, Office of Special Education Programs, Institute for Academic Access.

Bulgren, J. A., Sampson Graner, P., & Deshler, D. D. (2013). Literacy challenges and opportunities for students with learning disabilities in social studies and history. *Learning Disabilities Research & Practice, 28,* 17–27. doi:10.1111/ldrp.12003

Burden, R., Tinnerman, L., Lunce, L., & Runshe, D. (2010). Video case studies: Preparing teachers for inclusion. *TEACHING Exceptional Children Plus, 6*(4), 3.

Burns, E. (2006). *IEP-2005: Writing and implementing individualized education plans.* Springfield, IL: Charles C Thomas.

Callahan, R. (2005). Tracking and high school English learners: Limiting opportunity to learn. *American Educational Research Journal, 42*(2), 305–328.

Capizzi, A. M. (2008). From assessment to annual goals: Engaging a decision-making process in writing measurable IEPs. *Journal of Special Education, 33*(3), 166–176.

Capizzi, A. M., & Fuchs, L. S. (2005). Effects of curriculum-based measurement with and without diagnostic feedback on teacher planning. *Remedial and Special Education, 26*(3), 159–174.

Carlberg, C., & Kavale, K. (1980). The efficacy of special versus regular class placement for exceptional children: A meta-analysis. *Journal of Special Education, 14,* 295–309.

Carlo, M., August, D., McLaughlin, B., Snow, C., Dressler, C., Lippman, D., . . . White, C. (2004). Closing the gap: Addressing the vocabulary needs of English language learners in bilingual and mainstream classrooms. *Reading Research Quarterly, 39*(2), 188–206.

Carnahan, C. R., Williamson, P., Clarke, L., & Sorensen, R. (2009). A systematic approach for supporting paraeducators in educational settings: A guide for teachers. *TEACHING Exceptional Children, 41*(5), 34–45.

Carter, E., O'Rourke, L. O., Sisco, L. G., & Pelsue, D. (2009). Knowledge, responsibilities, and training needs of paraprofessionals in elementary and secondary schools. *Remedial and Special Education, 30*(6), 344–359.

Carter, E. W., Cushing, L. S., Clark, N. M., & Kennedy, C. H. (2005). Effects of peer support interventions on students' access to the general curriculum and social interactions. *Research and Practice for Persons With Severe Disabilities, 30*(1), 15–25.

Carter, N., Prater, M., Jackson, A., & Marchant, M. (2009). Educators' perceptions of collaborative planning processes for students with disabilities. *Preventing School Failure, 54*(1), 60–70.

Causton, J. (2011). *Effective inclusive practice.* Albany: College of St. Rose and New York State Task Force on Quality Inclusive Schooling, East Region.

Causton-Theoharis, J. H. (2009). *The paraprofessional's handbook for effective support in inclusive classrooms.* Baltimore, MD: Brookes.

Causton-Theoharis, J., Theoharis, G., Orsati, F. M., & Cosier, M. (2011). Does self-contained special education deliver on its promises: A critical inquiry into research and practices. *Journal of Special Education Leadership, 24*(2), 61-80.

Cho, H., Wehmeyer, M., & Kingston, N. (2011). Elementary teachers' knowledge and use of interventions and barriers to promoting student self-determination. *Journal of Special Education, 45*(3), 149–156.

Correa, V., & Wagner, J. (2011). Principals' roles in supporting the induction of special education teachers. *Journal of Special Education Leadership, 24,* 17–25.

Costa, A., & Garmston, R. (2002). *Cognitive coaching: A foundation for renaissance schools.* Norwood, MA: Christopher Gordon.

Cote Sparks, S., & Cote, D. L. (2012). Teaching choice making to elementary students with mild to moderate disabilities. *Intervention in School and Clinic, 47*(5), 290–296.

Council for the Accreditation of Educator Preparation. (2013). *CAEP accreditation standards.* Washington, DC: Author. Retrieved from http://caepnet.files.wordpress.com/2013/09/final_board_approved1.pdf

Council for the Accreditation of Educator Preparation. (n.d.). Glossary. Retrieved from http://caepnet.org/resources/glossary/

Council for Exceptional Children's position on special education teacher evaluation. (2013). *TEACHING Exceptional Children, 45*(3), 73–76.

Covey, S. (2007). *The 7 habits of highly effective people: Powerful lessons in personal change.* New York, NY: Free Press.

Culver, C. E., & Hayes, K. T. (2014). Beyond teacher evaluation: Prioritizing teacher instructional effectiveness with meaningful professional development. *School Improvement Network.* Retrieved from http://www.schoolimprovement.com/whitepapers/beyond-teacher-evaluation-prioritizing-teacher-instructional-effectiveness-with-meaningful-professional-development/

Cunningham, L., & McNally, K. (2003, November/December). Improving organizational and individual performance through coaching: A case study. *Nurse Leader,* 46–49.

Danielson, C. (2007). *Enhancing professional practice: A framework for teaching* (2nd ed.). Alexandria, VA: ASCD.

Danielson, C. (2011). The framework for teaching evaluation instrument. Retrieved from http://danielsongroup.org/download/?download=449

Darling-Hammond, L. (2014, Spring). One piece of the whole: Teacher evaluation as part of a comprehensive system for teaching and learning. *American Educator,* 1–13.

De Bortoli, T., Foreman, P., Arthur-Kelly, M., Balandin, S., & Mathisen, B. (2012). Mainstream teachers' experiences of communicating with students with multiple and severe disabilities. *Education and Training in Autism and Other Developmental Disabilities, 47*(2), 236–252.

de Jong, E., & Harper, C. (2008). ESL is good teaching "plus": Preparing standard curriculum teachers for all learners. In M. E. Brisk (Ed.), *Language, culture, and community in teacher education* (pp. 127–148). New York, NY: Erlbaum.

Deal, T. E., & Peterson, K. D. (2009). *Shaping school culture* (2nd ed.). San Francisco, CA: Jossey-Bass.

DeCapua, A., & Marshall, H. W. (2011). *Breaking new ground: Teaching students with limited or interrupted formal education in U.S. secondary schools.* Ann Arbor: University of Michigan Press.

Demchuk, L. (2000). *Children's perceptions and attitudes about special education* (Unpublished doctoral dissertation). University of Toronto, Toronto, Canada.

Department of Education of Hawaii v. Katherine D., 727 F. 2d 809 (HI 1984).

Diliberto, J. A., & Brewer, D. (2012). Six tips for successful IEP meetings. *TEACHING Exceptional Children, 44*(4), 30–37.

Downing, J., & Peckham-Hardin, K. (2007). Inclusive education: What makes it a good education for students with moderate to severe disabilities? *Research and Practice for Persons With Severe Disabilities, 32*, 16–30.

Doyle, L. H. (2004). Inclusion: The unifying thread for fragmented metaphors. *Journal of School Leadership, 14*, 352–377.

Dressler, C., & Kamil, M. L. (2006). First-and second-language literacy. In D. August & T. Shanahan (Eds.), *Developing literacy in second language learners: Report of the national literacy panel on language-minority children and youth* (pp. 197–238). Mahwah, NJ: Erlbaum.

Education for All Handicapped Children Act. (1975). P.L. 94-142.

Edwards, C., & Da Fonte, A. (2012). The 5-point plan: Fostering successful partnerships with families of students with disabilities. *TEACHING Exceptional Children, 44*(3), 6–13.

Edyburn, D. L. (2010). Would you recognize universal design for learning if you saw it? Ten propositions for new directions for the second decade of UDL. *Learning Disability Quarterly, 33*, 33-41.

Elbaum, B. (2002). The self-concept of students with learning disabilities: A meta-analysis of comparisons across different placements. *Learning Disabilities Research & Practice, 17*(4), 216–226.

Epstein, M., Munk, D., Bursuck, W., Polloway, E., & Jayanthi, M. (1999). Strategies for improving home-school communication about homework for students with disabilities. *Journal of Special Education, 33*, 166–176.

Esposito, A. (Director). (2004). *We can shine: From institutions to independence* [Documentary]. USA: Espocinema.

Etscheidt, S. (2005). Paraprofessional services for students with disabilities: A legal analysis. *Research and Practice for Persons With Severe Disabilities, 30*(2), 60–80.

Etscheidt, S. (2007). The excusal provision of the IDEA 2004: Streamlining procedural compliance or prejudicing rights of students with disabilities? *Preventing School Failure, 51*(4), 13–18.

Fenlon, A. (2011). Road map for a dream. *Educational Leadership, 68*(7), 23–26.

Ferguson, C. (2008). *The school–family connection: Looking at the larger picture.* Austin, TX: National Center for Community and Family Connections with Schools.

Flores, M. M., & Kaylor, M. (2007). The effects of a direct instruction program on the fraction performance of middle school students at-risk for failure in mathematics. *Journal of Instructional Psychology, 34*(2), 84–94.

Forte, E., & Faulkner-Bond, M. (2010). *The administrator's guide to federal programs for English learners.* Washington, DC: Thompson.

Francis, D. J., Rivera, M., Lesaux, N., Kieffer, M., & Rivera, H. (2006). *Practical guidelines for the education of English language learners: Research-based recommendations for instruction and academic interventions.* Portsmouth, NH: RMC Research Corporation, Center on Instruction. Retrieved from http://centeroninstruction.org/files/ELL1-Interventions.pdf

French, N. K. (2001). Supervising paraprofessionals: A survey of teacher practices. *Journal of Special Education, 35*, 41–53.

French, N. K. (2002). 20 ways to maximize paraprofessional services for students with learning disabilities. *Intervention in School and Clinic, 38*(1), 50–55.

Fry, R. (2008, June). *The role of schools in the English language learner achievement gap.* Washington, DC: Pew Hispanic Center. Retrieved from http://www.pewhispanic.org/files/reports/89.pdf

Fry, R., & Taylor, P. (2013). *Hispanic high school graduates pass whites in rate of college enrollment.* Washington, DC: Pew Hispanic Center. Retrieved from http://www.pewhispanic.org/files/2013/05/PHC_college_enrollment_2013-05.pdf

Fuchs, D., Mock, D., Morgan, P., & Young, C. (2003). Responsiveness-to-intervention: Definitions, evidence, and implications for the learning disabilities construct. *Learning Disabilities Research & Practice, 18*, 157–171.

Fuchs, L. S. (2003). Assessing intervention responsiveness: Conceptual and technical issues. *Learning Disabilities: Research and Practice, 18*(3), 172–186.

Gadow, K. D., DeVincent, C. J., Pomeroy, J., & Azizian, A. (2004). Psychiatric symptoms in preschool children with PDD and clinic and comparison samples. *Journal of Autism and Developmental Disorders, 34*, 379–393.

Gándara, R., Rumberger, R., Maxwell-Jolly, J., & Callahan, R. (2003). English learners in California schools: Unequal resources, unequal outcomes. *Education Policy Analysis Archives, 11*(36), 1–54.

Gardner, H. (1983). *Frames of mind.* New York, NY: Basic Books.

Genesee, F., Lindholm-Leary, K., Saunders, W., & Christian, D. (2006). *Educating English language learners.* New York, NY: Cambridge University Press.

Giangreco, M. F., Doyle, M. B., & Suter, J. C. (2012). Constructively responding to requests for paraprofessionals: We keep asking the wrong questions. *Remedial and Special Education, 33*(6), 362–373.

Goldenberg, C. (2008, Summer). Teaching English language learners: What the research does—and does not—say. *American Educator*, 8–44.

Gottlieb, M., & Ernst-Slavit, G. (2014). *Academic language in diverse classrooms: Definitions and contexts.* Thousand Oaks, CA: Corwin.

Gottlieb, M., Katz, A., & Ernst-Slavit, G. (2009). *Paper to practice: Using the English language proficiency standards in preK-12 classrooms.* Alexandria, VA: Teachers of English to Speakers of Other Languages.

Graham, S., & Harris, K. R. (2013). Common core state standards, writing, and students with LD: Recommendations. *Learning Disabilities Research & Practice, 28*(1), 28–37. doi:10.1111/ldrp.12004

Gronlund, N. E., & Waugh, C. K. (2009). *Assessment of student achievement* (9th ed.). Upper Saddle River, NJ: Pearson.

Haager, D., & Vaughn, S. (2013). The Common Core State Standards and students with learning disabilities: Introduction to the special issue. *Learning Disabilities Research & Practice, 28*, 1–4.

Hall, T. E., Wolfe, P. S., & Bollig, A. A. (2003). The home-to-school notebook: An effective communication strategy for students with severe disabilities. *TEACHING Exceptional Children, 36*(2), 68–73.

Hamayan, E. (2006). What is the role of culture in language learning? In E. Hamayan & R. Freeman (Eds.), *English language learners at school: A guide for administrators* (pp. 62–64). Philadelphia, PA: Caslon.

Hammond, S. A. (2013). *The Thin Book of appreciative inquiry.* Bend, OR: Thin Book.

Harlow, C. W. (2003). *Education and correctional populations* (Bureau of Justice Statistics Special Report). Washington, DC: Department of Justice, Bureau of Justice Statistics.

Haydon, T., Maheady, L., & Hunter, W. (2010). Effects of numbered heads together on the daily quiz scores and on-task behavior of students with disabilities. *Journal of Behavioral Education, 19*, 222–238.

Hendrickson, J. M., Shokoohi-Yekta, M., Hamre-Nietupski, S., & Gable, R. A. (1996). Middle and high school students' perceptions on being friends with peers with severe disabilities. *Exceptional Children, 63*, 19–28.

Hetherington, S. A., Durant-Jones, L., Johnson, K., Nolan, K. W., Smith, E., Tuttle J., & Taylor-Brown S. (2010). The lived experiences of adolescents with disabilities and their parents in transition planning. *Focus on Autism and Other Developmental Disabilities, 25*(3), 163–172.

Heward, W. L. (2003). Ten faulty notions about teaching and learning that hinder the effectiveness of special education. *Journal of Special Education, 36*, 186–205.

Heyward, S. (2009, April). *The ADA amendments: Do we really have to change the way we do business?* Paper presented at the eighth annual Disabilities Symposium, University of Pennsylvania, Philadelphia.

Heyward, W. L. (2009). *Exceptional children: An introduction to special education.* New York, NY: Pearson Education.

Hollenbeck, A. F. (2007). From IDEA to implementation: A discussion of foundational and future responsiveness-to-intervention research. *Learning Disabilities Research & Practice, 22,* 137–146.

Honigsfeld, A., & Dove, M. (2010). *Collaboration and co-teaching: Strategies for English learners.* Thousand Oaks, CA: Corwin.

Honigsfeld, A., & Dove, M. (2013, Winter). C3 = Common Core collaborations. *The Ri-Teller,* pp. 1, 4. Retrieved from http://ritell.org/Resources/Documents/RITELLER/RITELLER%202012-2013/3.1Riteller%20winter%2013.pdf

Houseman, N. G., & Martinez, M. R. (2002). *Preventing school dropout and ensuring success for English language learners and Native American students* (Report No. ED-99-CO-0137). Washington, DC: Office of Educational Research and Improvement.

Hudson, M. E., Browder, D., & Wakeman, S. (2013). Helping students with moderate and severe intellectual disability access grade-level text. *TEACHING Exceptional Children, 45*(3), 14–23.

Individuals with Disabilities Education Act of 2004, P.L. 108-446.

Individuals with Disability Education Act Amendments of 1997. (1997). Retrieved from http://thomas.loc.gov/home/thomas.php

Jones, N., Buzick, H., & Turkan, S. (2013). Students with disabilities and English learners in measures of educator effectiveness. *Educational Researcher, 42,* 234–241. doi:10.3102/0013189X12468211

Joo, B. (2005). Executive coaching: A conceptual framework from an integrative review of practice and research. *Human Resource Development Review, 4,* 462–490.

Kane, T. J. (2012). Capturing the dimensions of effective teaching. *Education Next, 12*(4), 34–41.

Kane, T. J., & Cantrell, S. (2012). *Learning about teaching: Initial findings from the measures of effective teaching project.* Seattle, WA: Bill use & Melinda Gates Foundation.

Kane, T. J., Taylor, E. S., Tyler, J. H., & Wooten, A. L. (2011). Identifying effective classroom practices using student achievement data. *Journal of Human Resources, 46*(3), 587–613.

Kao, G., & Thompson, J. S. (2003). Racial and ethnic stratification in education achievement and attainment. *Annual Review of Sociology, 29*(1), 417–442. doi:10.1146/annurev.soc.29.010202.100019

Keel, M. C., Dangel, H. L., & Owens, S. H. (1999). Selecting instructional interventions for students with mild disabilities in inclusive classrooms. *Focus on Exceptional Children, 31*(8), 1–15.

Kennedy, T., & Menten, T. (2010). Reading, writing, and thinking about disability: Five activities for the classroom. *English Journal, 100*(2), 61–67.

Kenyatta, C. P. (2012). From perception to practice: How teacher-student interactions affect African American male achievement. *Journal of Urban Learning, Teaching, and Research, 8,* 36–44.

Kozik, P. (2012). The AI-IEP protocol. In T. Armstrong (Ed.), *Neurodiversity in the classroom: Strength-based strategies to help students with special needs succeed in school and life* (pp. 000-000). Alexandria, VA: Association of Supervision and Curriculum Development.

Kozik, P., Osroff, P., Lee, S., & Marr, W. (2010). Listening first: Designing and implementing middle school inclusion. In M. Cianca & C. Freytag (Eds.), *Duets and dialogue: Voices on inclusive practices in our schools* [Monograph] (pp. 50–58). Albany, NY: New York State Education Department, Higher Education Support Center for Quality Inclusive Schooling. Available at http://www.inclusion-ny.org/files/Duets-and-Dialogue.pdf

Krashen, S. D. (1982). *Principles and practice in second language acquisition.* Oxford, UK: Pergamon.

Kurth, J., Gross, M., Lovinger, S., & Catalano, T. (2012). Grading students with significant disabilities in inclusive settings: Teacher perspectives. *Journal of the International Association of Special Education, 13*(1), 41–57.

Lai, S. A., & Berkeley, S. (2012). High stakes test accommodations: Research & practice. *Learning Disability Quarterly, 35*, 158–169.

Lane, K. L., Carter, E. W., & Sisco, L. (2012). Paraprofessional involvement in self-determination instruction for students with high-incidence disabilities. *Exceptional Children, 78*(2), 237–251.

Lecavalier, L. (2006). Behavioral and emotional problems in young people with pervasive developmental disorders: Relative prevalence, effects of subject characteristics, and empirical classification. *Journal of Autism and Developmental Disorders, 36*, 1101–1114.

Leithwood, K., Harris, A., & Hopkins, D. (2008). Seven strong claims about successful school leadership. *School Leadership and Management, 28*(1), 27–42.

Leithwood, K., & Mascall, B. (2008). Collective leadership effects on student achievement. *Educational Administration Quarterly, 44*, 529–561.

Lewis-Moreno, B. (2007). Shared responsibility: Achieving success with English-language learners. *Phi Delta Kappan, 88*(10), 772–775.

Liang, L. A., Peterson, C. A., & Graves, M. F. (2005). Investigating two approaches to fostering children's comprehension of literature. *Reading Psychology, 26*, 387–400.

Linquanti, R. (2011). Strengthening assessment for English learner success: How can the promise of the Common Core Standards and innovative assessment systems be realized? In Policy Analysis for California Education and Rennie Center for Education Research & Policy (Eds.), *The road ahead for state assessments* (pp. 13–25). Cambridge, MA: Rennie Center for Education Research & Policy. Retrieved from http://www.edpolicyinca.org/sites/default/files/2011_PACE_RENNIE_ASSESSMENT_REPORT.pdf

Liston, A. G., Nevin, A., & Malian, I. (2009). What do paraeducators in inclusive classrooms say about their work? Analysis of national survey data and follow-up interviews in California. *TEACHING Exceptional Children Plus, 5*(5), 2–17.

Lytle, R. K., & Bordin, J. (2001). Enhancing the IEP team: Strategies for parents and professionals. *TEACHING Exceptional Children, 33*(5), 40–44.

Madrid, E. M. (2011). The Latino achievement gap. *Multicultural Education, 19*(3), 7–12.

Magiera, K., & Zigmond, N. (2005). Co-teaching in middle school classrooms under routine conditions: Does the instructional experience differ for students with disabilities in co-taught and solo-taught classes? *Learning Disabilities Research and Practice, 20*(2), 79–85.

Maheady, L., Harper, G. F., & Mallette, B. (2001). Peer-mediated instruction and interventions and students with mild disabilities. *Remedial and Special Education, 22*(1), 4–14.

Malmgren, K. W. (1998). CL as an academic intervention for students with mild disabilities. *Focus on Exceptional Children, 31,* 1–8.

Malmgren, K. W., McLaughlin, M. J., & Nolet, V. (2005). Accounting for the performance of students with disabilities on statewide assessments. *Journal of Special Education, 39*(2), 86–96.

Marino, M. T. (2009). Understanding how adolescents with reading difficulties utilize technology-based tools. *Exceptionality, 17*(2), 88–102.

Marshall, K. (2012). Fine-tuning teacher evaluation. *Educational Leadership, 70*(3), 50–53.

Martin, J. E., Van Dycke, J. L., Christensen, W. R., Greene, B. A., Gardner, J. E., & Lovett, D. L. (2006). Increasing student participation in IEP meetings: Establishing the self-directed IEP as an evidence-based practice. *Exceptional Children, 72*(3), 299–316.

Martinez, D. C., Conroy, J. W., & Cerreto, M. C. (2012). Parent involvement in the transition process of children with intellectual disabilities: The influence of inclusion on parent desires and expectations for postsecondary education. *Journal of Policy and Practice in Intellectual Disabilities, 9*(4), 279–288.

Maryland State Department of Education (n.d.). *Co-teaching tools and resources.* Retrieved from http://marylandlearninglinks.org/1007

Marzano, R. J. (2002). Language, the language art, and thinking. In J. Flood, D. Lapp, J. R. Squire, & J. M. Jensen (Eds.), *Handbook of research on teaching the English language arts* (2nd ed., pp. 687–716). Mahwah, NJ: Lawrence Erlbaum.

Marzano, R. J. (2011). *Research base and validation studies on The Marzano evaluation model.* Retrieved from http://www.marzanoevaluation.com/files/Research_Base_and_Validation_Studies_Marzano_Evaluation_Model.pdf

Mastropieri, M. A., Scruggs, T. E., Norland, J. J., Berkeley, S., McDuffie, K., Tornquist, E. H., & Connors, N. (2006). Differentiated curriculum enhancement in inclusive middle school science: Effects on classroom and high-stakes tests. *Journal of Special Education, 40,* 130–137.

Maxwell, L. (2014, April 24). Test supports for ELLs: Differences between PARCC and Smarter Balanced [Blog post]. Retrieved from http://blogs.edweek.org/edweek/learning-the-language/2014/04/test_supports_for_english-lear.html

McLeskey, J. (2011). Supporting improved practice for special education teachers: The importance of learner-centered professional development. *Journal of Special Education Leadership, 24*(1), 26–35.

McTigue, E. M., & Rimm-Kaufman, S. E. (2011). The "responsive classroom" approach and its implications for improving reading and writing. *Reading & Writing Quarterly, 27*(1-2), 5–24.

Meadan, H., Shelden, D. L., Appel, K., & DeGrazia, R. L. (2010). Developing a long-term vision: A road map for students' futures. *TEACHING Exceptional Children, 43*(2), 8–14.

Measures of Effective Teaching Project. (2014). Project reports. Retrieved from http://www.metproject.org/reports.php

Minnici, A. (2014, Spring). The mind shift in teacher evaluation: Where we stand—and where we need to go. *American Educator,* 22–26.

Mooney, J. (2007). *The short bus: A journey beyond normal.* New York, NY: Holt.

Morcom, V. E., & MacCallum, J. A. (2012). Getting personal about values: Scaffolding student participation towards an inclusive classroom community. *International Journal of Inclusive Education, 16*(12), 1323–1334.

Murawski, W. W. (2012). Ten tips for using co-planning time more efficiently. *TEACHING Exceptional Children, 44*(4), 8–15.

Murawski, W. W., & Spencer, S. A. (2011). *Collaborate, communicate, and differentiate! How to increase student learning in today's diverse schools.* Thousand Oaks, CA: Corwin.

National Association for the Education of Young Children (2014). *Developmentally appropriate practice.* Retrieved from http://www.naeyc.org/DAP

National Center for Education Statistics. (2014). English language learners. In *The condition of education.* Retrieved from http://nces.ed.gov/programs/coe/indicator_cgf.asp

National Center for Public Policy and Higher Education. (2005). *Income of U.S. workforce projected to decline if education doesn't improve.* Retrieved from http://www.highereducation.org/reports/pa_decline/pa_decline.pdf#search=%22minorities%22

National Comprehensive Center for Teacher Quality. (2014). *Guide to evaluation products.* Retrieved from http://resource.tqsource.org/gep/gepsearchresult.aspx

National Council on Teacher Quality Teacher Prep Review. (2014). *2014 teacher prep review: A review of the nation's teacher preparations programs.* Retrieved from http://www.nctq.org/dmsView/Teacher_Prep_Review_2014_Report

National Drop-Out Prevention Center for Students with Disabilities. (2013). *An analysis of states' FFY 2011 annual performance report data for indicator B2 (dropout).* Washington, DC: Author. Retrieved from http://www.ndpc-sd.org/documents/NDPC-SD_FFY_2011_Indicator_B-2_summary.pdf

New York State United Teachers. (2012). *Teacher evaluation and development evaluation process workbook.* Latham, NY: Author.

New York State United Teachers. (2013). *NYSUT's teacher practice rubric.* Latham: NY: Author.

Nidus, G., & Sadder, M. (2011). The principal as formative coach. *Educational Leadership, 69*(2), 30–35.

No Child Left Behind Act of 2001, Pub. L. No. 107-110, 115 State 1425 et seq. (2001).

O'Brien, C. (2007). Using collaborative reading groups to accommodate diverse learning and behavior needs in the general education classroom. *Beyond Behavior, 16*(3), 7–15.

Ochoa, A., & Cadiero-Kaplan, K. (2004). Towards promoting biliteracy and academic achievement: Educational programs for high school Latino English language learners. *High School Journal, 87*(3), 27–43.

Olkin, R. (2002). Could you hold the door for me? Including disability in diversity. *Cultural Diversity and Ethnic Minority Psychology, 8,* 130–137.

Otis-Wilborn, A., Winn, J., Griffin, C., & Kilgore, K. (2005). Beginning special educators' forays into general education. *Teacher Education and Special Education, 28*(3/4), 143–152.

Palincsar, A. S., Magnusson, S. J., Cutter, J., & Vincent, M. (2002). Supporting guided-inquiry instruction. *TEACHING Exceptional Children, 34*(3), 88–91.

Palmer, D. S., Fuller, K., Arora, T., & Nelson, M. (2001). Taking sides: Parent views on inclusion for their children with severe disabilities. *Exceptional Children, 67*(4), 467–484.

PARC v. Commonwealth of Pennsylvania. (1972). Public Interest Law Center of Philadelphia. Retrieved from http://www.pilcop.org/pennsylvania-association-for-retarded-citizens-parc-v-commonwealth-of-pennsylvania/

Parrish, P., & Stodden, R. A. (2009). Aligning assessment and instruction with state standards for children with significant disabilities. *TEACHING Exceptional Children, 41*(4), 46–56.

Parrish, T. B., Merickel, A., Perez, M., Linquanti, R., Socias, M., & Spain, A. (2006, January). *Effects of the implementation of Proposition 227 on the education of English learners, K–12: Findings from a five-year evaluation* (Final Report for AB 56 and AB 1116). Washington, DC: American Institutes for Research.

Piaget, J. (2003). Part I: Cognitive development in children: Piaget development and learning. *Journal of Research in Science Teaching, 40*(S1), S8–S18.

Praisner, C. L. (2003). Attitudes of elementary school principals toward the inclusion of students with disabilities. *Exceptional Children, 69*(2), 135–145.

Pullin, D. (2005). When one size does not fit all: The special challenges of accountability testing for students with disabilities. *Yearbook of the National Society for the Study of Education, 104*(2), 199–222.

Purnell, P. G. (2007). Strategies for creating inclusive and accepting middle school classrooms. *Middle School Journal, 39*(1), 32–37.

Putnam, J., Markovchick, K., Johnson, D. W., & Johnson, R. T. (1996). Cooperative learning and peer acceptance of students with learning disabilities. *Journal of Social Psychology, 136,* 741–752.

Ragan, A., & Lesaux, N. (2006). Federal, state, and district level English language learner program entry and exit requirements: Effects on the education of language minority learners. *Education Policy Analysis Archives, 14,* 20.

Rea, P. J., McLaughlin, V. L., & Walther-Thomas, C. (2002). Outcomes for students with learning disabilities in inclusive and pullout programs. *Exceptional Children, 68,* 203–223.

Reardon, S. F., & Galindo, C. (2009). The Hispanic-White achievement gap in math and reading in the elementary grades. *American Educational Research Journal, 46*(3), 853–891.

Restrepo, M. A, Castilla, A. P., Schwanenflugel, P. J., Neuharth-Pritchett, S., Hamilton, C. E., & Arboleda, A. (2010). Effects of a supplemental Spanish oral language program on sentence length, complexity, and grammaticality in Spanish-speaking children attending English-only preschools. *Language, Speech, and Hearing Services in Schools, 41*(1), 3–13.

Rhode Island Federation of Teachers and Health Professionals. (2012). *Rhode Island Innovation Consortium Educator Evaluation & Support System innovation evaluation model descriptors of practice/rubrics.* Providence, RI: Author.

Rice, N., Drame, E., & Owens, L. (2007). Co-instructing at the secondary level: Strategies for success. *TEACHING Exceptional Children. 39*(6), 12-18.

Rivera, C., & Collum, E. (2004, January.). *An analysis of state assessment policies addressing the accommodation of English language learners.* Issue paper prepared for the National Assessment Governing Board, Washington, DC.

Robertson, K., & Ford, K. (2008). *Language acquisition: An overview.* Retrieved from http://www.colorincolorado.org article/26751/

Robertson, K., & Lafond, S. (2008). *Getting ready for college: What ELL students need to know.* Retrieved from http://www.colorincolorado.org/article/28377/

Rose, D., & Meyer, A. (2002). *Teaching every student in the digital age.* Alexandria, VA: ASCD. Available online at http://www.cast.org/teachingeverystudent/ideas/tes/

Sailor, W., Zuna, N., Choi, J., Thomas, J., McCart, A., & Roger, B. (2006). Anchoring schoolwide positive behavior support in structural school reform. *Research and Practice for Persons With Severe Disabilities, 31*(1), 18–30.

Salend, S. J. (2011). *Creating inclusive classrooms: Effective and reflective practices* (7th ed.). Columbus, OH: Pearson.

Scarcella, R. (2003). *Academic English: A conceptual framework* (Tech. Rep. No. 2003–1). Irvine: University of California, Linguistic Minority Research Institute.

Scarcella, R. (2008, August). *Defining academic English.* Webinar presented for the National Clearinghouse for English Language Acquisition. Retrieved from http://www.ncela.gwu.edu/webinars/event/1/

Schöen, D. (1984). *The reflective practitioner.* New York, NY: Basic Books.

Schultz, E. K., Simpson, C. G., & Lynch, S. (2012). Specific learning disability identification: What constitutes a pattern of strengths and weaknesses? *Learning Disabilities: A Multidisciplinary Journal, 18*(2), 87–97.

Scruggs, T. E., & Mastropieri, M. A. (2007). Science learning in special education: The case for constructed versus instructed learning. *Exceptionality, 15*(2), 57–74.

Seo, S., Brownell, M., Bishop, A., & Dingle, M. (2008). An examination of beginning special education teachers' classroom practices that engage elementary students with learning disabilities in reading instruction. *Exceptional Children, 75*(1), 97–122.

Shady, S. A., Luther, V. L., & Richman, L. J. (2013). Teaching the teachers: A study of perceived professional development needs of educators to enhance positive attitudes toward inclusive practices. *Education Research and Perspectives, 40*(1), 169–191.

Shanahan, T. (2013). *Letting the text take center stage.* Washington, DC: American Educator. Retrieved from http://www.aft.org//sites/default/files/periodicals/Shanahan.pdf

Sherwin, G. H., & Schmidt, S. (2003). Communication codes among African American children and youth: The fast track from special education to prison? *Journal of Correctional Education, 54*(2), 45–52.

Shevin, M., & Klein, N. K. (2004). The importance of choice-making skills for students with severe disabilities. *Research and Practice for Persons With Severe Disabilities, 29*(3), 161–168.

Shippen, M. E., Flores, M. M., Crites, S. A., Patterson, D., Ramsey, M. L., Houchins, D. D., & Jolivette, K. (2011). Classroom structure and teacher efficacy in serving students with disabilities: Differences in elementary and secondary teachers. *International Journal of Special Education, 26*(3), 36–44.

Shook, A. C., Hazelkorn, M., & Lozano, E. R. (2011). Science vocabulary for all. *Science Teacher, 78*(3), 45–49.

Shurr, J., & Taber-Doughty, T. (2012). Increasing comprehension for middle school students with moderate intellectual disabilities on age-appropriate texts. *Education and Training inAutism and Developmental Disabilities, 47*(3), 359–372.

Silva, J., & Contreras, K. (2011). The year we learned to collaborate. *Educational Leadership, 69*(2), 54–58.

Smith, T. J., Dittmer, K. I., & Skinner, C. H. (2002). Enhancing science performance in students with learning disabilities using cover, copy, and compare: A student shows the way. *Psychology in the Schools, 39*, 417–426.

Simkins, T., Coldwell, M., Caillau, I., Finlayson, H., & Morgan, A. (2006). Coaching as an in-school leadership development strategy: Experiences from leading from the middle. *Journal of In-Service Education, 32*, 321–340.

Staehr Fenner, D. (2013a, December 12). Deciding how much background knowledge to provide for ELLs [Blog post]. Retrieved from http://blog.colorincolorado.org/2013/12/12/determining-how-much-background-knowledge-to-provide-for-ells/

Staehr Fenner, D. (2013b, March 6). ELLs are everyone's kids: The role of collaboration in CCSS [Blog post]. Retrieved from http://blog.colorincolorado.org/2013/03/06/ells-are-everyones-kids-the-role-of-collaboration-in-the-ccss/

Staehr Fenner, D. (2013c, November 26). Your role in the Common Core: Advocating for ELLs [Blog post]. Retrieved from http://blog.colorincolorado.org/2013/11/26/your-role-in-the-common-core-advocating-for-ells/

Staehr Fenner, D. (2014). *Advocating for English learners: A guide for educators.* Thousand Oaks, CA: Corwin.

Staehr Fenner, D., & Snyder, S. (2014, February 27). Common Core curriculum rubric: Meeting the needs of ELLs [Blog]. Retrieved from http://blog.colorin

colorado.org/2014/02/27/common-core-curriculum-rubric-meeting-the-needs-of-ells/

Staehr Fenner, D., Kozik, P., & Cooper, A. (2014). Evaluating teachers of all learners. *Leadership, 43*(4), 8–12.

Stanovich, P. J., & Jordan, A. (1998). Canadian teachers' and principals' beliefs about inclusive education as predictors of effective teaching in heterogeneous classrooms. *Elementary School Journal, 98*(3), 221–238.

Staples, K. E., & Diliberto, J. A. (2010). Guidelines for successful parent involvement: Working with parents of students with disabilities. *TEACHING Exceptional Children, 42*(6), 58–63.

Stecker, P. M., Fuchs, L. S., & Fuchs, D. (2005). Using curriculum-based measurement to improve student achievement: Review of research. *Psychology in the Schools, 42,* 795–819.

Stronge, J. H., Ward, T. J., Tucker, P. D., & Hindman, J. L. (2007). What is the relationship between teacher quality and student achievement? *Journal of Personnel Evaluation in Education, 20*(3-4), 165–184.

Suarez-Orozco, C., Suarez-Orozco, M., & Doucet, F. (2004). The academic engagement and achievement of Latino youth. In J. Banks & C. Banks (Eds.), *Handbook of research on multicultural education* (pp. 420–437). San Francisco, CA: Jossey-Bass.

Suter, J. C., & Giangreco, M. F. (2009). Numbers that count: Exploring special education and paraprofessional service delivery in inclusion-oriented schools. *Journal of Special Education, 43*(2), 81–93.

Swail, W. S., Cabrera, A. F., Lee, C., & Williams, A. (2005). *Part III: Pathways to the bachelor's degree for Latino students*. Washington, DC: Educational Policy Institute.

Swedeen, B. L. (2009). Signs of an inclusive school: A parent's perspective on the meaning and value of authentic inclusion. *TEACHING Exceptional Children Plus, 5*(3), 1.

Tankersley, M., Niesz, T., Cook, B. C., & Woods, W. (2007). The unintended side effects of inclusion of students with learning disabilities: The perspectives of special education teachers. *Learning Disabilities: A Multidisciplinary Journal, 14,* 135–144.

Taylor, A. S., Peterson, C. A., McMurray-Schwartz, P., & Guillou, T. S. (2002). Social skills interventions: Not just for children with special needs. *Young Exceptional Children, 5*(4), 19–26.

Teachers of English to Speakers of Other Languages. (2010). *TESOL/NCATE standards for the recognition of initial TESOL programs in P–12 ESL teacher education*. Alexandria, VA: Author. Retrieved from http://www.tesol

Tharp, R. G., & Gallimore, R. (1988). *Rousing minds to life: Teaching, learning, and schooling in social context*. Cambridge, MA: Cambridge University Press.

Thomas, W. P., & Collier, V. P. (1997). *School effectiveness for language minority students*. Washington, DC: National Clearinghouse for Bilingual Education.

Thomas, W. P., & Collier, V. P. (2002). *A national study of school effectiveness for language minority students' long-term academic achievement*. Santa Cruz: University of California, Center for Research on Education, Diversity & Excellence.

Thompson, S. J., Johnstone, C. J., & Thurlow, M. L. (2002). *Universal design applied to large scale assessments* (Synthesis Report 44). Minneapolis: University of Minnesota, National Center on Educational Outcomes.

Thurlow, M. L., Lazarus, S. S., Thompson, S. J., & Morse, A. B. (2005). State policies on assessment participation and accommodations for students with disabilities. *Journal of Special Education, 38*(4), 232–240.

Timothy W. v. Rochester, New Hampshire, Sch. Dist., 875 F.2d 954 (1st Cir.), cert. denied, 493 U.S. 983 (1989).

Tinkler, B. (2002). *A review of literature on Hispanic/Latino parent involvement in K–12 education.* Retrieved from http://www.huildassest.org/products/latino-parentreport/latinopafentrept.htm

Tobin, R. (2007). Interactions and practices to enhance the inclusion experience. *TEACHING Exceptional Children, 3*(5), Article 5. Available at http://journals.cec.sped.org/tecplus/vol3/iss5/art5

Tschannen-Moran, M. (2009). Fostering teacher professionalism: The role of professional orientation and trust, *Educational Administration Quarterly, 45,* 217–247.

Tschannen-Moran, B., & Tschannen-Moran, M. (2010). *Evocative coaching.* San Francisco, CA: Jossey-Bass.

Tschannen-Moran, B., & Tschannen-Moran, M. (2011). The coach and the evaluator. *Educational Leadership, 69*(2), 10–16.

Turnbull, H. (2005). Individuals with Disabilities Education Act reauthorization: Accountability and personal responsibility. *Remedial and Special Education, 26,* 320–326.

U.S. Department of Education. (2009). *Race to the top* (Executive summary). Retrieved from http://www2.ed.gov/programs/racetothetop/executive-summary.pdf

U.S. Department of Education. (2010). *College- and career-ready standards and assessments.* Retrieved from http://www2.ed.gov/policy/elsec/leg/blueprint/faq/college-career.pdf

U.S. Department of Education. (2013). *The biennial report to Congress on the implementation of the Title III State Formula Grant Program, School Years 2008–10.* Retrieved from http://www.ncela.us/files/uploads/3/Biennial_Report_0810.pdf

U.S. Department of Education. (2014). *Consolidated state performance reports.* Retrieved from http://www2.ed.gov/admins/lead/account/consolidated/index.html#sy11-12

Understanding Language. (2012). *Persuasion across time and space: Analyzing and producing persuasive texts.* Retrieved from http://ell.stanford.edu/sites/default/files/ela_archives/understanding_language_materials_Jan2013.pdf

Valdés, G., Kibler, A., & Walqui, A. (2014, March). *Changes in the expertise of ESL professionals: Knowledge and action in an era of new standards.* Alexandria, VA: TESOL International Association.

Valle, J. W., & Connor, D. J. (2011). *Rethinking disability: A disability studies approach to inclusive practices.* New York, NY: McGraw-Hill

Voltz, D., & Collins, L. (2010). Preparing special education administrators for inclusion in divers, standard-based contexts: Beyond the council for exceptional children and the interstate school leaders licensure consortium. *Teacher Education Special Education, 33*(1), 70–82.

Vygotsky, L. S. (1978). *Mind and society: The development of higher mental processes.* Cambridge, MA: Harvard University Press.

Waldron, N. L., McLeskey, J., & Redd, L. (2011). Setting the direction: The role of the principal in developing an effective, inclusive school. *Journal of Special Education Leadership, 24*(2), 51–60.

Walqui, A. (2000). *Context counts in second language learning.* http://www.colorincolorado.org/article/99/

Wang, M. C., & Baker, E. T. (1985–1986). Mainstreaming programs: Design features and effects. *Journal of Special Education, 19,* 503–521.

Watkins, E., & Liu, K. K. (2013). Who are English language learners with disabilities? In K. Liu, E. Watkins, D. Pompa, P. McLeod, J. Elliott, & V. Gaylord (Eds.), *Impact: Feature issue on educating K-12 English language learners with disabilities, 26*(1). Retrieved from http://ici.umn.edu/products/impact/261/2.html

Weishaar, P. M. (2010). Twelve ways to incorporate strengths-based planning into the IEP process. *Clearing House: A Journal of Educational Strategies, Issues and Ideas, 83*(6), 207–210.

Whitehurst, G., Chingos, M., & Lindquist, K. (2014). *Evaluating teachers with classroom observations: Lessons learned in four districts.* Washington, DC: Brookings Institution, Brown Center on Education Policy.

Wiener, J., & Tardif, C. Y. (2004). Social and emotional functioning of children with learning disabilities: Does special education placement make a difference? *Learning Disabilities Research & Practice, 19*(1), 20–32.

Wiggins, G., & McTighe, J. (2005a). Backward design. In *Understanding by design* (2nd ed., pp. 13–34). Upper Saddle River, NJ: Pearson Education.

Wiggins, G., & McTighe, J. (2005b). Introduction. In *Understanding by design* (2nd ed., pp. 1–11). Upper Saddle River, NJ: Pearson Education.

Wiggins, G., & McTighe, J. (2005c). *Understanding by design* (2nd ed.). Alexandria, VA: Association of Supervision and Curriculum Development.

Will, M. (1986). Educating children with learning problems: A shared responsibility. *Exceptional Children, 52,* 411–415.

Williams, T., Hakuta, K., & Haertel, E. (2007). *Similar English learner students, different results: Why do some schools do better? A follow-up analysis based on a large-scale survey of California elementary schools serving low-income and EL students.* Mountain View, CA: EdSource.

Willingham, D. T. (2008). Should learning be its own reward? *American Educator, 31*(4), 29–35.

Willner, L. S., Rivera, C., & Acosta, B. D. (2008). *Descriptive study of state assessment policies for accommodating English language learners.* Arlington, VA: George Washington University Center for Equity and Excellence in Education.

Wilson, G. L., & Blednick, J. (2011). *Teaching in tandem.* Arlington, VA: Association of Supervision and Curriculum Development.

Winters, C. A. (1997). Learning disabilities, crime, delinquency, and special education placement. *Adolescence, 32*(126), 451–462.

Wonacott, M. E. (2003). *Employment of people with disabilities* (Eric Digest 247). Columbus, OH: Clearinghouse on Adult, Career, and Vocational Education. (ERIC Document Reproduction Service No. ED478950)

Wood, D. J., Bruner, J. S., & Ross, G. (1976). The role of tutoring in problem solving. *Journal of Child Psychiatry and Psychology, 17*(2), 89–100.

Zehler, A., Fleischman, H., Hopstock, P., Stephenson, T., Pendzick, M., & Sapru, S. (2003). *Descriptive study of services to LEP students and LEP students with disabilities* (Vol. I, Research Report). Arlington, VA: Development Associates.

Zepeda, S. J. (2007). *Instructional supervision: Applying tools and concepts.* Larchmont, NY: Eye on Education.

Index

A SAGE Company

Corwin is committed to improving education for all learners by publishing books and other professional development resources for those serving the field of PreK–12 education. By providing practical, hands-on materials, Corwin continues to carry out the promise of its motto: **"Helping Educators Do Their Work Better."**